AGRO-BIODIVERSITY
CONSERVATION AND SUSTAINABLE DEVELOPMENT

ENV BOOKS SERIES

AGRO-BIODIVERSITY
CONSERVATION AND SUSTAINABLE DEVELOPMENT

Editors

Dr. Pankaj Sharma
Sr. Scientific Professional
Himachal Pradesh State Biodiversity Board
State Council for Science, Technology & Environment
Shimla, Himachal Pradesh
(INDIA)

Dr. Narayan Singh
Manager
Corporate Social Responsibility
The Energy and Resources Institute (TERI)
Rampur, Shimla (Himachal Pradesh)
(INDIA)

&

Dr. Pawan Kumar 'Bharti'
Vice President (Executive)
Society for Environment, Health, Awareness
of Nutrition & Toxicology (SEHAT)
1775, Sohan Ganj, Near Clock Tower
Delhi - 110 007
(INDIA)
E-mail- gurupawanbharti@rediffmail.com

DPH

DISCOVERY PUBLISHING HOUSE PVT. LTD.
NEW DELHI-110 002

Published by:

Namit Wasan

DISCOVERY PUBLISHING HOUSE PVT. LTD.

4383/4B, Ansari Road, Darya Ganj
New Delhi-110 002 (India)
Phone : +91-11-23279245, 43596064-65
Fax : +91-11-23253475
E-mail : discoverypublishinghouse@gmail.com
namitwasan9@gmail.com
sales@discoverypublishinggroup.com

website: www.discoverypublishinggroup.com

First Edition: **2016**

ISBN: 978-93-5056-782-1

Agro-biodiversity: ***Conservation and Sustainable Development***

Printed at:
Infinity Imaging Systems
Delhi

ENV Books Series, India

Calls descriptive and error free chapters for upcoming volumes of books on various environmental issues. Send your manuscripts to envbooks@gmail.com

Founding Editor (Editor-in-Chief)

Dr. Pawan Kumar 'Bharti'

Society for Environment, Health, Awareness of Nutrition & Toxicology (SEHAT-India)
1775, Sohanganj, Near Clock Tower, Delhi - 7, India

E-mail: *gurupawanbharti@rediffmail.com*

Other Titles by Editor-in-Chief:

1. **Advances in Biotechnology and Ecological Sciences (2013)**
   Bharti, P.K., Chauhan, A. and Ray, J. (eds.)
   (ISBN: 978-93-5056-358-8).
2. **Advances in Agriculture and Ecology (2013)**
   Bharti, P.K., Chauhan, A. and Ezeaku Peter Ikemefuna (eds.)
   (ISBN: 978-93-5056-362-5).
3. **Agriculture Development and Sustainable Environment (2015)**
   Ray, J. and Bharti, P.K. (eds.)
   (ISBN: 978-93-5056-759-3).
4. **Agriculture, Environment and Nano-science (2015)**
   Bharti, Pawan K. (ed.)
   (ISBN: 978-93-5056-760-5).
5. **Agriculture Ecology and Environment (2014)**
   Bharti, P.K. and Olubukola O. Babalola (eds.)
   (ISBN: 978-93-5056-480-6).
6. **Agriculture and Environmental Biotechnology (2014)**
   Bharti, P.K. and Chauhan, A. (eds.)
   (ISBN: 978-93-5056-479-0).

7. **Agro-forestry and Climate Change (2014)**
Bharti, Pawan K. and Singh, Narayan (eds.)
(ISBN: 978-93-5056-514-8).

8. **Aquatic Biodiversity and Pollution (2013)**
Bharti, P.K., Chauhan, A. and Kaoud, H.A.H. (eds.)
(ISBN: 978-93-5056-359-5).

9. **Aquatic Ecology and Biotechnology (2014)**
Bharti, P.K. and Zaki, M.S.A. (eds.)
(ISBN: 978-93-5056-451-6).

10. **Aquatic Environment and Toxicology (2013)**
Bharti, Pawan K. (ed.)
(ISBN: 978-93-5056-236-9).

11. **Aquaculture and Fisheries Environment (2014)**
Gupta, S.K. and Pawan K. Bharti (eds.)
(ISBN: 978-93-5056-408-0).

12. **Biodiversity, Biotechnology and Environmental Conservation (2015)**
Bharti, P.K. and Bhandari, G. (eds.)
(ISBN: 978-93-5056-750-4).

13. **Biotechnological Approaches and Water Ecosystem (2016)**
Zaki S.A. Mona and Pawan K. 'Bharti' (eds.)
(ISBN: 978-93-5056-779-1)

14. **Biotechnology, Agro-ecology and Environment (2015)**
Avnish Chauhan and Bharti, P.K. (eds.)
(ISBN: 978-93-5056-757-9).

15. **Biodiversity of Aquatic Ecosystem: *Significance, Threat and Conservation* (2013)**
Bharti, P.K. and Kaoud, H.A.H. (eds.)
(ISBN: 978-93-5056-297-0).

16. **Clean Technology for Environmental Protection (2015)**
Chauhan, A., Sharma, S. and Bharti, P.K. (eds.)
(ISBN: 978-93-5056-731-9).

17. **Climate Change and Biodiversity (2013)**
Bharti, P.K., and Chauhan, Avnish (eds.)
(ISBN: 978-93-5056-360-1).

18. **Climate Change and Agriculture (2012)**
Bharti, P.K. and Chauhan, Avnish (eds.)
(ISBN: 978-93-5056-148-5).

19. **Conservation and Cultivation of Medicinal Plants (2015)**
Narayan Singh and Bharti, P.K. (eds.)
(ISBN: 978-93-5056-740-1).

20. **Eco-toxicology and Eco-technology (2013)**
Bharti, P.K. and Zaki, M. (eds.)
(ISBN: 978-93-5056-313-7).

21. **Environmental Biotechnology and Application (2013)**
Bharti, P.K. and Chauhan, Avnish (eds.)
(ISBN: 978-93-5056-262-8).

22. **Environmental Conservation and Biotechnology (2014)**
Chauhan, A. and P.K. Bharti (eds.)
(ISBN: 978-93-5056-512-4).

23. **Environmental Health and Problems (2013)**
Bharti, P.K. and Gajananda, Kh. (eds.)
(ISBN: 978-93-5056-263-5).

24. **Environmental Pollution and Biodiversity (2012)**
Bharti, P.K., Chauhan, Avnish and Kumar, P. (eds.)
(ISBN: 978-93-5056-149-2).

25. **Fish Habitat and Aquaculture (2015)**
Gupta, S.K. and Bharti, P.K. (eds.)
(ISBN: 978-93-5056-744-9).

26. **Fisheries and Toxicology (2014)**
Zaki, M.S.A., Bharti, P.K. and Chauhan, A. (eds.)
(ISBN: 978-93-5056-452-3).

27. **Freshwater Ecosystem and Xenobiotics (2013)**
Bharti, P.K., Zaki, M. and Chauhan, A. (eds.)
(ISBN: 978-93-5056-299-4).

28. **Limnology and Aquatic Science (2015)**
Sharma, S. and Bharti, P.K. (eds.)
(ISBN: 978-93-5056-735-7).

29. **Medicinal Plants: *Status, Distribution and Significance* (2015)**
Sharma, P., Bharti, P.K. and Narayan Singh (eds.)
(ISBN: 978-93-5056-734-0).

30. **Microbial Applications and Environment (2014)**
Bharti, Pawan K. (ed.)
(ISBN: 978-93-5056-515-5).

31. **Microbial Ecology and Habitat (2014)**
Bharti, Pawan K. (ed.)
(ISBN: 978-93-5056-514-8).

32. **Natural Ecosystem and Climate Change (2015)**
Bharti, P.K. and Gajananda, Kh. (eds.)
(ISBN: 978-93-5056-749-0).

33. **Prakriti me Aushadhi (*in Hindi*) (2012)**
Singh, J.R., Bharti, P.K. and Bharti, B.
(ISBN: 978-93-5056-200-0).

34. **Seed Technology, Plant Growth and Cropping System (2015)**
Tyagi, P.K. and Bharti, P.K. (eds.)
(ISBN: 978-93-5056-738-8)

35. **Soil Contamination and Conservation (2015)**
Ezeaku, P.I. and Bharti, P.K. (eds.)
(ISBN: 978-93-5056-737-1).

36. **Soil Characteristics and Agro-ecology (2015)**
Avnish Chauhan and Bharti, P.K. (eds.)
(ISBN: 978-93-5056-758-6).

37. **Soil Quality and Contamination (2013)**
Bharti, P.K. and Chauhan, Avnish (eds.)
(ISBN: 978-93-5056-361-8).

38. **Waste Disposal and Management (2015)**
Bharti, P.K., Tabassum, B. and Bajaj, P. (eds.)
(ISBN: 978-93-5056-729-6).

39. **Waste Management and Environmental Health (2016)**
Tabassum B; Bajaj Priya and Bharti, P.K. (eds.)
(ISBN: 978-93-5056-777-7)

40. **Water Resources and Agriculture (2014)**
Bharti, P.K. and Ezeaku Peter Ikemefuna (eds.)
(ISBN: 978-93-5056-481-3).

Preface

The Earth's biological diversity has agonized massive losses in recent decades, putting the resources vital to life on the planet at great risk. The Convention on Biological Diversity (CBD), which was adopted at the 1992 UNCED Earth Summit and to which India and most other countries of the world are signatories, sets out three main goals *i.e.,* conservation of biological diversity; sustainable use of its components; fair and equitable sharing of benefits arising out of the utilization of genetic resources. Biodiversity refers to the Earth's diverse life forms, ecosystems and species, and genetic variability within species. It plays a pivotal role in the life-giving systems that make up the biosphere and is thus vital to human survival. It is also indispensable in the processes of evolution and adaptation to changing conditions. Primarily, agricultural biodiversity is understood to be the diversity in life forms used or able to be used directly or indirectly by human kind in efforts to secure the resources vital to survival: crops (including their wild relatives), forest plants, livestock, wildlife that can be hunted or otherwise made use of, fish and other aquatic life forms, microorganisms used in food technology and other processes, and other small life forms.

Services provided by species and ecosystems, such as: carbon storage and regulation of water and energy supply, can make a significant contribution to harnessing climate change. Sustainable production systems can serve to reduce greenhouse gas emissions in agriculture. Also, long-term storage of carbon reserves in forests and in farmed soil harbours potential for emission reductions. Apart from serving climate change mitigation, such measures are environmentally sound and contribute to biodiversity conservation. For energy, climate, forestry and agricultural policy reasons, renewable resources play a key role, not least because they can be used as a substitute energy source in place of fossil fuels. The use of these life forms in agriculture, forestry and fisheries, hereafter described as 'agricultural practice', manifests itself in management systems which involve many different actors ranging from producers to consumers. These management systems are embedded into the surrounding ecosystems in a variety of ways and with varying degrees of intensity. The life forms used interact with others and work in conjunction with the surrounding ecosystems, *e.g.*, soil organisms that aid soil fertility, promotion of beneficial animals and insects, and pollination of plants by insects. For this reason, apart from the diversity of used and usable species and their genetic diversity, agricultural biodiversity also includes the associated biodiversity that fulfils the various functions on which its use depends.

The climate change represents one of the greatest environmental, social and economic threats facing the planet today. In developing countries, climate change will have a significant impact on conditions of the poor people who rely heavily on the natural resource base for their livelihoods. Livestock is a global resource or both developing and industrialized societies. They provide multiple benefits that include food and clothing, fuel, nutrients cycling for soils, draught, and a means of insurance weather risk management, income and employment. The hot environment impairs the livestock production, reproductive performance, metabolic and health status, immune response. Climate change affect the pasture by affecting its productivity, quality of forage, change in spp. Composition, biodiversity loss and carrying capacity of pasture. In the present scenario, agroforestry play a significant role in mitigating the atmospheric accumulation of greenhouse gases, it also has a role to play in helping small-holder farmers adapt to climate change. Agroforestry is recognized as an important component in climate-smart agriculture for both its adaptation and mitigation roles. Agroforestry is an attractive and promising option for sequestering carbon on agricultural land because it can sequester significant amounts of carbon while leaving the bulk of land for agricultural production. Agroforestry has such a high potential, not because it is the land use Practice with highest carbon density but also because of such a large area is susceptible for the land use change.

This book updates the subject matter and issues related to agro-biodiversity, its conservation, sustainable development in the present scenario of climate change. Thanks are due to contributors from various institutions and publisher for their interest in this book. We hope this book will definitely provide a multidisciplinary forum to explore emerging areas in the field of agro-biodiversity, biotechnology, environmental conservation and pollution. Editors also hope that this publication will be of immense help to researcher, students, teachers, conservationists, policy-makers/planners, foresters, farmers and other interested to undertake studies/work on agro-biodiversity and related areas.

– Editors

(envbooks@gmail.com)

Contents

Pages: 1-27

AGRO-BIODIVERSITY: *CONSERVATION AND SUSTAINABLE DEVELOPMENT*
Edited by: Dr. Pankaj Sharma; Dr. Narayan Singh & Dr. Pawan Kumar 'Bharti'
ISBN: 978-93-5056-782-1
Edition: 2016
Published by: Discovery Publishing House Pvt. Ltd., New Delhi (India)

1

Ethnic Fermented Foods of India
The Rich Treasure Houses of Microbial Diversity

Nivedita Sharma* and
Shweta Handa

ABSTRACT

Indian fermented foods are an intrinsic part of the diet of ethnic tribes and being the oldest and most economic methods for developments of a diversity of aroma, flavour, texture, food preservation and biological enrichment of food products by the manipulation of different microbial population. Preparation and use of fermented foods and beverages using local food crops and other biological resources is very common amongst the high Landers of Himalayas, though the name of the products and the base material vary from region to region. Ethnic foods are fermented naturally, except the alcoholic beverages which are produced by usinginocula of consortia of different microorganisms in the form of dry, cereal based starters. Different groups of food grade microbes have been isolated from the traditional fermented foods. They include: bacteria, fungi and yeasts. Some groups of microbes are common while a few have been found unique inhabitants of different food items depending upon the variation in food ingredients, their preparation method as well as change in geographic location. Diversity within the species of Lactic acid bacteria and *Bacilli* has imparted different sensory characteristics to the ethnic foods.

Microbiology Research Laboratory, Department of Basic Sciences, Dr. YS Parmar University of Horticulture and Forestry, Nauni - Solan - 173230, Himachal Pradesh, India.

It has been demonstrated that functional microorganisms present in the ethnic fermented foods have many biological functions contributing to enhance the health promoting benefits, bio-preservations of perishable foods, bio enrichments of their nutritional values, protective properties and therapeutic values.

***Keywords*:** Microbial diversity, ethnic, fermented food, traditional, beverages

INTRODUCTION

A rich legacy of consuming varieties of fermented food in different states of India since ages might be due to its geographical as well as climatic conditions. Being a hilly and having a cold weather for most of the year in most of the states, probably renders this pre-digested food easier for digestion besides providing high nutritional value to the hard working people of India. Within the states, one can find local variation due to the pattern of food production and altitudinal variation, *e.g.*, in the barren region of Lahaul Spiti and Kinnaur, people consume products having coarse grains (buchwheat, millet, barley) as the main substrate, while in the lower areas of the state *i.e.*, Mandi, Kangra, Hamirpur, Bilaspur, people prefers roties made mostly of wheat and rice or maize flour. These traditional/indigenous foods are prepared according to the traditional methods using simple equipment's and under natural conditions from the staple material and other ingredients (Sharma *et al.* 2013).

Fermented foods rich in fermenting microbe's *viz;* lactic acid bacteria, yeasts and other bacteria have played an important role in human health for hundreds of years. Societies known for their long lives have been noticed to eat some form of fermented food regularly. Fermented foods, whether from plant or animal origin, are an intricate part of the diet of people in all parts of the world. Fermentation is a well-known method used for preserving the foods and beverages. It has been practiced for over thousands of years by the primitive people (Borgstorm, 1968). It is a procedure used for preparing consumable food products by the utilization of various microorganisms (Wood, 1998). It is the diversity of raw materials used as substrates, methods of preparation and sensory qualities of finished products that are so astounding as one begins to learn more about the eating habits of various cultures. The preparation of many indigenous or 'traditional' fermented foods and beverages remains today as a household art. They are prepared by using relatively simple procedures and equipments (Battcock and Azam-ali, 1998; Sankaran, 1998; Aidoo *et al.* 2006). Fermented foods are receiving worldwide consideration due to their health encouraging effects. Enhancement of flavor, manifestation, nutritional worth and storage stability with reduction in cooking time are the additional benefits of fermented foods.

Fermented foods are prepared by the action of microorganism(s), either naturally fermented or by adding starter culture(s), which modify the substrates biochemically and organoleptically into edible products, and are thus generally palatable, safe, and nutritious (Simango, 1997, Steinkraus, 1983). During the course of fermentation, a group of metabolites such as: lactic acid, alcohol, enzymes, antimicrobial substances, aromatic compounds, and organic acids are produced, which enrich the quality of products in respect to availability of nutrients and therapeutic potentials (Steinkraus, 1983).

Definition of Fermented Food

Campbell-Platt (1987) has defined fermented foods as those foods which have been subjected to the action of microorganisms or enzymes so that desirable biochemical changes cause significant modification to the food. However, to the microbiologist, the term 'fermentation' describes a form of energy-yielding microbial metabolism in which an organic substrate, usually a carbohydrate, is incompletely oxidised, and an organic carbohydrate acts as the electron acceptor (Adams, 1990). Whichever definition used, foods submitted to the influence of lactic acid producing microorganisms is considered a fermented food.

Microflora – Main Vehicles for Fermentation

A variety of microorganisms are responsible for carrying out fermentation in the fermented products by playing an essential role in bringing out the biochemical changes during fermentation (Basappa and Venkataramu, 1994). Use of microorganisms in preparing foods from locally available plants is a traditional practice since pre-historic times (Ross *et al*. 2002). Microorganisms associated with traditional fermented foods are present either in or on the ingredients, in the environment and are selected through adaptation to the substrate and fermentation conditions (Soni and Sandhu, 1990). The indigenous natural fermentation carried out by a mixed colony of micro-organisms such as: moulds, bacteria and yeasts generally in successions.

By tradition, lactic acid bacteria (LAB) are the most commonly used microorganisms for preservation of foods. Their importance is associated mainly with their safe metabolic activity while growing in foods utilising available sugar for the production of organic acids and other metabolites. Their common occurrence in foods and feeds coupled with their long-lived use contributes to their natural acceptance as GRAS (Generally Recognised As Safe) for human consumption (Aguirre and Collins, 1993). However, there are many kinds of fermented foods in which the dominating processes and end products are contributed by a mixture of endogenous enzymes and other microorganisms like yeast and mould. Very often, a mixed culture originating from the native microflora of the raw materials is in action in most of the food fermentation processes. However, in an industrial scale a particular defined starter culture, which has been developed under controlled conditions, is of first preference so that the qualities of the finished product could be consistently maintained day after day. Moreover, modern methods of gene-technology make it possible for the microbiologists to design and develop starter cultures with specific qualities.

In India, mostly due to wide variation in agro-climatic conditions and diverse form of dietary culture of the various ethnical groups, the following three major types of microorganisms are recorded with the traditional fermented foods and beverages (Sharma *et al.* 2013; Tamang 1998; Joshi, 2000):

1. ***Filamentous Fungi:*** Species of *Aspergillus, Amylomyces, Actinomucor, Monascus, Mucor, Neurospora, Penicillium* and *Rhizopus.*
2. ***Yeasts:*** *Debaromyces, Candida, Geotrichum, Hansenula, Kluyveromyces, Pichia, Saccharomyces, Saccharomycopsis, Torulopsis* and *Zygosaccharomyces.*
3. ***Bacteria:*** Species of lactic acid bacteria (LAB); *Lactobacillus, Lactococcus, Leuconostoc, Enterococcus, Tetragenococcus* and *Streptococcus* and species of *Klebsiella, Acetobacter, Citrobacter, Bacillus, Brevibacterium* and *Propionibacterium.*

Traditional Starter Cultures

Using native knowledge of locally available raw materials from the plant or animal sources, people across the globe produce this type of food and drink either naturally or adding starter cultures that contain microorganisms. Microorganisms transform these raw material both biochemically (*i.e.*, the nutrients) and organolaptically (*i.e.*, the taste/texture/odour) into edible products that are culturally acceptable to the maker and consumer (Tamang, 2010). Fermented foods preparations generally require some starter culture for their fermentation. Some of the fermented foods are naturally fermented while most of the foods are having some inocula added. Inoculum refers to the addition of microorganisms to the medium for the production of conversion of the new product. Some of the traditional mixed starter cultures are enlisted in Table 1.1 and Figure 1.1.

An Insight of Traditional Fermented Foods of India

Indigenous fermented foods have been prepared and consumed for thousands of years, and are strongly linked to culture, traditions and reveal the intellectual richness of indigenous people of the country in terms of their ability to prepare microbial products for varied purposes in addition to food and beverages (Sekar and Mariappan, 2007). However, the preparation of indigenous or 'traditional' fermented foods and beverages remain as a household art today (Larry and Beuchat, 2008). The indigenous fermented food is prepared utilizing different substrates and non-pathogenic microorganisms as starter and processing culture to be sold at the local markets for local consumption.

Table 1.1: Traditional mixed starter cultures of fermented foods and beverages of India

Starter	Substrate	Nature of Product	Microflora
Marcha	Rice, wild herbs, spices	Dry, flattened, ball like, white starter	Mold, yeast, LAB
Malera	Wheat	Dry, granular, starter	Mold, yeast, LAB
Mana	Wheat, herbs	Dry, granular-type starter	*Aspergillus oryzae*
Treh	Wheat	Slurry	Mold, yeast, LAB
Phagli	Wheat, herbs	Dry, granular-type starter	Mold, yeast, LAB
Manapu	Rice-wheat, herbs	Dry, flattened, ball like, white starter	Yeast and Mold
Phab	Wheat, wild herbs	Dry, flattened, ball like, brownish starter	Mold, yeast and LAB
Daheli	Wheat, wild herbs	Dry, flattened, ball like, white starter	Mold, yeast and LAB
Buth/ Thanbum	Rice, wild herbs	Dry, flattened, ball like, white starter	Mold, yeast and LAB
Hamei	Rice, wild herbs	Dry, ball like white starter	Mold, yeast and LAB
Humao	Rice, barks of wild plants	Dry, flat cake like starter	Mold, yeast and LAB
Chol	Rice, wild plants	Dry, flat, starter	Mold, yeast and LAB
Thiat	Rice-herbs	Dry, flat like white starter	Mold, yeast and LAB
Pham	Rice-herbs	Dry, flattened, ball like, white starter	Mold, yeast and LAB
Bhakhar	Wheat, wild herbs	Dry, flattened, ball like, white starter	Mold, yeast and LAB
Khekhrii	Rice, wild plants	Dry, flattened, ball like, white starter	Mold, yeast and LAB

Fermented foods are found either in solid or liquid state (Figure 1.2). Most of the traditional fermented foods are cereal-based (wheat/barley/buckwheat) and among these, some of the products like: *Bhaturu, Siddu, Chilra, Marchu, Manna, Dosha, Pinni/Bagpinni, Seera* etc., are unique to Himachal Pradesh (Sharma *et al*. 2013; Kanwar *et al*. 2007). In the tribal districts of Himachal Pradesh, large variety of fermented foods are prepared either daily, during special occasions or for the consumption during journey (Sharma *et al*. 2013). Traditional starter cultures like *'Malera'* and *'Treh'* are used as inocula in these fermented foods. However, the natural fermentation method is also used in the production of several products like: *Seera, Sepubari, Borhe* etc. (Thakur *et al*. 2004).

(1a) (1b)

(1c) (1d)

Fig. 1.1: **Some of the traditional starter cultures (1a) Phab (1b) Dhaeli (1c) Phagli (1d) Marcha**

Kinema, hawaijar, tungrymbai, bekang, aakhone, and peruyaan are naturally fermented ethnic soybean foods of India; they are popular among the Mongolian-origin races in the Eastern Himalayas. Ethnic fermented vegetable products are very famous in India. Vast varieties of these fermented vegetable products in the form of fermented soups, pickles are famous among Indians. North east part of India is generally a large producer of these fermented vegetables products. Gundruk, sinki, anishi, maseura, goyang, Ziangsang ae the famous fermented plant based foods of eastern Himalayas (Gautam and Sharma, 2014). Mostly are prepared from bamboo. Meat and fish products like: ngari, tungtap, hentak, kargyongare also famous among these ethnic tribes of India.

These products are made during various occasions like parties and ceremonies or may be prepared with the purpose of their preservation for long time. Long time preservation of these fermented foods is a necessity of the tribal folks due to their climatic conditions. The diversity of fermenting microbes enlisted in Table 1.2.

Table 1.2: Microbial diversity found in traditional fermented foods of India

Fermented Food	Substrate	Microorganisms Responsible for Fermentation	States in India	References
1	2	3	4	5
Bhaturu, Babroo Marchu, siddu and *Chilra*	*Wheat flour*	*Lactobacillus plantarum, L. acidophilus, Leuconostoc, Bacillus sp., Lactococcuslactis, S. cerevisiae, Debaromyceshansenii*	Himachal Pradesh	Kanwar *et al*. 2007; Sharma *et al*. 2013
Sepu Badi, Mash badi, Lasudabadi	*Pulses*	*Lactobacillus plantarum, L. acidophilus, Leuconostoc, Bacillus sp., Lactococcuslactis, Pediococcusacidilactici*	Himachal Pradesh	Sharma *et al*. 2013; Sharma *et al*. 2011
Soibum		*Enterococcus durans, Streptococcus lactis, Bacillus subtilis, B. licheniformis, B. coagulans, Candida sp., Saccharomyces sp., Torulopsis sp.*	Himachal Pradesh	Tamang and Tamang, 2009
Seera	*Wheat Grains*	*Lactobacillus plantarum, L. acidophilus, Leuconostoc, Bacillus sp., Lactococcuslactis*	Himachal Pradesh	Sharma *et al*. 2008; Sharma *et al*. 2013; Handa *et al*. 2012
Aakhone	*Soybean*	*B. subtilis, Proteus mirabilis*	Nagaland	Singh *et al*. 2014
Bekang	*Soybean*	*B. subtilis, B. brevis, B. circulans, B. coagulans, B. licheniformis, B. pumilus, B. sphaericus, Lysinibacillus fusiformis*	Mizoram	Chettri and Tamang, 2015
Hawaijar	*Soybean*	*B. subtilis, B. licheniformis, B. amyloliquefaciens, B.cereus, Staph. aureus, Staph. sciuri, Alkaligenessp., Providenciarettgers, Proteus mirabilis*	Manipur	Jeyaram *et al*. 2008; Singh *et al*. 2014
Kinema	*Soybean*	*B. subtilis, B. licheniformis, B. cereus, B. circulans, B. thuringiensis, B. sphaericus, Ent. faecium, Cand.parapsilosis, Geotrichumcandidum*	Sikkim, Darjeelinghills, Assam	Sarkar *et al*. 1994; Tamang, 2003
Peruyaan		*B. subtilis, B. amyloliquefaciens, Vagococcuslutrae, Ped. acidilactici, Ent. faecalis*	Arunachal Pradesh	Singh *et al*. 2014

Contd…

1	2	3	4	5
Tungrymbai		*B. subtilis, B. licheniformis, B. pumilus*	Meghalaya	Chettri and Tamang, 2015
Gundruk	Pickle	*L. spicheri, L. plantarum*	Sikkim	Gautam and Sharma, 2014
Dhulliachar	Pickle	*Lactobacillus bervis*	Sikkim	Gautam and Sharma, 2014
Nagari	Fermented fish	*Lactococcusplantarum and Lactobacillusplantarum, Bacillus subtilis, B.pumilus* and *Miocrococcus sp., Enterococcus faecium*	North-east India	Thapa *et al*. 2004
Hentak	Fermented Fish Paste	*Bacillus cereus, B. subtilis, Staphylococcusaureus, Enterococcus faecium, Candida sp.*	North-east India	Thapa *et al*. 2004
Tungtap	Fermented fish	*L. lactissubsp. cremoris, Lactococcusplantarum, E. faecium, Lactobacillus fructosus, L. amylophilus and L. corneformis*	Meghalaya	Thapa *et al*. 2004
Kargyong	Fermented Meat	*L. brevis, L. plantarum, L. carnis, Leu. mesenteroides*	North-east India	Rai *et al*. 2010
Humao	Rice, barks of wild plants	*P. pentosaceous B. polymyxa, B. licheniformis B. stearothermophilus*	Assam	Chakrabarty *et al*. 2014
Tuaithur	Bamboo shoot	*L. plantarum, L. brevis, P. pentosaceou, Lectococcuslactis Bacillus circulans, B. firmus, B. sphaericus, B. subtilis*	Assam	Chakrabarty *et al*. 2014
Tuairoi	Bamboo shoot	*L. plantarum, E. faecium, P. pentosaceous, L. mesenteroides B. laterosporus, B. circulans, B. stearothermophilus, B. firmus, B. cereus*	Assam	Chakrabarty *et al*. 2014

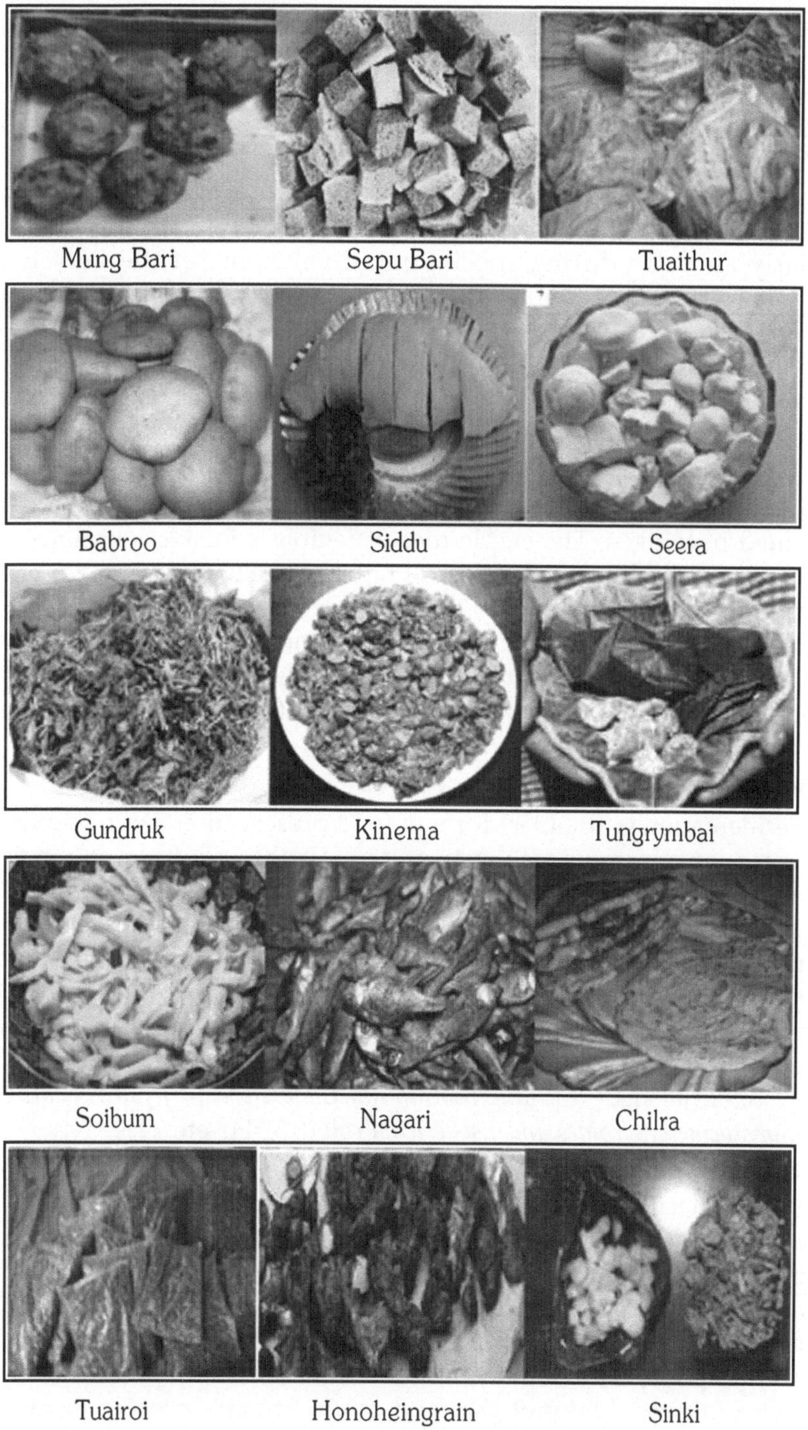

Fig 1.2: **Famous traditional fermented foods of India**

Traditional Fermented Beverages of India

India is a country of tradition. A number of traditional fermented non-alcoholic and alcoholic drinks are made here from the past many decades. Fermented non-alcoholic beverages are made from milk fermentation. A number of cereals (rice/barley), fruits (grapes/wild apricot/apple), jaggery and millet-based indigenously made fermented beverages are popular among the people of India. These fermented beverages are prepared and consumed regularly and also during special occasions. Some of the very common traditional fermented beverages are: *Sura, Chhang/Lugri, Daru/Chakti, Angoori/ Kinnauri, Chulli, Arak/Ara* and *Behmi, Haria,* Bhaatijaanr, Makai kojaanr, Gahoonkojaanr, Simaltarulkojaanr, Jaokojaanr, Faaparkojaanr, Poko, Raksi, Arak, Chyang (Kanwar *et al.* 2007). In the preparation of these fermented beverages (except *Sura*), an inoculum is used for their fermentation, but, *Sura*is a product made by natural fermentation (Thakur *et al.* 2004).

Ladakh region of Jammu and Kashmir is also well known for its fermented beverages. The staple diet of region is huskless barley, or grim, which is roasted and ground for use as flour for Tsampa (Tibetan) or namphey (Ladakh) or for making the local beer brew, Chhang. Paba, Tangthur, Zathuk, Nettle, Markhu are some other famour fermented food products of J&K. People in Ladakh believe that the great Tibetan yogi Milarepa survived while mediating in the mountains by eating Nettle (Zathuk) thus confirming its nutritional benefits (Angchok *et al.* 2009).

Fermented Foods and Bio-preservatives

Fermentation is an oldest form of food preservation. Fermentation leads to suppression of various pathogens and producing various compounds which lead in the increase in shelf life of food. The organoleptic and chemical changes which occur during fermentation like bacteriocin productions, low pH and organic acids production causing acidic environment by microflora helps in increase in shelf life. The recent increasing trend of consumption of pre-cooked food has led to food borne illness worldwide. The bacterial pathogens that account for many of these cases mainly include: *Listeria monocytogenes, Staphylococcus aureus, Clostridium botulinum, Campylobacter jejuni, Bacillus cereus, Leuconostocmesenteroides and Escherichia coli* 0157:H7 etc. (Fig. 1.4).

Until now, approaches to seek suppression of these pathogens have relied upon the search for more efficient chemical preservatives or on the application of more drastic physical treatments. Nevertheless, these types of preservatives have many drawbacks *viz;* the proven toxicity of commonest chemical preservatives, the alteration of the organoleptic and nutritional properties of foods, and especially recent consumer trends in purchasing and consumption, with demands for safe but minimally processed products without additives. Many of the food grade bacteria present in fermented food have the capability to produce proteinaceous compound - bacteriocin.

Table 1.3: Microflora associated with traditional fermented beverages of India

Beverage	Substrate	Starter	State	References
Bhaati Jaanr	Glutinous rice	*March (mixed culture of yeasts, filamentous molds, lactic acid bacteria)*	Eastern Himalayan regions of Nepal, India, and Bhutan	Tamangand Thapa, 2006
Chaang/Lugri, Daru, Angoori	Rice/wheat grains, grapes	*Lactobacillus plantarum, L. acidophilus, Leuconostoc, Bacillus sp., Lactococcuslactis, S. cerevisiae,*	Himachal Pradesh	Sharma and Sharma, 2014; Savitri and Bhalla, 2007; Handa and Sharma, 2012
Chuu	Milk		Bhutan	
Judima	Rice	*P. pentosaceous B. circulans, B. laterosporus, B. pumilus, B. firmus*	Assam	Chakrabarty *et al.* 2014
Sujen	Rice + husk + medicinal plants + charcoal	*Mod pitha (natural starter)*	Assam, India	Deori *et al.* 2007
Tai Ahom	Rice (Bora variety)	*Vekurpitha (yeast + leaves of some ethnomedicinal plants)*	Assam, India	Saikia *et al.* 2007
Apong (white)	Boiled rice	*Ipoh (yeast)*	Arunachal Pradesh, India	Tiwari and Mahanta, 2007
Ennog (black)	Boiled rice + burned rice husk	*Ipoh (yeast)*	Arunachal Pradesh, India	Tiwari and Mahanta, 2007
Zutho	Whole sprouted rice + unhulled sprouted rice	*Piazu*	Nagaland, India	Das *et al.* 2012
Haria	Boiled Rice	*Bakhar*	West Bengal and East-Central India	Ghosh *et al.* 2014
Churpa	Yak Milk	*L. plantarum, L. curvatus, L. fermentum, L. paracasei subsp. Pseudoplantarum, Leuconostocmesenteroides*	Himachal Pradesh	Tamang *et al.* 2009
Daru and Jann	Wheat	*S. cerevisiae, Candida famata, C. valida, Kluveromycesmaxianus, Saccharomycopsisfibuligera*	Himachal Pradesh	Thakur *et al.* 2004; Das and Pandey, 2007
Zathuk	Butter milk	*L. plantarum, L. curvatus, L. fermentum, L. paracasei subsp. Pseudoplantarum, Leuconostocmesenteroides*	Jammu and Kashmir	Angchok *et al.* 2009

Chhang Angoori Haria

Fig 1.3: **Traditonal fermented beverages of India**

These compounds have found to be an effective bio-preservative effect on processed foods as they have broad spectrum of antagonism against various foodborne pathogens (Fig. 1.5).

Today, bacteriocidal peptides or proteins produced by bacteria are typically referred to as bacteriocins. Usually, to demonstrate the proteinaceous nature of a newly characterized bacteriocin, sensitivity to proteolytic enzymes such as: trypsin, _chymotrypsin, and pepsin is an expected demonstration (Fig. 1.6). Evaluation for use as a food additive requires estimation of its heat resistance and pH given the widespread use of thermal processing in food production (Fig. 1.7 and 1.8).

Bacteriocins are classified into four main groups which include class I that contains Bacteriocin (Lantibiotics). These are small peptides that undergo extensive post translational modification to produce active peptide. *Nisin* the most studied bacteriocin belong to Class I bacteriocin which are active against broad spectrum of food spoilage and pathogenic bacteria including *L. monocytogenes* (Maisnier *et al.* 1992). Class II bacteriocins are heat stable, low molecular weight membrane active protein. Class II bacteriocin members are generally large heat labile proteins. Whereas, Class IV complex bacteriocin are placed that require non protein moieties for activity (Klaenhammer, 1993).

Nisin is a one of the bacteriocin which so far has commercially been used in bio-preservation of various milk products. It is a peptide composed of 34 amino acid residues, with a molecular mass of 3.5 kDa, and is classified as a class-Iabacteriocin or lantibiotic (Hurst, 1981). It is produced by strains of *Lactococcuslactis* subsp. *lactis* isolated from milk and vegetable-based products and its importance is due to its wide spectrum of activity against Gram-negative and Gram-positive bacteria. The use of nisin as a biopreservative has been widely investigated in a large variety of fresh and processed foods (Jung *et al.* 1992). Consequently, it was admitted into the European food additive list, where it was assigned the number E234 (EEC, 1983). Because it was thoroughly studied and formed part of the human diet, nisin was also approved by the Food and Drug Administration (1988)

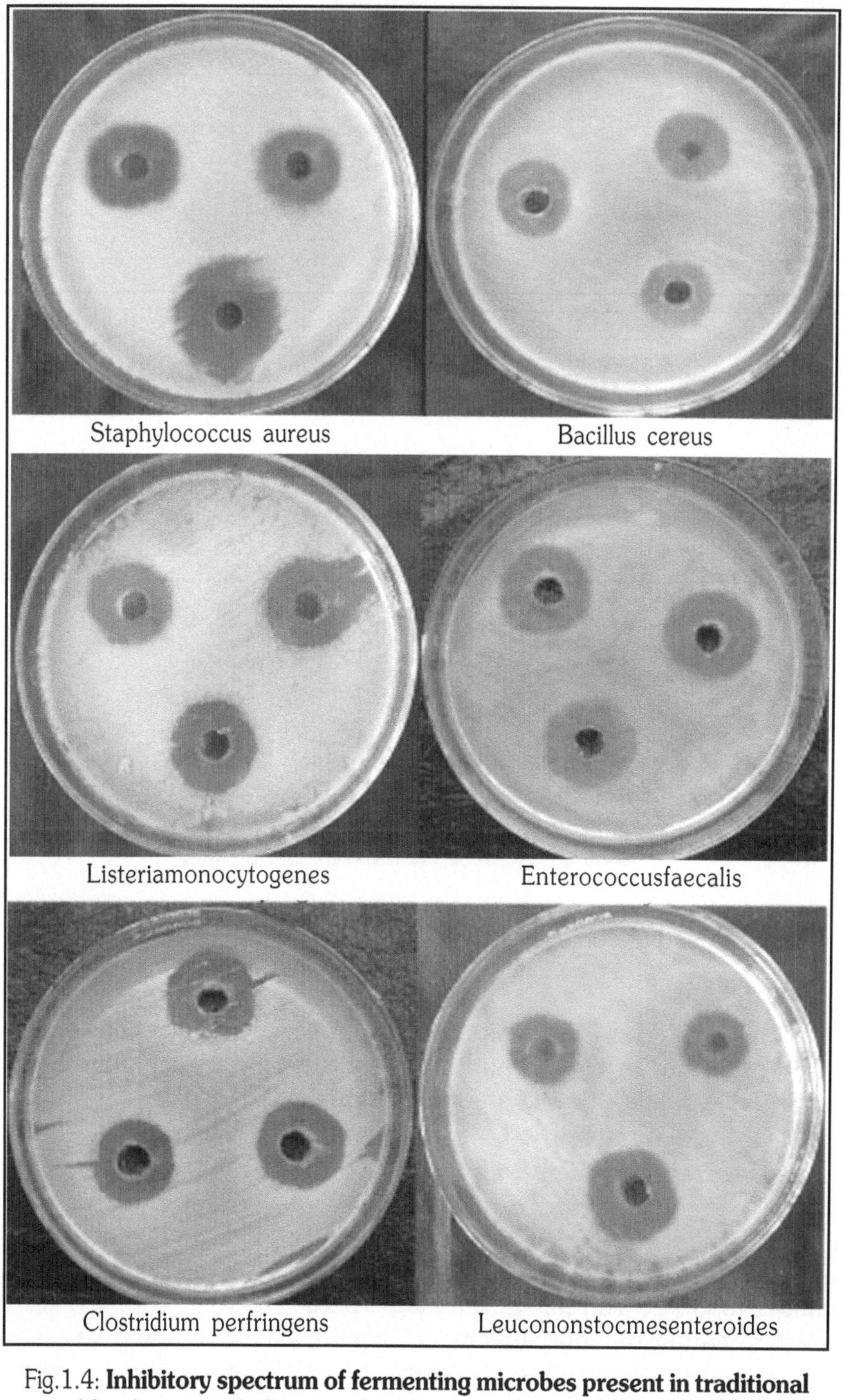

Fig.1.4: **Inhibitory spectrum of fermenting microbes present in traditional fermented food against challenging food borne pathogens by well diffusion method**

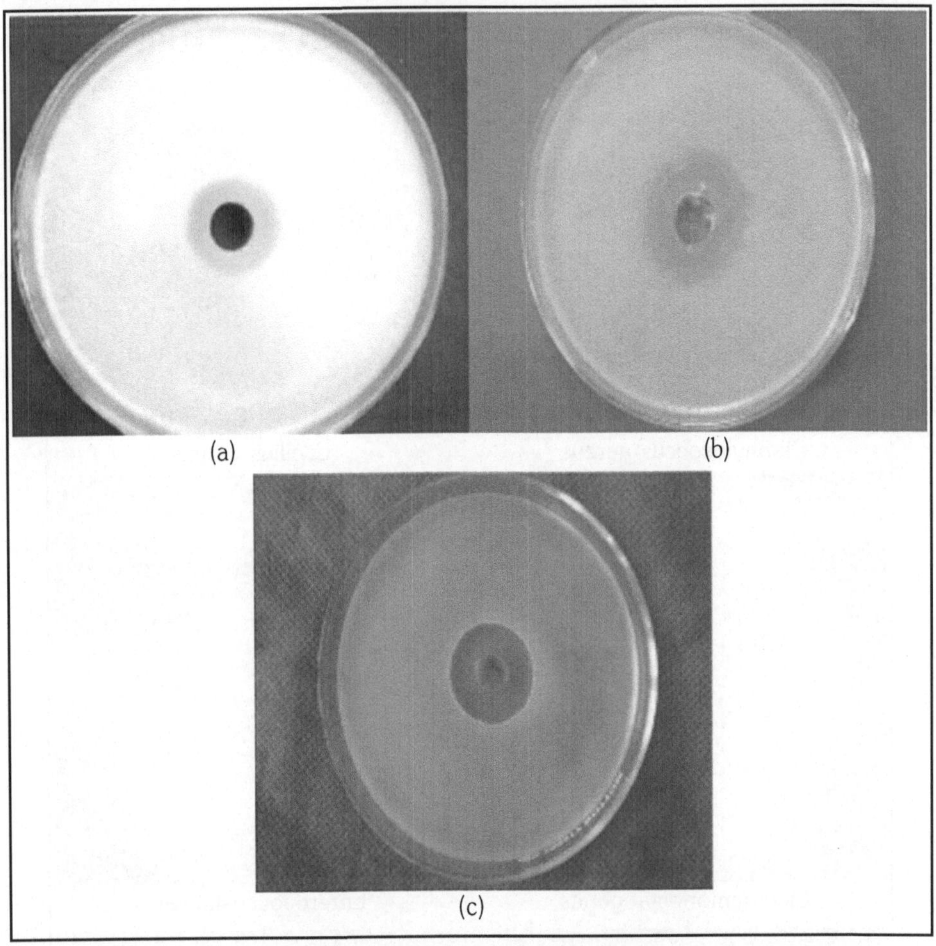

Fig.1.5: **Antimicrobial activity of bacteriocin (a) Lecticin (b) Bacicin (c) Brevicin against *L. monocytogenes***

in the USA as GRAS; to date, it is the only bacteriocin that has been approved by the World Health Organization for use as a food preservative and it is commercialized as a dried concentrated powder.

The use of natural preservative i.e. bacteriocins is becoming an efficient way of extending food safety without causing any health hazards and altering the nutritional quality of food products. Many successful experiments have been conducted in our research laboratory showing higher preservation qualities as compared to commercial chemical preservatives of bacteriocin mediated food *viz;* fruit juices, milk and cheese etc. (Fig. 1.10, 1.11 & 1.12). Many fermenting microorganisms *i.e.*, bacilli, LAB and some yeasts have been reported to produce broad spectrum bacteriocin to control food borne illness/pathogenicity.

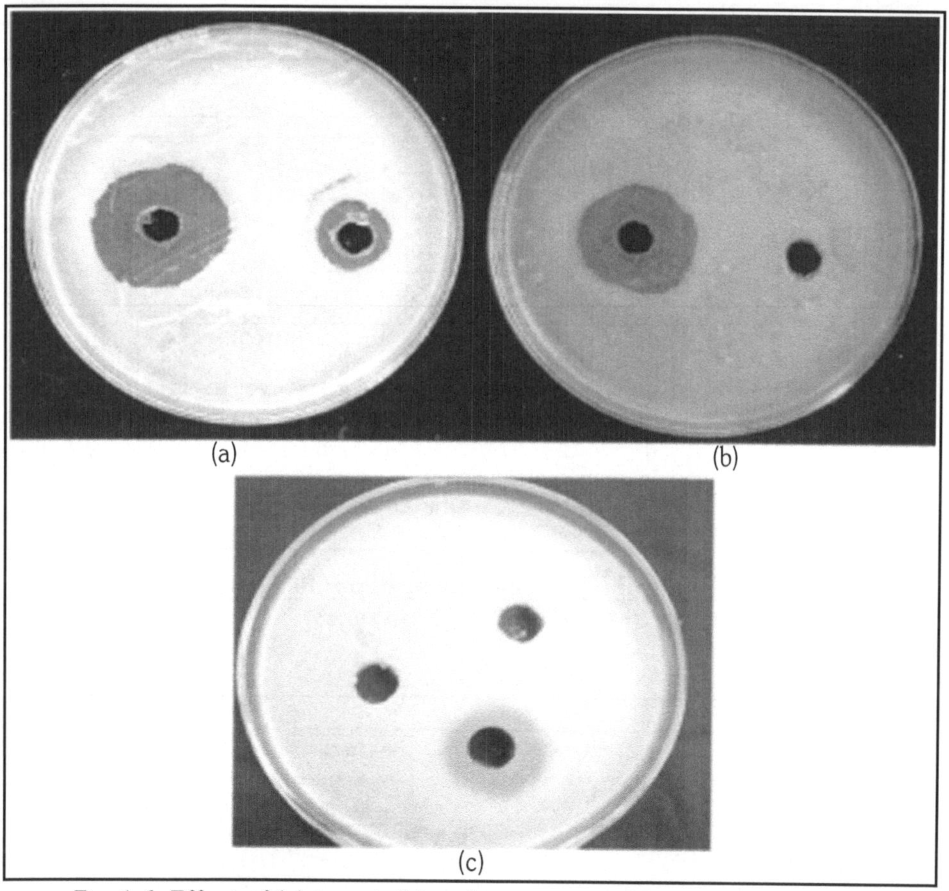

Fig. 1.6: **Effect of (a) trypsin(b) α chymotrypsin (c) papain on activity of Purified bacteriocinlecticin against *Staphylococcus aureus*.**

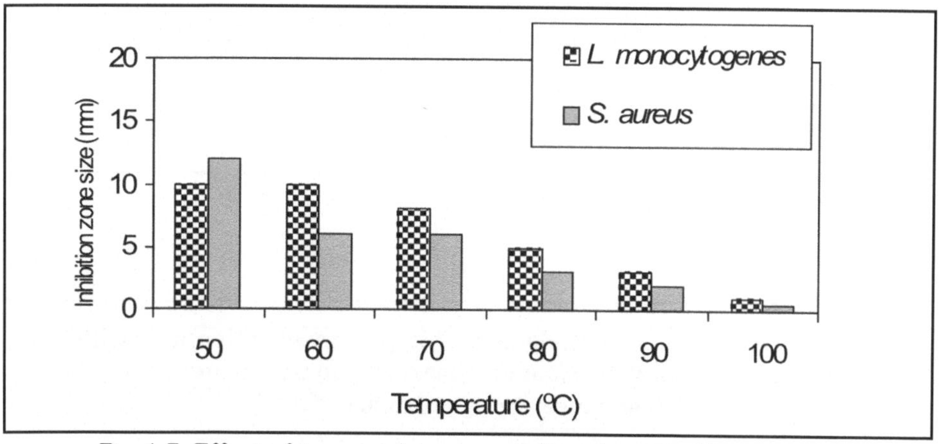

Fig. 1.7: **Effect of temperature on activity of purified bacteriocin (in terms of inhibition zones)**

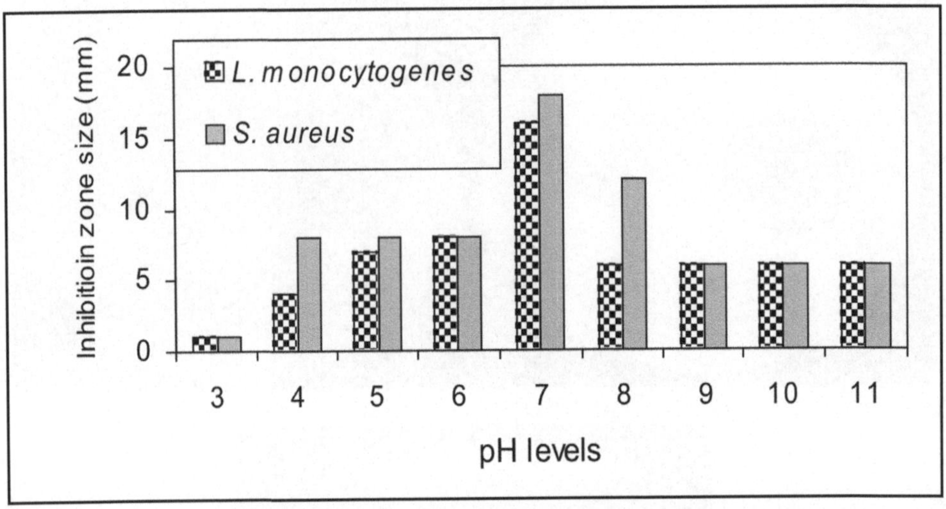

Fig. 1.8: **Effect of pH on the activity of purified bacteriocin (in terms of inhibition zones)**

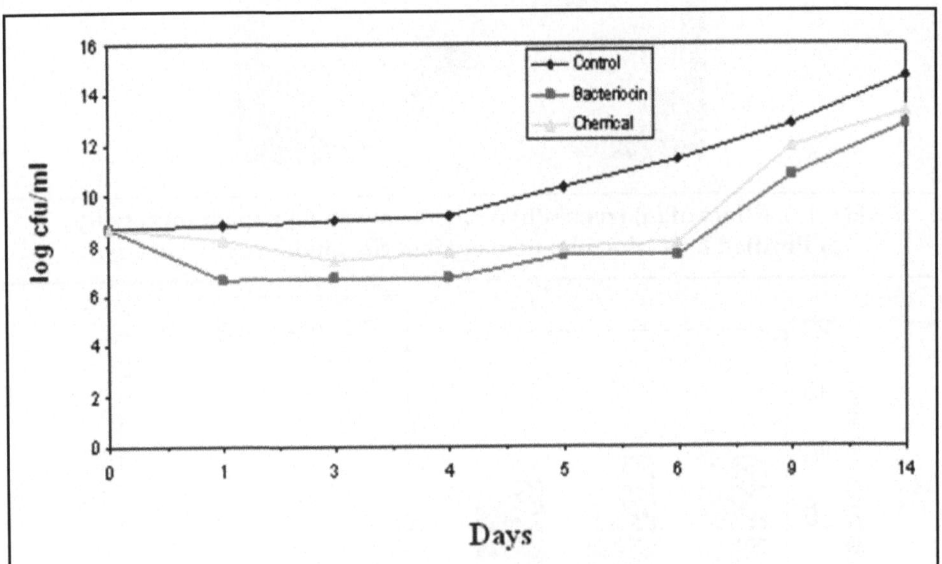

Fig.1.9: **A comparative study to use bio-preservative (*lenticin*) with chemical preservative (sodium benzoate) against *S. aureus* to enhance storage of milk (4°C)**

Fig. 1.10: **Effect of Brevicin inenhancing the shelf life of fruit juice**

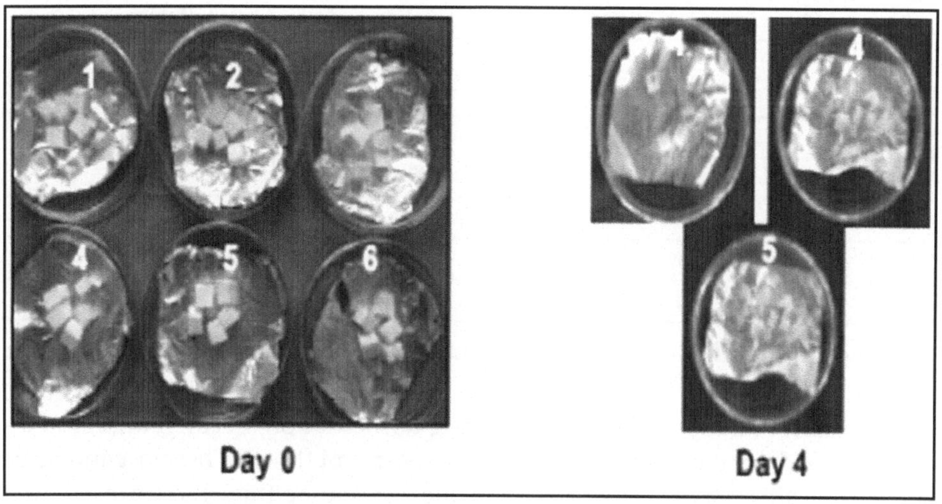

Fig.1.11: **Effect of partially purified bacteriocin and purified bacteriocin in cheese inoculated with *Listeriamonocytogens* at 4°C as compared to nisin, sodium banzoate and control**

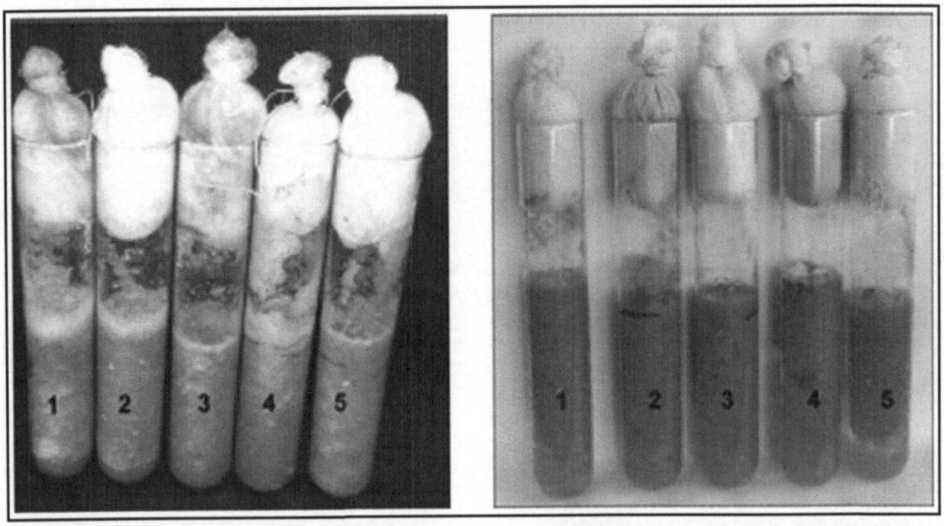

Fig.1.12: **Effect of partially purified bacteriocin and purified bacteriocin in tomato paste inoculated with *L. monocytogens* at 4°C as compared to nisin, sodium banzoate and control**

Table 1.4: Potential bacteriocinogenic bacteria from ethnic fermented foods and their sources

Producer Organism	Name of Bacteriocin	Source	Reference
B. lentus	Lanticin	Dough	Sharma *et al.* 2007; Sharma *et al.* 2006
L. brevis	Brevicin	Kandal Vari	Gautam and Sharma, 2009
Bacillus sp. A12	Bacicin A12	Whey	Sharma *et al.* 2011
B. subtilis	Subtilin R75	Mung Bari	Sharma and Gautam, 2007
B. mycoides	Mycosin	Whey	Sharma *et al.* 2009
Lactobacillus sp. A75	Lacticin A75	Dal Bari	Sharma *et al.* 2008

Traditional Health Benefits of Fermented Foods on the Indian Population

1. *Nutritional Enrichment*: Generally, a significant increase in the soluble fraction of a food is observed during fermentation. Fermentation makes the food palatable by enhancing its aroma and flavor. These organoleptic properties make fermented food more popular than the unfermented one in terms of consumer acceptance (Blandino *et al.* 2003). The quantity as well as quality of the food proteins as expressed by biological value, and often the content of water soluble vitamins is generally increased, while the antinutritional factors show a decline during fermentation (Paredes-López & Harry, 1988). Fermentation results in a lower

proportion of dry matter in the food and the concentrations of vitamins, minerals and protein appear to increase when measured on a dry weight basis (Adams, 1990). Single as well as mixed culture fermentation of pearl millet flour with yeast and *lactobacilli* significantly increased the total amount of soluble sugars, reducing and non-reducing sugar content, with a simultaneous decrease in its starch content (Khetarpauland Chauhan, 1990). Koozhu is included in the daily diet of rural and agricultural workers of Tamil Nadu and is claimed to be a nourishing health food (Antony and Chandra, 1997). There is an increase in thiamine, riboflavin and niacin contents during its fermentation (Aliya and Geervani, 1981; Rajyalakshmi and Geervani, 1990). Koozhu is given to children at weaning age (Mbithi-Munikya *et al.* 2002). Kodokojaanr, Bhati-Jannar, Zutho, is a famour traditional fermented beverage of north east India, due to its high calorie content, it is consumed by post-natal women to regain the strength (Tamang and Thapa, 2006). The fermenting microorganisms present it leads to the fermentation of grains and synthesize new vitamins which are not present in grains itself.

2. *Elimination of Anti Nutritional Factors:* Fermentation cause degradation of grain compounds, especially starch and soluble sugars by both grain and fermented media enzyme. Finger millet known as ragi in India a source of carbohydrate, protein and mineral that is comparing to other common cereal grain antinutrients like phytate and tannin reduce the nutrient bioavailability which can be improved by suitable processing methods such as: germination and fermentation. Combination of cooking and fermentation improved the nutrient quality of all tested sorghum seeds and reduced the content of antinutritional factors to a safe level in comparison with other methods of processing (Obizoba & Atii, 1991). Fermented cereal products are widely consumed in India and many countries of central and Southern Africa.
3. *Traditional Medicine*: Indian fermented foods are consumed by the local population not just as a diet but as traditional medicine too. Many of the foods were observed to have beneficial effect during ailment by the local people and they are used as a special diet or medicine for ages. Fermented food idli is easily digested and often used as food for infant and invalids. It is a prescribed diet in the hospitals for patients undergoing treatment (Steinkraus 1996). Fermented milk dahi can be used to cure intestinal disease such as: diarrhoea (Agarwal and Bhasin, 2002); intake of dahi has anti-cholesteremic (Sinha and Sinha, 2000), anticarcinogenic (Arvind *et al.* 2010), anti-diabetic (Yadav *et al.* 2007), angiotensin-converting enzyme inhibition effect (Harun-ur-Rashid *et al.* 2007) and anti-atopic dermatitis effect (Watanabe *et al.* 2009). Chass a

fermeted buttermilk of Gujarat helps in prevention of Diarrhoea. Various fermented foods of Himachal Pradesh like seera, jholangoori/lugri helps in health benefits. Seera is known to protect from various gynae ailments, jhol in digestion and angoori/lugri helps tribal people to survive in extreme cold climate. The above properties are validated by in vivo experiments. Certain fermented vegetable products (gundruk, sinki and iniziangsang) are said to be good appetizers, and the ethnic people use these foods for remedies from indigestion (Tamang and Tamang, 2009). Bhutia women use gundruk soup and give it to breast-feeding mothers to improve milk efficiency. It is considered as a tonic for old age people (Singh *et al.* 2007). Fermented radish root pieces are called sinki. It is very effective in curing diarrhoea and stomach pain, and is consumed mostly during lean period. Iromba is prepared from tree bean (*Perkiaroxburgii*) and is considered an appetizer (Singh *et al.* 2007b). Fermented rai helps in curing stomach pain and gas trouble, and significantly improves digestion (Singh *et al.* 2007).

Kanjika or kanji is a lactic fermented rice product of North East India. It has been prescribed for a number of chronic diseases by Indian ayurvedic practitioners (Reddy *et al.* 2007). Carrot Kanji is considered to have high nutritional value and cooling and soothing properties (Sura *et al.* 2001). Beetroot kanji is considered to have potential to prevent infection and malignant disease (Kingston *et al.* 2010). Fermented BS juice has preservation property similar to vinegar. Meat, fish or vegetables are cooked with it to have longer shelf-life (Mao and Odyuo, 2007). Handua or Kardi is used as medicine against any digestive problems, particularly against constipation in North East states of India. The Meitei community in Northeastern India use fermented Soibum along with fermented fish against the plague disease (Singh *et al.* 2007). Ngari-dry fish of Puntus breed Phutunis or Eromusdandricus is mixed with Iromba (fermented Soibum) and this dish called Yongchak. Iromba is considered as an appetizer and is well known to the old age women of the Meitei community (Singh *et al.* 2007). Hentak is consumed as curry as well as condiment with boiled rice. Sometimes, it is given to the mothers during confinement and patients during convalescence (Sarojnalini and Singh, 1988).

Paba, Tangthur, Zathuk, Nettle, Markhu are some other famour fermented food products of J&K. People in Ladakh believe that the great Tibetan yogi Milarepa survived while mediating in the mountains by eating Nettle (Zathuk) thus confirming its nutritional benefits (Angchok *et al.* 2009).

4. *Fermenting Microflora as Source of Probiotics*: Fermented food is having beneficial fermenting microorganisms which act as good probiotics once the food is being consumed in terms imparting many additional health benefits. Microflora associated with the fermented foods has been found

to possess probiotic properties and help to fight various diseases. Generally fermented foods contain Lactic acid bacteria and yeast which have been used as a probiotics from last many years. Probiotics are beneficial microorganisms which when consumed gave beneficial health nutritive and disease fighting effect. Lactic acid bacteria are a major probiotic recommended till today. Various fermented foods like: Seera, Malera, bhaturu, Chilra, gundruk, selroti, dhulliachar etc., contains beneficial microflora which not only add taste after fermentation but also exert probiotic effects after consumption to the folks of India. These microflora help in fighting various diseases like: Diarrhoea, Cancer, chronic disorders, hypersensitivity, obesity etc. Various commercially applied probiotic microbes are enlisted in Table 1.5 and therapeutic properties of probiotic bacteria are enlisted in Table 1.6.

Table 1.5: Microorganisms added in probiotic products

Lactobacillus Species	*Bifidobacterium* Species	Others	References
L. acidophilus *L. casei* *L. delbrueckii* subsp. *bulgaricus* *L. plantarum* *L. salivarus* *L. johnsonii* *L. plantarum* *L. fermentum* *L. spicheri*	*B. bifidum* *B. animalis* *B. breve* *B. infantis* *B. longum* *B. lactis*	*Enterococcus faecalis* *Enterococcus faecium* *Streptococcus salivarus* subsp. *thermophilus* *Lactococcuslactis* subsp. *lactis* *Lactococcuslactis* subsp. *cremoris* *Pediococcusacidilactici* *Saccharomyces boulardii*	Sharma, (2014); Gautam and Sharma, (2012); Gautam and Sharma, (2013), Gautam *et al.* (2012); Handa, (2012); Kore *et al.* (2012); Kanwar *et al.* (2011)

Conclusion

The knowledge of traditional foods harboured by the tribal communities is rich in terms of its capacity cure diseases. Fermented foods are encountered worldwide and their origin is due to their prolonged shelf life (through lactic acid, alcohol, acetic acid and alkaline fermentations), reduced volume, shorter cooking times and superior nutritive value as compared to the non-fermented ingredients, biological enrichment of food substrates with protein, essential amino acids, essential fatty acids, and vitamins and elimination of anti-nutrients. Fermented foods have and enhance the flavor and aroma of food. The process also increases digestibility and exert health promoting benefits. Fermentation may assist in the destruction or detoxification of certain undesirable compounds which may be present in raw foods. Other health benefits include cholesterol control, anti-cancer effects, immunity, longevity, anti-hypertensive effect, and anti-diabetic effect. This information behoves us to turn back to the traditional ways in preparing our daily food menu; to consume more fermented foods and not rely as heavily on refrigeration and

Table 1.6: Various special therapeutic/prophylactic properties of specific probiotics (Parvez *et al.* 2006)

Microflora	Associated Actions	Reference
Bifidobacteria species	Reduced incidence of neonatal necrotizing enterocolitis	Caplan and Jilling (2000)
Enterococcus faecium	Decreased duration of acute diarrhoea from gastroenteritis	Marteau *et al.* (2001)
Lactobacillus strains	Administration of multiple organisms, predominantly Lactobacillus strains shown to be effective in ameliorating pouchitis Lactose digestion improved, decreased diarrhoea and symptoms of intolerance in lactose intolerant individuals, children with diarrhoea, and in individuals with short-bowel syndrome Microbial interference therapy – the use of non-pathogenic bacteria to eliminate pathogens and as an adjunct to antibiotics Improved mucosal immune function, mucin secretion and prevention of disease	Vanderhoof (2000) Marteau *et al.* (2001) Bengmark (2000)
Lactobacillus acidophilus	Significant decrease of diarrhoea in patients receiving pelvic irradiation Decreased polyps, adenomas and colon cancer in experimental animals Prevented urogenital infection with subsequent exposure to three ropathogens Escherichia coli, Klebsiellapneumoniae, Pseudomonas aeruginosa. Lowered serum cholesterol levels	Marteau *et al.* (2001) Gorbach *et al.* (1987) Sanders and Klaenhammer (2001) Ouwehand *et al.* (2002)
Lactobacillus plantarum	Reduced incidence of diarrhoea in daycare centres when administered to only half of the children Especially effective in reducing inflammation in inflammatory bowel; *e.g.*, enterocolitis in rats, small bowel bacterial over-growth in children, pouchitis. Reduced pain and constipation of irritable bowel syndrome. Reduced bloating, flatulence, and pain in irritable bowel syndrome in controlled trial. Positive effect on immunity in HIV+ children	Vanderhoof (2000) Schultz and Sartor (2000); Vanderhoof (2000) Vanderhoof (2000) Nobaek *et al.* (2000) Walker (2000)
Lactobacillus reuteri	Shortened the duration of acute gastroenteritis Shortened acute diarrhoea.	Marteau *et al.* (2001) Shornikova *et al.* (1997a,1997b)
Lactobacillus rhamnosus	Enhanced cellular immunity in healthy adults in controlled trial.	Tomioka *et al.* (1992)
Lactobacillus salivarius	Suppressed and eradicated Helicobacter pylori in tissue cultures and animal models by lactic acid secretion.	Aiba *et al.* (1998)
Bacteroides species	Chronic colitis, gastritis, arthritis (increased bacterial urease activity in chronic juvenile arthritis).	Vanderhoof (2000)
Saccharomyces boulardii (yeast)	Reduced recurrence of Clostridium difficile diarrhoea Effects on C. difficile and Klebsiellaoxytoca resulted in decreased risk and/or shortened duration of antibiotic-associated diarrhoea Shortened the duration of acute gastroenteritis. Decreased only functional diarrhoea, but not any other symptoms of irritable bowel syndrome.	Pochapin (2000) Marteau *et al.* (2001) Marteau *et al.* (2001) Marteau *et al.* (2001)

freezing of our food supply as a means of preserving food. Mankind has been eating fermented food for millennia; it's time to get back to practicing the same healthy ways of preparing family foods.

REFERENCES

Adams, M. R. (1990). Topical Aspects of Fermented Foods. Trends in Food Science and Technology 1: 141-144.

Aguirre, M. and Collins, M. D. (1993). Lactic acid Bacteria and Human Clinical Infection. *Journal of Applied Bacteriology*, 75: 95-107.

Aiba, Y. Suzuki, N. Kabir, A. M. Takagi, A. and Koga, Y. (1998). Lactic Acid-mediated Suppression of Helicobacter pylori by the oral Administration of Lactobacillus salivarius as a probiotic in a gnotobiotic murine model. *American Journal of Gastroenterology*, 93: 2097-2101.

Aidoo, K. E. Rob, N. M. J. and Sarkar, P. K. (2006). Occurrence and Function of yeasts in Asian Indigenous Fermented Foods, *FEMS Yeast Research*, 6 (1): 30-39.

Aliya, S. and Geervani, P. (1981). An Assessment of the Protein Quality and Vitamin B Content of Commonly used Fermented Products of Legumes and Millets. *Journal of Science and Food Agriculture*, 32: 837-842.

Angchok, D. Dwivedi, S. K. and Ahmed, Z. (2009). Traditional Foods and beverages of Ladakh. *Indian Journal of Traditional Knowledge*, 8(4): 551-558.

Antony, U. and Chandra T. S. (1997). Microbial Population and Biochemical changes in Fermenting Finger millet (Eleusinecoracana). *World Journal of Microbiology and Biotechnology*, 13: 533-537.

Arvind, K. Nikhlesh, K.S. Pushpalata, R.S. (2010). Inhibition of 1,2-dimethylhydrazine induced colon genotoxicity in rats by the administration of probiotic curd. *Molecular Biology Research*, 37:1373-1376.

Battcock, M. and Ali-Azam, S. (1998). Fermented Fruits and Vegetables. A Global Perspective, Bulle-tinof FAO Agricultural Services for United Nations, Rome.

Bengmark, S. (2000). Colonic Food: Pre- and probiotics. *American Journal of Gastroenterology*, 95: S5-S7.

Blandino, A. Al-Aseeri, M. E. Pandiella, S. S. Cantero, D. and Webb, C. (2003). Cereal-based Fermented Foods and Beverages. *Food Research International*. 36(6):527-543.

Borgstrom, G. (1968). Principals of Food Science, *Food Microbiology and Biochemistry*, (Macmallin, New York).

Campbell-Platt, G. (1987). Fermented Foods of the World - A Dictionary and Guide. London, Butterworths.

Caplan, M. S. and Jilling, T. (2000). Neonatal necrotizing enterocolitis: Possible Role of Probiotic Supplementation. *Journal of Paediatrics and Gastroenterology Nutrition*, 30: S18-S22.

Chakrabarty, J. Sharma, G. D. and Tmang, J. P. (2014). Traditional Technology and Product Characterization of some Lesser-Known Ethnic Fermented Foods and Beverages of North Cachar Hills District of Assam. *Indian Journal of Traditional Knowledge*, 13(4): 706-715.

Chettri, R. (2011). Microbiological Evaluation of Turangbai and Bekang, Ethnic Fermented Soybean Foods of North East India, PhD. Thesis, Food Microbiology Laboratory, Sikkim Government College, Gangtok, (North Bengal University).

Deori, C. Begum, S. S. and Mao, A. A. (2007). Ethnobotany of Sujen - A Local Rice beer of Deori Tribe of Assam. *Indian Journal of Traditional knowledge*, 6(1): 121-125.

European Economic Community. (1983). EEC Commission Directive 83/463/EEC.

Gautam, N. and Sharma, N. (2009). Purification and Characterization of Purified Bacteriocin of *Lactobacillus brevis* isolated from Traditional Fermented food of H.P. *Indian Journal of Biochemistry and Biophysics*, 46: 337-341.

Gautam, N. Sharma, N. and Ahlawat, O. P. (2013). Purification and Characterization of Bacteriocin Produced by *Lactobacillus brevis* UN isolated from Dhulliachar: A Traditional Food Product of North East India. *Indian Journal of Microbiology*, 54(2): 185-189.

Gautam, N. Sharma, N. and Ahlawat, O. P. (2013). Purification and Characterization of Bacteriocin Produced by *Lactobacillus brevis* UN isolated from Dhulliachar: A Traditional Food Product of North East India. *Indian Journal of Microbiology*, 54(2): 185-189.

Gorbach, S.L. Chang, T.W. and Goldin, B. (1987). Successful Treatment of Relapsing Clostridium Difficile colitis with Lactobacillus GG. Lancet, 2: 1519.

Gosh, K. Maity, C. Adak, A. Halder, S. K. and Jana, A. (2014). Ethnic Preparation of a Rice based Fermented Beverage Haria in Province of lateritic West, Bengal, India, Ethnobotany Research Applications, 12.

Handa. S. (2012). Isolation of Lactic Acid Bacteria and to Study its Potential as probiotics. M. Sc. Thesis, UHF, Nauni, 315 p.

Harun-ur-Rashid, M. Togo, K. Useda, M. Miyamoto, T. (2007). Probiotic Characteristics of Lactic Acid Bacteria Isolated from Traditional Fermented milk 'Dahi' in Bangladesh. *Pakistan Journal of Nutrition*, 6: 647-652.

Hurst, A. (1981). Nisin. In D. Perlman, and A. I. Laskin (Eds.), Advances in Applied Microbiology. Academic Press, New York, USA. pp. 85-123.

Jeyaram, Mohendro, Singh, K. Premarani, W. Ranjita, T. Devi, A. Selina Chanu, K. Talukdar, N.C. and Rohinikumar, S.M. (2008). Molecular identification of dominant microflor aassociated with Hawaijar – A Traditional Fermented Soybean (*Glycinemax* (L.) Food of Manipur, India. *International Journal of Food Microbiology*, 122: 259-268.

Joerger, M.C. and Klaenhammer, T. R. (1986). Characterization and Purification of Helveticin J and Evidence for a chromosomally determined bacteriocin produced by *Lactobacillus helveticus* 481. *Journal of Bacteriology*, 167: 439-46.

Jung, D.S. Bodyfelt, F. W. and Daeschel, M. A. (1992). Influence of fat and emulsifiers on the Efficacy of nisin in inhibiting Listeria monocytogenes in fluid milk. *Journal of Dairy Science*, 75: 387-393.

Kanwar, S.S. Gupta, M.K. Katoch, C. Kumar, R. and Kanwar, P. (2007). Traditional Fermented Foods of Lahaul and Spiti area of Himachal Pradesh. *Indian Journal of Traditional knowledge*, 6 (1): 42-45.

Kanwar, S.S. Gupta, M.K. Katoch, C. Kumar, R. and Kanwar, P. (2007). Traditional Fermented Foods of Lahaul and Spiti area of Himachal Pradesh. *Indian Journal of Traditional knowledge*, 6 (1): 42-45.

Kanwar, S.S. Gupta, M. K. Chhaya, Katoch. and Kanwar, P. (2011). Cereal based Traditional alcoholic beverages of Lahaul and Spiti area of Himachal Pradesh. *Indian Journal of Traditional Knowledge*, 10(2): 251-257.

Khetarpaul, N. and Chauhan, B. M. (1990). Fermentation of pearl millet flour with yeasts and lactobacilli: in vitro digestibility and utilisation of fermented flour for weaning mixtures. *Plant Foods for Human Nutrition*, 40: 167-173.

Kingston, J.J. Radhika, M. Roshini, P.T. Raksha, M.A. Murali, H. S. and Batra, H. V. (2010). Molecular Characterization of Lactic Acid Bacteria Recovered from Natural Fermentation of beet root and carrot Kanji. *Indian Journal of Microbiology*, 50: 292-298.

Klaenhammer, T.R. (1993). Genetics of Bacteriocin Produced by Lactic acid Bacteria. FEMS *Microbiological Review*, 12 : 39-86.

Kore, K.B. Pattanaik, A.K. Sharma, K. and Mirajkar, P.P. (2012). Effect of Feeding Traditionally Prepared Fermented milk dahi (curd) as a probiotics on nutritional status, hindgut health and haematology in dogs. *Indian Journal of Traditional Knowledge*, 11(1): 34-39.

Mao, A. A. and Odyuo, N. (2007). Traditional Fermented Foods of the Naga Tribes of Northeastern India. *Indian Journal of Traditional Knowledge*, 6(1): 37-41.

Maisnier, P.S. Deschamps, N. Tatini, S. R. and Richard, J. (1992). Inhibition of *Listeria monocytogenes* in commembert cheese made with a nisin producing starter. Lait, 72: 249-263.

Marteau, P. de Vrese, M. Cellier, C. J. and Schrezenmeir, J. (2000). Protection from gastrointestinal diseases with the use of probiotics. *American Journal Clinical Nutrition*, 73: 430S-436S.

Mbithi-Mwikya, S. Camp, J. V. Mamiro, P. R. S. Ooghe, W. Kolsteren, P. Huyghebaert, A. (2002). Evaluation of the Nutritional Characteristics of a Finger Millet based Complementary Food. *Journal of Agriculture and Food Chemistry*, 50: 3030-3036.

Nobaek, S. Johansson, M. L. and Molin, G. (2000). Alteration of Intestinal Microflora is Associated with Reduction in Abdominal Bloating and Pain in Patients with Irritable bowel syndrome. *American Journal of Gastroenterology*, 95: 1231-1238.

Obizoba, I. C. and Atii, J. V. (1991). Effect of Soaking, Sprouting, Fermentation and Cooking on Nutrient Composition and some Anti-nutritional Factors of sorghum (Guinesia) seeds. Plant Foods for Human Nutrition, 41: 203-212.

Ouwehand, A. C. Salminen, S. and Isolauri, E. (2002). Probiotics: An Overview of Beneficial Effects. Antonie Van Leeuwenhoek, 82: 279-289.

Paredes-López, O. and Harry, G. I. (1988). Food Biotechnology Review: Traditional Solid-state Fermentations of Plant Raw materials – Application, Nutritional Significance and Future Prospects. *Critical Reviews in Food Science and Nutrition*, 27: 159-187.

Pochapin, M. (2000). The Effect of probiotics on Clostridium Difficile Diarrhea. *American Journal Gastroenterology*, 95: S11-S13.

Rai, A. K, Tamang, J. P. and Palani, U. (2010). Microbiological Studies of Ethnic Meat Products of the Eastern Himalyas. *Meat Science* 85: 560-567.

Rajyalakshmi, P. and Geervani, P. (1990). Studies on Tribal Foods of South India: Effect of Processing Methods on the Vitamin and in-vitro Protein digestibility of cereals, millets and legumes. *Journal of Food Science and Technology*, 27: 260-263.

Reddy, K.B. P.K. Raghavendra, P. Kumar, B.G. Misra, M.C. and Prapulla, S.G. (2007). Screening of probiotic properties of lactic acid bacteria isolated from Kanjika, an ayruvedic lactic acid fermented product: an in-vitro evaluation. *Journal of Genetics and Applied Microbiology*, 53: 207-213.

Saikia, Tag, B. H. and Das, A.K. (2007). Ethnobotany of Foods and Beverages among the Rural Farmers of Tai Ahom of North Lakhimpur District, Asom. *Indian Journal of Traditional Knowledge*, 6:126 132.

Sanders, M.E. and Klaenhammer, T.R. (2001). Invited Review: The Scientific basis of Lactobacillus acidophilus NCFM Functionality as a Probiotic. *Journal of Dairy Science*, 84: 319-331.

Sarojnalini, C. and Singh, W. V. (1988). Composition and Digestibility of Fermented Fish Foods of Manipur. *Journal of Food Science and Technology*, 25: 349-351.

Savitri, and Bhalla, T. C. (2007). Traditional Foods and Beverages of Himachal Pradesh. *Indian Journal of Traditional Knowledge*, 6 (1): 17-24.

Schultz, M. and Sartor, R. B. (2000). Probiotics and Inflammatory bowel Diseases. *American Journal Gastroenterology*, 95: 19S-21S.

Sekar, S. and Mariappan S. (2007). Traditionally Fermented Biomedicines, Arishtas and asavas from Ayurveda. *Indian Journal of Traditional knowledge*, 7(4): 548-556.

Sharma, R. (2014). Isolation and Screening of Potential Microorganisms from Traditional Fermented Foods and to Study their Probiotic Attributes, M. Sc. Thesis, UHF, Nauni, 417 p.

Sharma, N. and Gautam, N. (2007). Use of Bacteriocin as Potential Bio-preservative in Milk, Cheese and Apple Juice. *Beverages and Food World*, 34: 44-47.

Sharma, N. Attri, A. Gautam, N. and Gupta, R. K. (2012). Role of Lenticin – A Bacteriocin as Bio-preservative in Different Food Products to Enhance their Safety. *Beverages and Food World*, 39(2): 23-27.

Sharma, N. Gautam, N. and Sharma, H. K. (2009). Bacteriocin: Food Preservative. *Food Science and Technology*, 137-167.

Sharma, N. Handa, S. and Gupta, A. (2013). A Comprehensive Study of Different Traditional Fermented Foods/Beverages of Himachal Pradesh to Evaluate their Nutrition Impact on Health and Rich Biodiversity of Fermenting Microorganisms. *International Journal of Research in Applied, Natural and Social Sciences*, 1(3): 19-28.

Sharma, N. Kapoor, G. and Neopaney, B. (2006). Characterization of a New Bacteriocin Produced from A Novel Isolated Strain of *Bacillus lentus* NG121. Antonie Van Leeuwenhoek, 89: 337-343.

Sharma, N. Kapoor, R. Gautam, N. and Neopaney, B. (2008). Purification and Characterization of Natural Food Bio-preservative Produced from *Lactobacillus* sp. A75 isolated from Traditional Fermented Food of India, Presented in Natural Product Discovery and Production, Whistler BC Canada.

Sharma, N. Kapoor, R. Gautam, N. and Kumari, R. (2011). Purification and Characterization of Bacteriocin Produced by *Lactobacillus* sp. A75 isolated from Fermented chunks of *Phaseolus radiate*. *Food Technology and Biotechnology*, 49(2), 169-176.

Shornikova, A.V. Casas, I.A. and Isolauri, E. (1997). Lactobacillus reuteri as a therapeutic agent in acute Diarrhea in Young Children. *Journal of Paediatrics Gastroenterology Nutrition*, 24: 399-404.

Singh, A. Singh, R.K. and Sureja, A.K. (2007). Cultural Significance and Diversities of Ethnic Foods of Northeast India. *Indian Journal of Traditional Knowledge*, 6(1):79-94.

Sinha, P.R. and Sinha, R.N. (2000). Importance of Good Quality dahi in Food. *Indian Dairyman* 52:45-47.

Soni S.K. and Sandhu, D.K. (1989). Biochemical and Nutritional changes Associate with Indian Punjabi warri fermentation. *Journal of Food Science and Technology*, 27: 82.

Steinkraus, K.H. (1996). Handbook of Indigenous Fermented Food, 2nd edn. New York: Marcel Dekker.

Sura, K. Garg, S. and Garg, F. C. (2001). Microbiological and Biochemical Changes during Fermentation of Kanji. *Journal of Food Science and Technology*, 38: 165-167.

Tamang, B. and Tamang, J. P. (2009). Traditional Knowledge of Bio-preservation of Perishable Vegetable and Bamboo Shoots in Northeast India as food Resources. *Indian Journal of Traditional Knowledge*, 8 (1): 89-95.

Tamang, B. and Tamang, J. P. (2009). Traditional Knowledge of Bio-preservation of Perishable Vegetables and Bamboo Shoots in Northeast India as food Resources. *Indian Journal of Traditional Knowledge*, 8(1): 89-95.

Tamang, B. and Tamang J.P. (2011). Lactic Acid Bacteria Isolated fromindigenous fermented bamboo Products of Arunachal Pradesh in India and their Functionality, *Food Biotechnology*, 23: 133-147.

Tamang, J. P. and Thapa, S. (2006). Fermentation Dynamics during Production of Bhatijaanr, A Traditional fermented Rice Beverage of the Eastern Himalyas. *Food Biotechnology*, 20(3): 251-261.

Tamang, J.P. Tamang, N. Thapa, S. Dewan, S. Tamang, B. Yonzan, H. Rai, A.K. Chettri, R. Chakrabarty, A. and Kharel, N. (2012). Microorganisms and Nutritional value of Ethnic fermented Foods and Alcoholic Beverages of North East India. *Indian Journal of Traditional Knowledge*, 11 (1): 7-25.

Thakur, N. Savitri, and Bhalla, T.C. (2004). Characterization of some Traditional Fermented Foods and Beverages of Himachal Pradesh. *Indian Journal of Traditional Knowledge*, 3: 325-335.

Thapa, N. Pal, J. and Tamang, J. P. (2004). Microbial Diversity in ngari, hentak and tungtap, fermented fish products of northeast India. *World Journal of Microbiology and Biotechnology*, 20(6): 599-607.

Tiwari, S.C. and Mahanta, D. (2007). Ethonological Observations on fermented food Products of Certain Tribes of Arunachal Pradesh, *Indian Journal of Traditional Knowledge* 6:126 132. 6(1), 106-110.

Tomioka, H. Tomioka, K. Sato, K. and Saito, H. (1992). The Protective Activity of immune stimulants against Listeria monocytogenes infection in mice. *Journal of Medical Microbiology*, 36: 112-116.

Vanderhoof, J. A. (2000). Probiotics and Intestinal inflammatory Disorders in Infants and Children. *Journal of Paediatrics and Gastroenterology Nutrition*, 30: S34-S38.

Vaughan, E.E. Daly, C. and Fitzgerald, G.F. (1992). Identification and Characterization of Helveticin V-1829, A Bacteriocin Produced by *Lactobacillus helveticus*1829. *Journal of Applied Bacteriology*, 73: 299-308.

Walker, W.A. (2000). Role of Nutrients and Bacterial Colonization in the Development of Intestinal Host Defense. *Journal of Paediatrics and Gastroenterology Nutrition*, 30: S2-S7.

Watanabe, T. Hamada, K. Tategaki, A. Kishida, H. Tanaka, H. Kitano, M. (2009). Oral Administration of Lactic Acid Bacteria isolated from Traditional South Asian Fermented milk 'Dahi' inhibits the Development of Atopic Dermatitis in NC/Nga mice. *Journal of Nutrition Science and Vitaminology*, 55:271-278.

Wood, J. B (1998). Microbiology of Fermented Foods, (BlackieAcademic Press, Glesgow, UK).

Yadav, H. Jain, S. and Sinha, P. R. (2007). Antidiabetic Effect of Probiotic dahi containing *Lactobacillus acidophilus* and *Lactobacillus casei* in high fructose fed rats. Nutrition, 23:62-68.

Pages: 28-37

AGRO-BIODIVERSITY: *CONSERVATION AND SUSTAINABLE DEVELOPMENT*
Edited by: Dr. Pankaj Sharma; Dr. Narayan Singh & Dr. Pawan Kumar 'Bharti'
ISBN: 978-93-5056-782-1
Edition: 2016
Published by: Discovery Publishing House Pvt. Ltd., New Delhi (India)

Male *vs*. Female Food Pattern System of Male and Female Along an Altitudinal Gradient in Kuloor Watershed of Kumaun Himalaya, India

2

P.S. Bungla[1]; Lalit M. Tewari[1]*; Kamal Kishor[1]; Brij M. Upreti[1]; Mamta Bharti[1]; Neetu Bora[1]; R.S. Rawal[2] and I.D. Bhatt[2]

ABSTRACT

Food habit of people depends largely on availability of crops and available fertile lands in surroundings. Seasonality of agriculture production affects local food availability and consumption. In order to assess diversity in food systems between male and female genders in Kuloor watershed. Information was collected from selected 15 villages during July 2007 to February 2010 using structured questionnaire and informal interviews. The study reveals that the inhabitants of the watershed exhibit considerable diversity in food habits and consequent intake of nutrients. Patterns of gender nutritional intake, per meal basis, have been evaluated from villages of different altitudinal zones in Kuloor watershed.

Keywords: Kuloor watershed, food system, altitudinal gradient, female *vs* male

INTRODUCTION

It is stated that "Food is essential for the survival of the creatures. But the importance of the food is just not limited to the purpose of survival; it is also

1. Department of Botany, D.S.B. Campus, Kumaun University, Nainital - 263 002, Uttarakhand, India.
2. G.B. Pant Institute of Himalayan Environment and Development, Kosi-Katarmal, Almora - 263 643, Uttarakhand, India.

a source of pleasure, comfort and security. It has its value as a symbol of hospitality social status and also has a ritualistic significance. The selection of food to eat, the manner in which it is prepared and served and even the manner in which we eat are all the factors which are deeply influenced by our individual cultural heritage" (Shahnnaz, 1988). For instance, the superiority of diets of Northern India over those in the southern and eastern part of country are often referred (Stiebeling, 1939). To appreciate the importance of nutrition to human life, one needs to look back to get the proper perspective. While, human is the combined product of inheritance and environment (Stanley, 1939), nutrition affects humans health, ability to work, behaviour and the learning ability. The body requires food energy for resting metabolism, synthesis of body tissues, physical activity, and excretory processes and to maintain thermal balance. Food energy is supplied by the different nutrients in approximately the ratio of carbohydrate: fat: protein as 1:2.5:1 (Krammer, 1980).

The food habit of people depends largely on what they grow and raise in their surroundings. Seasonality of agriculture production affects local food availability and consumption. In many areas of Himalaya consumption of wild foods has been reported as a coping mechanism to address food shortage (Jenny and Egal, 2002)· An attempt has been made to measure the magnitude of mal nutritional chronic energy deficiency among the women samples (Pant, 2008).

Besides diversity of crops in agricultural systems, diversification of food recipes is a major specialty of Kumaun Himalaya. There are many recipes used as a substitute of the items, which are meagerly produced in the region. Traditional farming system, identification of wild plant species for their food importance, diversification of food items and value addition in local recipes are of paramount importance to secure the food availability in the region. Consequently local communities cultivate around 100 crop species and their numerous varieties and identified and equal number of wild plant species, which are also utilized as food (Mehta *et al*. 2010).

Investigation on the food system in Kumaun Himalaya started long back when detailed documentation of traditional foods of Kumaun was done (Atkinson, 1882). Similarly, some Kumauni food stuffs and their local name were described in the book Kumaun Ka Itihas (Pandey 1937). More recently, various types of traditional diets of Kumaun and their ingredients were described (Bhatt, 2008; ICMR, 2010).

Material and Methods

Study Areas

The study area, Kuloor watershed, forms a part of Sarju catchment in the western section of the middle Himalaya in Kumaun and ranges between an altitudes of 700-2361 m asl. Administratively, the Kuloor watershed includes part of Gangolihat and Berinag developmental blocks in district Pithoragarh and Kanda tehsil of Bageshwar district. The watershed broadly extends from Bansikhet (in West) to Dharichaura (in East) and from Baraun Malla (in North) to Neoliasera (in South) and lies between 79°46′-80°1′E longitudes and 29°30′-29°55′ N latitudes. The area covered by the watershed is approximately 228 km^2.

Diversity of Food Systems

In order to assess diversity in food systems in Kuloor watershed, information was collected from selected 15 villages situated at different altitudinal zones of watershed. For collection of information surveys were conducted during July 2007 to February 2010 using structured questionnaire and informal interviews. In each village, 5 households were randomly selected and each household both male as well as female was interviewed for their food systems. Among others, schedule caste (SC) and other backward classes (OBC) villages were also included in surveys to capture maximum diversity of food systems in the watershed.

The information on food system of each village was obtained in local units and subsequent by converted into standard units as 1 roti = 50 gm of wheat, 1 plate rice = 100 gm of rice. The nutritional value and composition of these items was taken from the health bulletin no. 23 in the form of energy, protein, fat, carbohydrate, minerals and vitamins (Gopalan *et al.* 1980). The value obtained for each item were summed and categorised into breakfast, lunch and dinner accordingly. Based on the information obtained for 5 samples in each village mean values per unit were calculated for the village. The cumulative value obtained for 5 persons were then calculated for each village. Data from villages were pooled for generating mean value for each of the altitude zone. Cumulative data of different altitudes were used for representing food system of the watershed. While describing per day nutritional intake, the mean value for one meal has been considered after pooling values for three meals in a day. However, comparison with national standards have been made on per day intake basis (*i.e.*, sum of intake through three meals).

Statistical Analysis

Analysis of variance and significant difference among means were tested as Fisher's Least Significance Differences (F-LSD) on mean values by one way ANOVA; using SPSS (version for window). Correlation coefficients (r) and co-efficients of determination were calculated using Microsoft Excel 2007. Statistical analysis of the data was performed using SPSS version 7.5.

Results and Discussions

The traditional food system of the Kuloor watershed is as diverse as its cropping diversity. While exploring this diversity is interesting it also imposes many challenges. The food systems in the study area vary amongst societal groups depending on the climate condition of the village location, economic status of a particular family, distance from main road, availability of market and access to modern amenities etc.

Food Consumption and Nutritional Intake

All the 15 villages fall within the altitudinal range of 700-2361 m asl. As for the diversity of the cropping systems and types, the inhabitants of the watershed exhibit considerable diversity in their food habits and types. This diversity usually follows diversity of traditional crops. In general, three meals – breakfast, lunch and dinner are common all through the watershed. Breakfast usually includes: milk, tea, paratha/roti and vegetable. Butter milk also forms a common ingredient of breakfast. During the lunch, rice forms the main food item along with many traditional food items such as: dubke, fana, dal (Lentil, Soyabean, Gahat, Urd etc.,) and vegetables (Pumpkin, torai, radish, pinalu, etc.). Dinner mostly includes: roti, beru roti, poori and vegetables. Curd, Ghee, Butter also form major constituents of dinner. Meat, Fish, Chicken and egg occasionally supplement the food mainly during dinner. Among others, few traditional foods such as: Madira ka bhat, Koni ki kheer, Bhat ki bhatwani and churkani, Gahat ki dal, Mandua ki roti and Gaderi ka sag are common in the watershed.

The mean nutritional intake through food (*i.e.,* per meal basis) was analyzed among the people of 15 villages of the study area using the Duncan multiple range test. Moisture content among the villagers ranged from 94.99±15.89 (Sukna) to 151.71±27.17g (Dharichaura). Protein content was ranging from 15.37±3.53g to 20.73±3.58g. The lowest protein intake was detected in the people of Sukna whereas the highest in Dharichaura. The fat intake across villages ranged from 3.30±0.84g (Rawatsera) to 6.27±1.80g (Gwasikot) while fiber content varied from 2.39±0.59g to 3.82±0.58g. It was found that the highest fiber content in food was present in Kimtola and the lowest in Nayal. Intake of carbohydrate content was significantly ($p<0.05$) higher in Dharichaura village (124.03±31.95) while minimum (68.86±8.40g) in Gwasikot. The calcium content in food across villages ranged from 0.17±0.04g to 0.63±0.34g, with lowest value for Pilkhi village and highest for Simalta. Intake of Phosphorus content was significantly higher in Gwasikot (1.00±0.66g) and minimum (0.27±0.06g) in case of Nayal and Rawatsera. The iron content in food across villages ranged from 5.87±1.44 mg (Nayal) to 32.98±12.60 mg (Kimtola). Total average calorie thus received through one meal by villagers in studied ranged from 383.93±52.55 Kcal to 459.80±43.18 Kcal. The minimum per meal calorie intake was recorded in Kimtola whereas maximum for Bayati. The carotene content of food varied from 92.15±27.40 mg to 556.87±376.89 mg. The maximum carotene was present in food of Bansikhet while minimum in case of Pilkhi. The highest (0.40±0.09 mg) thiamine content intake through food was for Dharichaura and the lowest (0.29±0.08 mg) for Rawatsera. The niacin content was recorded significantly ($p<0.05$) higher (5.63±1.99 mg) in the case of food consumed by people at Dharichaura and minimum (1.61±0.35 mg) in Rawatsera. Riboflavin content of food ranged between 0.19±0.04 mg (Nayal) to 0.26±0.04 mg (Dharichaura and Sartola). Ascorbic acid was recorded lowest (2.50±1.85 mg) in food takeb by Pilkhi villagers and highest (11.41±3.48 mg) in Dharichaura. In general, significant ($p<0.05$) variation was observed in case of per meal carbohydrate, phosphorus and niacin intake.

Food Structure Across Altitude Zones

Diet composition did not vary greatly among the altitudinal zone in the watershed *i.e.*, lower (<1000 m asl), middle (1000-2000 m asl) and high (>2000m asl). Duncan Multiple Range Test reveals a significantly ($p<0.05$) higher value of carbohydrate intake in low altitude villages as compared to middle and high altitude villages. The lowest per meal moisture content (128.96±9.06g) was found in upper altitude zone and highest (133.30±9.56g) in lower altitude zone. Protein intake varied from 16.58±1.62g (middle altitude) to 18.27±1.53g (higher altitude). The fat ranged from 4.59±0.64 g to 4.66±0.59g across altitude zones. Fiber content ranged from 4.59±0.30g to 4.87±0.68g and highest content was recorded at lower altitude zone was and lowest in case of villages of upper altitude zone. Carbohydrate content observed in all altitudes and ranged from 76.76±4.34g to 92.83±7.19g. The highest carbohydrate content present in lower altitude zone and the lowest in higher altitude zone. Per meal calcium content ranged from 0.26±0.03g to 0.43±0.12g. The lowest calcium content was recorded for the food of higher altitude villages whereas the highest in lowest altitude. Phosphorus ranged from 0.32±0.03g (high altitude) to 0.45±0.13g (mid altitude). The intake of iron for each meal ranged from 15.07±3.46 mg to 22.51±4.69 mg in middle and upper region, respectively. The calorie intake among the people of different altitudinal zones, as a result of each meal, varied between 416.36±23.21 Kcal (higher) to 446.68±21.00 Kcal (lower).

Nutritional Intake at Overall Watershed Level (female vs. male)

No significant variation ($t=1.195$; $p>0.253$) was detected in nutritional composition of female and male in the study area using pair t-test. Per meal moisture content intake by female was 128.05±8.47g while it remained 131.27±6.95g for male. Female protein intake was found 16.28±1.35g and it was 18.24±1.18g for male. The female fat intake was recorded as 4.33±0.56g, for male it was 4.95±0.48g. Fiber intake for female was observed 3.19±0.24g was and 2.92±0.22g for male. Per meal carbohydrate taken by female was 78.99±3.68g, which was slightly more 84.18±4.61g for male. The female and male were respectively taking 0.30±0.02g and 0.43±0.08g calcium for one meal. Phosphorus intake by female was 0.50±0.11g while it remained as 0.32±0.02g for male. Similarly, the iron intake per meal was relatively more for female (20.01±3.93 mg) then male (17.03±2.86 mg). While comparing total calorie intake, female with 416.30±19.96 Kcal receive less calorie than males (430.55±17.29 Kcal). Details of variations in nutritional intake by male and female villages basis, has been shown (Table 2.2).

Composition of Diet Chart of Kuloor Watershed with the National Diet Chart

According to the national diet chart (Nutritional chart of Indian Council of Medical Research, 2010, New Delhi) the recommended daily allowances (RDA) for female is as follows – Calorie (1900-3490 Kcal), protein (55-82.2 gm.), fat (20-30 gm.), calcium (0.6-1.2 gm.), iron (21-35 mg.), carotene (480-760 mg.), thiamine (1.0-2.2 mg.), riboflavin (1.1-4.1 mg.), niacin (12-51 mg.) and ascorbic acid (40-80 mg.). While in case of male the recommended daily allowances (RDA) is – Calorie (2320-3490 Kcal.), protein (60 gm.), fat (25-40 gm.), calcium (0.6 gm.), iron (17 mg.), carotene (480 mg.), thiamine (1.2-1.7 mg.), riboflavin (1.4-2.1 mg.), niacin (16-21 mg.) and ascorbic acid (40 mg.) (Table 2.3).

The average per person dietary intake through traditional food system on per day basis across the altitudinal zones of watershed is presented in (Table 2.3). In the overall watershed, female average dietary food system of per day is as follows – Calorie (1339 Kcal.), protein (60.4 gm.), fat (13.3 gm.), calcium (1.44 gm.), iron (41.3 mg.), carotene (962 mg.), thiamine (1.26 mg), niacin (9.9 mg.), riboflavin (0.72 mg.) and ascorbic acid (37.4 mg.). While in the case of male the average dietary food system of each adult person on per day basis includes: Calorie (1326 Kcal.), protein (56.7 gm.), fat (12.8 gm.), calcium (1.52 gm.), iron (41 mg.), carotene, (1051 mg.), thiamine (1.16 mg.), niacin (8.5 mg.), riboflavin (0.69 mg.) and ascorbic acid (33.6 mg.). The detailed composition of dietary system on per day basis female and male in the watershed has been included Table 2.4 and 2.5.

Both male and female inhabitants in the watershed lag far behind of national standard on per day calorie intake (Figure 2.1). This clearly suggests the prevalence of poverty in the watershed. While for females the intake more or less remained unchanged it declined amongst male of high altitude zone.

Conclusion

Food security and nutrition clearly remain core issues in sustainable development in the study area. It is important to raise awareness at all levels. It is high time when decision-makers, both within national government and international donor agencies, need to be equipped with the information and knowledge to develop appropriate policies to support the study areas development through appropriate agricultural intervention to strong the traditional agricultural and use in food habits of local inhabitants.

Table 2.1: Difference in mean nutritional intake of the female *vs.* male (per meal basis for overall watershed)

Sex (♀/♂)	Moisture (g)	Protein (g)	Fat (g)	Fibre (g)	Carbohydrate (g)	Calcium (g)	Phosphorus (g)	Iron (mg)	Calorie (Kcal)	Carotene (mg)	Thiamine (mg)	Niacin (mg)	Riboflavin (mg)	Ascorbic-acid (mg)
Female	128.05 ±8.47	16.28 ±1.35	4.33 ±0.56	3.19 ±0.24	78.99 ±3.68	0.30 ±0.02	0.50 ±0.11	20.01 ±3.93	416.30 ±19.96	237.32 ±91.17	0.47 ±0.03	2.63 ±0.31	0.36 ±0.02	7.74 ±1.13
Male	131.27 ±6.95	18.24 ±1.18	4.95 ±0.48	2.92 ±0.22	84.18 ±4.61	0.43 ±0.08	0.32 ±0.02	17.03 ±2.86	430.55 ±17.29	350.39 ±93.68	0.35 ±0.03	3.13 ±0.44	0.23 ±0.01	6.95 ±0.90

No significant difference (t-1.195 $p>0.253$)

Table 2.2: Mean daily nutritional intake through local foods in the watershed and altitude zones

Altitude Level	Height (m)	Moisture (g)	Protein (g)	Fat (g)	Fibre (g)	Carbohydrate (g)	Calcium (m)	Phosphorus (g)	Iron (mg)	Calorie (Kcal)	Carotence (mg)	Thiamine (mg)	Niacin (mg)	Riboflavin (mg)	Ascorbic-acid (mg)
Lower	<1000	376.2	67.7	13.8	10.1	279.4	1.08	0.99	71	1340	440	1.27	9.9	0.81	35.10
Middle	1000-2000	376.3	59.3	15.9	8.2	247.7	1.30	1.08	33.9	1349	1122	1.22	8.02	0.72	26.1
Higher	>2000	388.3	54.4	10.2	8.8	251.4	1.08	0.92	19	1338	1325	1.31	12.05	0.63	51.15
Overall watershed	**700-2361**	**380.2**	**60.4**	**13.3**	**9.0**	**259.5**	**1.44**	**0.99**	**41.3**	**1342**	**962**	**1.26**	**9.9**	**0.72**	**37.4**

Table 2.3: Diet chart (female) of Kuloor watershed compared with the national diet chart

Parameters	Requirement of Nutrients	Watershed (700-2361m)	Low Altitude (<1000m)	Mid Altitude (1000-2000m)	High Altitude (>2000m)
Protein (gm.)	55-82.2	60.4	67.7	59.3	54.4
Fat (gm.)	20-30	13.3	13.8	15.9	10.2
Calcium (gm.)	0.6-1.2	1.44	1.08	1.30	1.95
Iron (mg.)	21-35	41.3	71	33.9	19
Carotene (mg.)	480-760	962	440	1122	1325
Thiamine (mg.)	1.0-2.1	1.26	1.27	1.22	1.31
Riboflavin (mg.)	1.1-2.0	0.72	0.81	0.72	0.63
Ascorbic acid (mg.)	40-80	37.4	35.1	26.1	51.1
Niacin (mg.)	12-25	9.9	9.9	8.02	12.05
Calories (Kcal.)	1900-3490	1339	1340	1349	1338

Table 2.5: Diet chart (male) of Kuloor watershed compared with the national diet chart

Parameters	Requirement of Nutrients	Watershed (700-2361m)	Low Altitude (<1000m)	Mid Altitude (1000-2000m)	High Altitude (>2000m)
Protein (gm.)	60	56.7	59	62	49
Fat (gm.)	25-40	12.8	9.3	16.8	12.3
Calcium (gm.)	0.6	1.52	0.96	1.3	2.3
Iron (mg.)	17	41	60	35	30
Carotene (mg.)	480	1051	337	1149	1669
Thiamine (mg.)	1.2-1.7	1.16	1.17	1.29	1.02
Riboflavin (mg.)	1.4-2.1	0.69	0.69	0.75	0.65
Ascorbic acid (mg.)	40	33.6	34.8	29.9	36.4
Niacin (mg.)	16-21	8.5	8.7	8.8	8.1
Calories (Kca.l)	2320-3490	1326	1359	1389	1229

A dialogue must be established between watershed people and external stakeholders. In this context, nutrition education and capacity building is important at both the community level and the technical level to orient people decisions about production and utilization of produce appropriately.

For example, Jaun, Bajra, Koni and Ganera; all were having much higher protein and carbohydrate contents as compared to most of the studied landraces of paddy. This proves the case of lesser known traditional crops for promotion. Unfortunately, with the changing mindsets of peoples these crops are finding very rare introduction in food. People in the watershed are more interested in inclusion of PDS (Public Distribution System) based

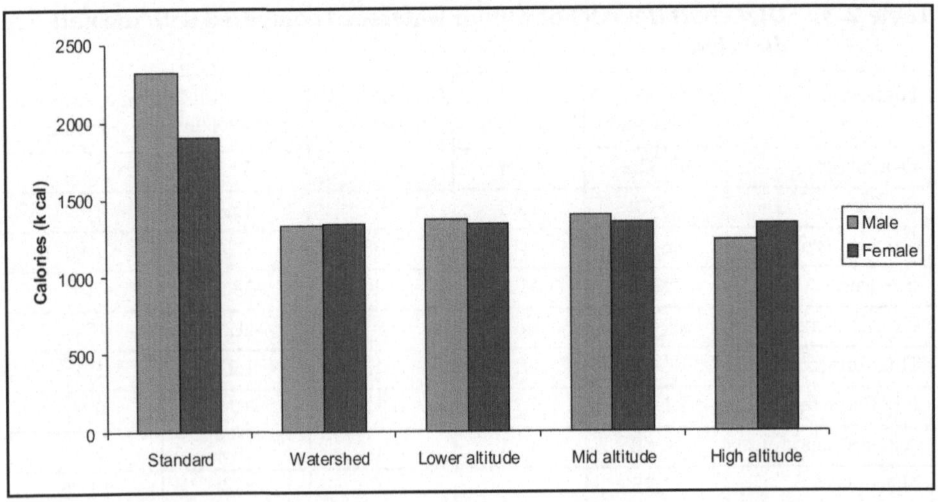

Fig. 2.1: **Calorie intake by male and female in the watershed as compared to national standard**

grains and vegetables supplied from outside the region. As a result, the nutritional and energy intake of the watershed invariably falls short of the national standard. Take an example of per day calorie intake, as against the Recommended Daily Allowances (RDA) of 2320-3490 K cal. for male and 1900-3490 K cal. for female, the watershed people on an average were having per day intake of 1342 K cal. only. This is much lower than the desired. This, in general, indicate overall nutritional deficiency among watershed people. While comparing the per day intake of calorie by inhabitants of watershed with that of national standard, it was invariably less than the national standard. The calorie intake by females in the watershed more or less remained unchanged across the altitude zones. However, males in high altitude zone were having relatively low calories through per day food consumption.

The study reveals that the inhabitants of the watershed exhibit considerable diversity in food habits and consequent intake of nutrients. Patterns of nutritional intake, per meal basis, have been described for studied villages as well as for altitude zones. Also, it has been analyzed separately for male and female inhabitants. No significant difference ($p<0.05$) was observed across altitude zones or gender categories.

REFERENCES

Bhatt J.C. (2008). Pithoragarh Champawat-supplement-1. (Pahar 16-17). Parikarma, Talladanda, Tallital, Nainital. pp. 25-208.

Goplan C., Ramasastri B.V, *et.al.* (1980). Nutritive Value of Indian Foods, Health Bulletin No. 23, Indian Council of Medical Research, National Institute of Nutrition.

ICMR, (V). (2010). Revised Recommended Dietary Allowance for Indian. National Institute of Nutrition, Hyderabad, India.

Kramer A. (1980). We eat to live. Food and the consumer. Eastern graphics INC, Old Saybrook, Connecticut, USA. pp. 18-23.

Mehta P.S., Negi K.S., *et.al*. (2010). Native Plant Genetic Resources and Traditional Foods of Uttarakhand Himalaya for Sustainable Food Secutity and Livelihood. *Indian Journal of Natural Products and Resources*, 1(1): 89-96.

Pandey B.D. (1937). Kumaun ka itihas. Shayam Prakashan, Almora Book Depot, Almora, India. (In Hindi).

Pant B.R. (2008). Women and Nutrition in Himalayan Region: A Case Study, http://www.gbpihed.gov.in/ envis/HTML/vol161/B.R.%20Pant.pdf.

Shannaz A. (1988). Food intake system. Nutritional Problems in Rural India. Northern Book Centre, New Delhi.

Stanley L. (1939). From Tradition to Science. Food and Life. The Superintendent of Document Washington, D. C.

Stiebeling H.K. (1939). Food Habits, old and New. Adequate Diets for Families with Limited Incomes. US Department of Agriculture, Miscellaneous Publication No. - 113.

Pages: 38-55

AGRO-BIODIVERSITY: *CONSERVATION AND SUSTAINABLE DEVELOPMENT*
Edited by: Dr. Pankaj Sharma; Dr. Narayan Singh & Dr. Pawan Kumar 'Bharti'
ISBN: 978-93-5056-782-1
Edition: 2016
Published by: Discovery Publishing House Pvt. Ltd., New Delhi (India)

Agriculture in Hills

At a Glance

3

Meenakshi Jalal[1*] and
Deeksha Nautiyal[2]

ABSTRACT

Agricultural is term as backbone of Indian economy especially a source of living for hilly people. Traditional knowledge system has been a key to the survival of the hill society, be it in cropping, forestry or health. It has not only ensured continuous livelihood of farm households but also ecological sustainability. Farming in the hills is highly interdependent with forestry and animal husbandry, and women have been the backbone to this totally integrated system. They have a high workload but have successfully preserved transformed and carried traditional agricultural knowledge from generation to generation. However, over the last few decades, this entire knowledge system has been threatened due to various reasons. Modern agriculture practises has given tough completion to hilly agriculture and due to inaccessibly of things, lack of knowledge and poverty people of hills still relying on their in hold system result for this is agriculture started dying in hilly villages of Uttarakhand and man-power started migrating in search of job. The present communication is the representation of a study carried out in 7 villages in the hills of Uttarakhand: north India state. It studies hilly agriculture and highlighted the positive and negative aspect of living of hilly peoples.

Keywords: Agricultural, traditional, animal husbandry, migration, Uttarakhand

1. WWF Field Office, Haldwani, Address - P.O.- Chakuluwa, Vill. Devipura, Kaladungi, Nainital 263 140, Uttrakhand, India.
2. Department of Forestry, D.S.B Campus, Kumaun University, Nainital 263 002, Uttrakhand, India.

INTRODUCTION

Agriculture helps to meet the basic needs of human and their civilization by providing food, clothing, shelters, medicine and recreation. Hence, agriculture is the most important enterprise in the world. It is a productive unit where the free gifts of nature namely: land, light, air, temperature and rain water etc., are integrated into single primary unit indispensable for human beings. Secondary productive unitsnamely animals including: livestock, birds and insects, feed on these primary units and provide concentrated products such as: meat, milk, wool, eggs, honey, silk and lac.

Agriculture is derived from Latin words Agerand Cultura. Agermeans land or field and cultura means cultivation. Therefore the term agriculture means cultivation of land *i.e.,* the science and art of producing crops and livestock for economic purposes. It is also referred as the science of producing crops and livestock from the natural resources of the earth. The primary aim of agriculture is to cause the land to produce more abundantly, and at the same time, to protect it from deterioration and misuse. It is synonymous with farming – the production of food, fodder and other industrial materials.

Agriculture is not only a means of survival but also a way of life. The application of high input technologies in intensive agriculture has undoubtedly increased agricultural production, but, now realizing the plateau in the growth, there is serious concern over their adverse effects on environment quality. Sustainable agriculture aims at achieving permanence through utilization of renewable resource (Joshi and Singh 2004). Indigenous knowledge is the knowledge acquired by the local people through their past experience, evolved over the time under the influence of traditional knowledge, external factors and agents, and individual innovations Simpson B (1994). Knowledge, skill and survival strategy of farmers operating with low external inputs have often been ignored to promote modern agriculture Haverkort and Zeeuw (1992) Farmers-based indigenous/traditional knowledge has scientific rationale and great deal of relevance for agricultural productivity and sustainability. Various scholars have highlighted the importance of indigenous knowledge in developing low cost, location specific and appropriate technology for resource poor farmers Padaria and Singh (1990); Gupta and Rajput (2001).

Agricultural in itself has many different branches. According to Wikipedia branches of agriculture broadly classify into two parts – on the basis of life form produced or harvested and on the basis of industry. Some of its sub-branches are highlighted below in a block diagram

Agriculture, directly or indirectly, has continued to be the main source of livelihood for the majority of the population in India. In one term we can say agriculture form back bone of Indian economy. The censuses indicate that 70 per cent of the population is supported by agriculture. These censuses

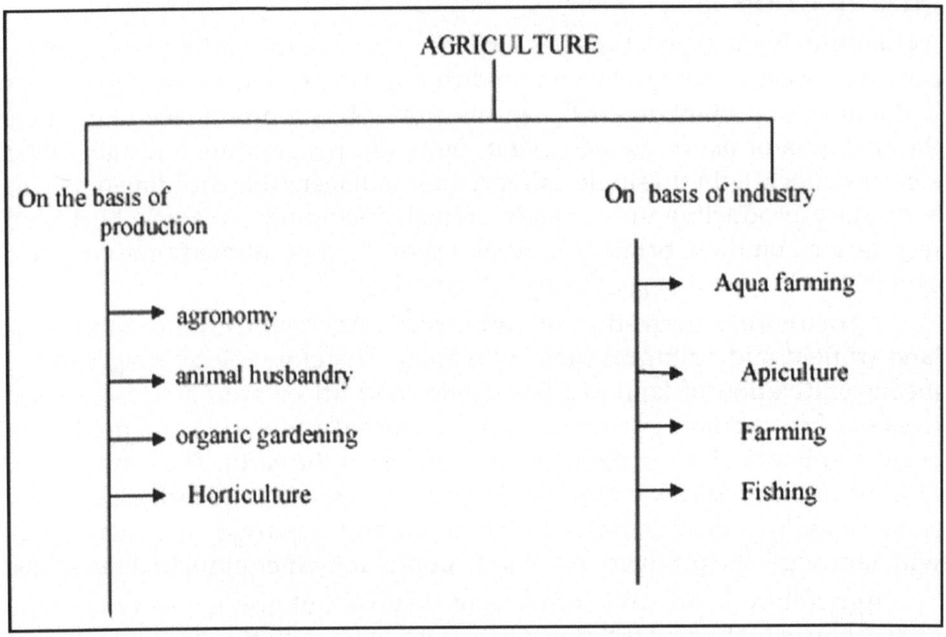

show that an overwhelming majority of workers have been engaged in cultivation in India. The geographical condition provides favorable condition to grow and produce all the year round just there is a need of proper management. In India at present there are 29 state which depend on agriculture directly or in-directly and there are different type of agriculture which practice in each state some are rich for cereals, other for spices and there are states which are hub of cash crops animal husbandry etc.

This chapter mainly focuses on the agriculture in hilly areas of Uttarakhand. Uttarakhand State is small state in India, carved out from the state of Uttar Pradesh on November 9, 2000. It is divided into two broad regions: *(i)* Garhwal and *(ii)* Kumaon. The state is comprised of 13 districts, namely: Chamoli, Pauri, Tehri, Uttarkashi, Dehradun, Haridwar and Rudraprayag in the Garhwal region and Nainital, Almora, Pithoragarh, Udham Singh Nagar, Champawat and Bageshwar in the Kumaon region. Of these 13 districts, four districts (Nainital, Haridwar, Dehradun and Udham Singh Nagar) have large areas in the plains, whereas the other nine districts comprise the hill region of the state.

Out of the total population, more than 75 per cent people are engaged either with the main occupation as agriculture or its allied practices, dominated by traditional subsistence cereal farming (Sati, 2005). The terraced slopes covering 85 per cent of total agricultural land are largely rain fed, while the valleys, covering 15 per cent of the area, are irrigated (Palni *et al.* 1998; Maikhuri *et al.*). The farming of crops is mostly traditional and overall cropping pattern of the mountain region of central Himalaya is typically of an underdeveloped agricultural economy. The traditional crop diversity and their landrace in agricultural land use in Himalayas have great significant for long-term sustainability of agro ecosystem along with conservation and management surrounding landscape (Negi. *et al*. 2001).

Within Uttarakhand there is a geographical inequality between the hills and the plains that divides the state critically. Districts in the plains are far ahead on various development indicators. The hill region districts are less developed interms of infrastructure, *i.e.,* electricity, roads and irrigation. The inter-district inequality in infrastructure leads to increasing disparity in terms of income and livelihood between the hills and the plains. Low levels of income not only result in low levels of consumption and material deprivation, but also constrain human potential by restricting access to education and health facilities, thereby creating a vicious cycle of poverty. In hills of Uttarakhand the land holdings are small and fragmented, and irrigation facilities limited these farmers are usually practicing traditional ways of cultivation which adds very little to the input. A farmer who is only dependent on agriculture hardly secures his family food and nutritionally (Roy. *et al*. 2013). Soil and water conservation is another issue for inclusive development. As a result, the majority of the rural population in the hills either survives on subsistence agriculture or migrates to other parts of the country for employment.

In the rural areas of Uttarakhand, adult male members of the families usually migrated to towns of plains in India for service and other earning sources, keeping behind the women and children all alone, sometimes with old aged diseases parents. The woman of such families heads the family and carried out dual work of man and woman all alone. Even where men reside with families, it is the women and girls children who look the agriculture and the cattle. The situation is that the women contributing 90 per cent of the total agricultural and cattle rearing work in rural areas of the states (Dang, *et. al*). The men folk only plough in the agricultural field, rest of the agricultural operation like: making of compost, sowing, harvesting, winnowing, picking and cleaning all work done by female folk only. Sometimes women are taking up plough also especially in female headed house hold, single women houses and among nuclear families (USNPSS, 2005).

This paper mainly focused on the living and earning of hilly areas people highlighting difficulty which they are facing to earn living. It also concentrates on the condition of women in hills and reasons of migration of people living behind their land to be left barren.

Material and Methods

The study was conducted in Nainital district of Uttarakhand. It has an area of 3422 sq.km. The district is located between Longitude 80°14'E and

78°80′ E and Latitude 29° 05′ N and 29°05′N in the Kumaon area and spread over hilly as well as the plains area. The specific areas where the pattern of agricultural notice were hilly villages of Kotabagh, Betalghat and Bhimtal block *i.e.,* Bagad, Maherora in kotabgh block; Pangot in Betalghat block and Khurpatal, Jungaliya gaun and Songaon in Bhimtal block.

Data is collected in the year 2013 in kotabagh block and Betalghat block and 2014 in Bhimtal block. These villages are surveyed for their livelihood pattern and socio-economic condition through PRA and particular household survey through the study agricultural in hilly areas is derived and separated as a chapter.

(a) Field Work and Site Selection

Reconnaissance survey was carried out at different attitudinal zones having agricultural as a main occupation. The information was collected on the basis of kind of agriculture they practice and difficulty they are facing in practicing traditional method of farming and reason of migration of people to plains in search of living .Particular site is selected for study because these are sites lies in periphery of tourist spot and is affected by tourism directly and indirectly. The sites have different infrastructure along with transportation difficulties in some of the area but the basic occupation in all of the villages is farming.

(b) Observation Recorded

The following information was recorded to fulfill the requirement of topic:

Main Parameter		Sub-parameter
1.	Agricultural practice	Farming, horticulture, animal husbandry, apiculture, pollutary management etc.
2.	Difficulty they are facing	Old method of farming, wildlife conflict, ill-transportation etc.
3.	Reasons of migration from hills	Small land holding, weak market, schooling problem, various environmental crisis.
4.	Are they getting good money in terms of their hard work.	Description of market and procedure they are adopting to reach that market.
5.	Roles of women and men's in maintain their occupation	In what content they are contributing to their agricultural fields, and occupation they are adopting.
6.	Aids provide by government in hills to stop migrating them.	Is there any scheme given to villagers by the government to stop them from migration.

The information collected is based on secondary data as well as primary data.

Results

The villages selected for study lies in outskirt of hot tourist spot of Uttarakhand *i.e.,* Nainital. Some villages are in periphery of Nainital which form a good tourist attraction which give them hike in economy like: Khurpatal and Pangot but as a distance of Villages from main tourist spot increases their income decreases and they have to find alternate to survive.

In hills land are small and mostly terrace farming is practiced. People hardly secure for their family instead of doing tones of hard work. Human and wildlife conflict is high which force them to leave some land as barren. Old traditional methods are use in fields due to lack of money and education although a good networks of road is present which are seasoned road but still lack of good market for sale of products. Women mostly head of every work from household chore to agricultural fields still they are in bad conditions and girl child mortality is high in hills.

1. Agricultural Practiced in Hills

In hilly areas people have small land holding which are measured in Naali (12 naali = 1 bigha) and lands are mostly terraced type. The hilly people are shifting to other modes of agricultural like: Animal husbandry, horticulture, pollutary farming etc., besides. Farming which is previously traditionally practice all over India.

Terrace Farming in Hills

A. *Farming*

Technique of growing crop and raw material come under farming. It is a part of agriculture. Mostly cultivation of cereals crops like: wheat, bajra, rice, millets maize and growing of pulses come under this category although no specific division is done.

Due to change in scenario of human cereals cultivation is decreases in hilly areas now cereals are marked as a plains crop. In hilly areas people hardly grow cereals, if they grow them they grow for household consumption only few families are such in which cereals consumption is nil.

Pulses growing is also decreases in large extent in comparison to past but still they grow and sell in local markets. According to some village seniors now days pulses are grown only when lands are free otherwise it not necessary grow as a part of routine.

Table 3.1 (a): To represent Cereals and pulse consumption in hills

Name of the Village	Cereals/Pulses Cultivated	Area
Pangot	Wheat, gram and udad	Wheat in 9-10% household for hosehold. consumption. Gram and udad 15% for sell.
Bagad	Wheat, bajra, gram udad and masur	Wheat 30% in total Gram, masur, Udad 20-40%.
Mahrora	Gram, wheat	Only for consumption 1-2% people grow wheat also.
Khurpatal	Wheat, jai, gram and masor	40-30% for consumption purpose 5-6% use it for sell also.
Soangaon	Wheat, Gram, masor, goht	70% people cultivate wheat and sell in little extent. 30-40% families grow pulses.
Jungaliya gaon	Wheat, gram, black, maize, masor, udad	30-40% people grow cereals like: wheat, bajra and maize for consumption. Pulses are consumed as well as sell.

Reason of drifting people from farming to other methods:

- Due to adverse weather condition these crop face much loss compare to others as lands in hills are mostly rain fed.
- Wildlife including birds harm in farming 50 per cent more compare to other methods of agricultural.
- Risky to cultivate as need more investment and less return.
- Engage land 4 more than 6 month, with less income and high hard work.
- Due to old farming techniques threshing of crops still done by hands or by bullock which cause much crop loss and time consuming.
- Low connectivity and bad marketing is main reason for drifting of people toward other agricultural practices.

Pulses and Cereals Crop in Hills

B: Horticulture

The horticulture which includes: fruits, vegetable, spices, flowers, medicinal and ornamental plants has proved beyond doubt its potentiality for gainful diversification. The emerging trend worldwide and also in the country is indicative of paradigm shift in dietary needs of the people with the rice in the income, which demand for more horticulture produce.

In horticulture, the vegetable crops have been identified as the most remunerative crops for replacing subsistence farming in rain fed, dry land, hills, arid and coastal agro ecosystems. Being short duration crops and fewer requirements for capital, vegetables are also best suited in the crop rotation. Such a diversification in favor of vegetable is sweeping across the nation.

Besides the vegetables hilly people are also grow fruits tree in bunds of their lands or in fields where irrigation is not possible. They grew fruit like: plum, apricot etc.

Reason for people to shift to horticulture:

- The varied climate of the region makes it an ideal location for growing temperate, subtropical and tropical fruits that fetch a high value in the domestic urban markets and international markets.
- The climate also allows these regions to grow off season vegetables that get a high price for these in the plains.
- Horticulture crops are of less duration which give opportunity to farmers to grow quarterly crops.
- It is easy to cultivate vegetables in the poly-houses.

Table 3.1 (b): To represent vegetable and fruits consumption in hills

Name of the Village	Vegetable/fruits Cultivated	Area
Pangot	Potatoes, radish, carrot, coriander and cabbage. Apricot, pears	Vegetables are sell in market. Fruits are also selled but in less quantity.
Bagad	Peas, Potatoes, radish, carrot, coriander and cabbage Pears, apricot	Vegetable for sell and fruits localy sell.
Mahrora	Potaote, coriander, Peas Lemon and pears	Both are foe sell.
Khurpatal	Potao, raddish, carrot, Peas, coriander, pyaz, beetrrot tomatoe etc. No fruit	For sell.
Soangaon	Potato, raddish and Peas Plum, apricot and lemon	For sell in local market and in main market Haldwani.
Jungaliya gaon	Potaoe, peas, raddish, Lemon, plum, pears, apple	For sale.

Reason which sometime put challenges with the farmers depending on horticulture:

- The relatively small size of each farmers produce and the distance of their villages from roads and mandis makes the process of marketing their products too costly to be profitable.
- They do not have easy access to storage and warehousing facilities.
- Finally, they do not have ready access to information about potential markets for their produce. As a result of this lack of marketing facility, a large part of the total horticultural crops produced by the state of Uttarakhand is wasted each year.

C: *Animal Husbandry*

Like agriculture, small scale livestock rearing is an important livelihood activity in the hilly region. Most households keep cattle, goats or chickens for milk, manure, eggs or meat. Previously in hills desi cow and buffaloes are reared but now due to the increment in the dairy business American and jersey cows are preferred which give good output. Beside dairy business government is also providing aids for pollutary farming and fisi-culture.

Positive aspect of Animal husbandry:

- These are a good source of alternate income beside agriculture.
- It requires comparatively less man-power than farming.
- Animal husbandry can't affected by adverse effects of climate.
- Marketing value of animal husbandry product is almost fixed which make good marketing for layman also.

Table 3.1 (c): To represent animal husbandry practice in hills

Name of the Village	Animals	Purpose
Pangot	Dairy farming, goats	More for personnel consumption and less for sale.
Bagad	Dairy farming, Pollatry hens and goats	For market sale.
Mahrora	Dairy business and Polatry hens	For sale less and for consumption more.
Khurpatal	Dairy business, poluutary for pig and hens, goats	Highly sale in market.
Soangaon	Dairy business and hen	Good sell in market.
Jungaliya gaon	Dairy business and goats	Good market sell.

Domesticated Animals by Villager's

However, milk yields for cattle in some region are very low, for a variety of reasons. *First* of all, the indigenous breeds of cattle are inherently lower milk yielding than many hybrid varieties. *Secondly*, access to adequate nutritious fodder to feed the cattle is a constraint for many farmers, especially in the winter months. *Thirdly*, the farmers are often not well informed and educated on animal health and rearing practices.

2. Difficulty Hilly People are Facing

People in the hilly areas face many difficulties to earn their living from the inaccessibility to natural calamities all things bring them down. The area deprivation in the present sense is not only the lack of economic resources but also the lack of infrastructural development and presence of environment susceptibility of these areas.

Some highlighting features that makes hilly farming difficult:

- Farming is not a profitable means of employment in this hilly district due to its uneven geographical conditions, small terraced fields and non-availability of proper irrigation facilities.
- Rain fed farming communities across Uttarakhand is today struggling with the vagaries and unpredictability of changing swinging climate to which they have made virtually no contribution.
- The relatively small size of each farmers produce and the distance of their villages from roads and mandis makes the process of marketing their products too costly.
- Irrigation facilities is vey less in villages they do not have tube well and tanks constructed in fields.
- They do not have easy access to storage their products.
- They do not have ready access to information about potential markets for their produce.
- They still depend on traditional technique of farming due to inaccessibility, illiteracy and poverty they still do no cope with the present world and government scheme are running still only in papers in many villages.
- Cultivation techniques are primitive and simple. In other words there is a total absence of modern equipments like: tractors and farm inputs like: chemical fertilizers, insecticides and pesticides.
- Over the years rates of farm inputs have increased manifold. Farm inputs include: fertilizer, insecticide, pesticides, HYV seeds, farm labour cost etc. Such an increase puts low and medium land holding farmers whose ratio is high in hills at disadvantage.
- On the basis of higher priority, the respondent of district Nainital were largely faced problems related with production *e.g.*, lack of irrigation, lack of information, manpower, finance/credit, inputs, production levels, insect/pest, diseases, poor linkages with extension agencies inadequate soil testing facilities, risk aversion.

- Problems related to marketing included transportation standardization and grading, infrastructure, unfair deductions, storage, market related information, bargaining and low price received by the farmers for the produces.
- There were also other, less important problems. Farmers were aware about most of problems but unfortunately they had no access by which they could overcome these constraints.
- Last but least problem which is faced by the farmers are Human - wildlife conflict which is high in respected hilly areas.

Beside this there might be many problems which hilly people are facing to earn their living.

Table 3.2: To represent problem face by people in hills

Name of the Village	Problems
Pangot	Lack of irrigational water, lack of marketing, small land holding and Danger of wild animals monkey tiger etc.
Bagad	Lack of irrigation, traditional method of farming, Crop every year affected by disease.
Mahrora	Lack of irrigation, in accessibility of roads, area in between of hill and terrain face much climate fluctuation. Nearby market is too far, People are unawre of modern agricultural. Danger of tiger, pig etc.
Khurpatal	Traditional method of farming, danger of wild animal like: pig, shaul. Transportation facility is costly.
Soangaon	Lack of irrigation, inaccessibility of roads, danger of pig, shaul, tiger. Crop mostly affect by disease.
Jungaliya gaon	Nearby mark is far, transportation is too costly, water problem fluctuate, wild animals like: pig, tiger, rabbit and sahul raided crop mostly.

3. Reasons of Migration from Hills

The hilly Uttarakhand economy is very poor due to the higher percentage of migration from the rural areas of the state or to the urban centres of other states. This push migration from these regions is mainly attributed to the poor development status of these regions which is reflected in the lack of basic infrastructural abilities of health, education, employment etc.

- The natural and geographical settings of these regions have indirectly enacted in path of the growth of employment opportunities in these regions as they are not conducive for industrial development. This has always led to the problem of lack of employment opportunities in these regions which is further been accentuated by the poor infrastructural development of these regions.

- The hill rural regions of Uttarakhand are poor in every basic facility which has failed to help in making its inhabitants life and living easy. Majority of villages have still the *kuccha* road, they have water problems, irrigation system is poor and villagers have to depend on the far areas for the health facilities.
- The other major problem, with which, these regions of the state has to deal every year is of uncertain extreme weather conditions and the natural havoc it causes. The natural disasters not only adversely affect the agriculture development but also directly affect the normal living and working conditions of the inhabitants of these regions.
- Their crop is mostly facing adverse affect of climate and wild animals. Their net input is too high in comparison to net output. In such circumstances it is not possible to rely on agricultural fields therefore people are migrating to urban areas to providing their children better education and for searching jobs.
- In spite of doing plenty of hard work they hardly save for their family, there in accessibility to resources make them hard to compete with modern word. They are not getting any fame, popularity and reorganization in their field. They want their children to cope out of this and want them to stand in this modern world which is now the main reason of migration of hilly inhabitant.

All these adversities have led to far spread absolute poverty and to small extent relative poverty when we consider it within these areas but it is much significant when compared to urban areas of the district or of the state.

4. Is Hard Work Getting Pay

It is not enough just produce the products it must be produced efficiently and marketed successfully but in hilly areas they are not doing so as they unaware of many things which need to be good producers. No hilly people are not getting the pay for their hard work reason for this might be:

- *Using Traditional Variety:* Hilly people mostly unaware of breeding varieties which provide them good income in both agricultural as well as animal husbandry.
- *Lack of Market Knowledge*: Hilly people are unaware of market rate, as there is no organization or offices which take their product in government rate. Monopoly is also not present in village market therefore the fluctuation in every households income.
- *Lack of Storage Facility*: These people have lack of medium to store crop therefore they face loss in large extent in their crops.
- *Present of Series of People between Buyer and Seller*: In between buyer and seller there are 3-4 traders in between which earn their good commission beside of poor condition of producers.

Table 3.3: To represent problem face by people in hills

Name of the Village	Migration Present	Reasons
Pangot	Yes, for education less extent for job Because it is a tourist place in itself. People got employment in village	No good education institute in village; for higher study people have to move out. 10% people migrate for job also as they want to give good life to their families. 5% of people regularly do up down from nearest town.
Bagad	Yes, for education less extent for job	Education is higher problem to cope with world people send their children in hostels or 1 family member migrate with children, 20% or somewhat more people are away from home for job. There are 3 families in village which total migrate and their lands are barren.
Mahrora	Yes, High amount	The village is very inaccessible in terms of roads and basic necessity of life. People still have their journey in horses and have no l.p.g connection. These are reason enough to migrate to cities for good life. There are 5-6 family which migrate permently fro village. Education is another issue which force migration.
Khurpatal	Yes, very little	The third generation is now migrating in search of job as they want to compete with world. For education migration is negligible people do up-down in local cabs for schools.
Soangaon	Yes, negligible	The migration is present in village but it is negligible in comparison of total population. People are employ in nearby town cities and do regular up-down.
Jungaliya gaon	Yes	30% people migrated in search of job and higher education.

- *Due to Inaccessible area the cost of Transportation is High:* The cost of transportation or making product to sell in the market is too high. This force people sell their product to local vender who come to take their product at cheaper rate from home.

5. Role of Women in Hills

Women's role becomes all the more important in the traditional society of Kumaon Hills, located in the mountainous region of the Himalayas, where the livelihood of the people is still dependent on the sound management of its natural resources and their sustainable utilisation. Women's knowledge has been the mainstay of crop production, animal husbandry, dairy and forestry.

The most important feature of a woman's life in Kumaon Hills is her workload. Women are expected right from girlhood to do all the household chores and contribute substantially to agriculture.

Except for ploughing and harrowing, which are predominantly male activities, as well as sowing and occasionally harvesting wheat and *mandua* (a coarse grain) there is domination/dominance of women's labour in land levelling, manuring, planting and sowing, weeding, harvesting and post harvesting activities like sun drying the stalks, winnowing, pounding, separating the husks from grains again and again. Some of the operations such as: manuring, weeding, harvesting, transplanting are quite old, and different from those carried out in the plains such as: the land levelling exercise. Even in male dominated operations, women perform a supportive role.

Women are fully dependent on men to initiate the crop production cycle. Interestingly in almost all the crop operations where males perform a dominant role, draught animals are deployed, while women always depend on manual labour.

Women are also well aware of the traditional techniques and methods of preparing highly energetic food from pulses and grains. These homemade concentrates are fed to animals for enhancing milk yield, provide them energy especially during field working activities such as: ploughing etc. Besides, cattle and goats are traditionally fed a very healthy and nutritious home-made concentrate after the delivery and in the days following it. Since most of the land is small and fragmented with hardly any space for growing fodder trees, the significance of homemade concentrates and thereby traditional crop residues becomes all the more important.

Women in hills are solely responsible for collecting fuel wood and fodder from the nearby forest. In short those are the women who are responsible for completing house hold chore from maintain house to maintain off filed.

Women's doing Various Work in Villages

6. Aids Provided by Government in Hills

There are various government scheme provided by the government in hills region all over the Uttarakhand. It's all about people and authorities to use them efficiently. Scheme launched by government in hills through various blocks are:

- Scheme for employment.
- Scheme for tank construction.
- Scheme for C.C roads.
- Scheme for child education.
- Scheme for child delivery and human welfare.
- Scheme for providing subsidy in business establishment like: poultry farm, polyhouses andpig farm.

There are various schemes running at particular village and block level for the welfare of society.

Conclusion

The study clearly reveled that agricultural in hills are facing many problems which need to be cope up with proper planning and management. It is necessary to improve the marketing system and to aid development for two reasons; *firstly,* it may work as a tool to increased production; *secondly*, if the market does not supply consumers with produce at reasonable prices and at the time and place needed, and then the increased production has no meaning in a welfare society.

Peoples in hills should be encouraged to practice modern way of agricultural proper management, training and facilities must be given to them to increase yield and proper market should be develop to sell their products.

Reason of migration of people for job should be eliminated by government, Ngo's and other welfare working teams. A help to start a business, an employment in village should be provided. Women are backbone of hilly agricultural as state above by the studies that women do lots of household chore still not getting proper respect.

As government solely not responsible for everything the peoples also should have to put their foot forward to fight their problems and cope up with each and every little difficulty putting them backward in this era of world.

REFERENCES

Dang J.P., Malhotra K. and Ghai D. (2009). Uttarakhand Women Entrepreneurs "The Hand that Rocks the Cradles Rules the World" *In Political Economy Journal of India,* July - Dec, 2009.

Gupta R.K, and Rajput R. (2001). Indigenous Nutrient Management Practices in Madhya Pradesh, in Indigenous Nutrient Management Practices – Wisdom Alive in India, ed Acharya C L, Ghosh P.K., and Rao A., (Indian Institute of Soil Science, Nabibagh, Bhopal), 205-228.

Haverkort B. and De Zeeuw H. (1992). Development of Technologies towards Sustainable Agriculture: Institutional Implications. In: W.M. Rivera and D.J. Gustafson (eds.) Agricultural Extension: Worldwide Institutional Evolution and Forces for Changes, (Elsevier Science Publishing Company, New York), 231-242.

Maikhuri R.K., Rao K.S., and Semwal R.L. (2001). Changing Scenario of Himalayan Agroeco-sytem: Loss of Agro-biodiversity, An Indicator of Environmental Change in Central Himalaya, India. *The Environmentalist*, 20, 23-39.

Negi Vikram., Maikhuri R.K., Rawat L.S. and Phondan, P.C. (2010). Current Status and Future Potential of Fiber Yielding Crop *Hibiscus cannabinus* L. in Mountain Region of Central Himalaya, India. *Environ. We Int. J. Sci. Tech. 5* pp. 87-96.

Padaria R.N. and Singh R.P. (1990). Risk Adjustment and Traditional Wisdom in Dry Land Farming, *Indian J. Ext Edu*, 26 (3&4), 1-7.

Palni L.M.S., Maikhuri R.K. and Rao K.S. (1998). Conservation of the Himalayan Agroeco-system: Issues and Priorities. Technical paper V. In. Eco-regional Co-operation for Biodiversity Conservation in the Himalaya. United Nations Development Programme (UNDP), pp. 253-290.

Roy M.L., Chandra N., Kharbikar H.L., Joshi P., Jethi R. (2013). Socio-economic Status of Hill Farmers: An Exploration from Almora District. *International Journal of Agriculture and Food Science Technology*. ISSN 2249-3050, Volume 4, Number 4, pp. 353-358.

Sati V.P. (2005). System of Agriculture Farming in the Uttaranchal Himalaya, *India. Journal of Mountain Science,* 2, pp. 76-85.

Simpson B. (1994). Systematic Integration of Knowledge System: An Underutilized Potential for Agricultural Development in Marginal Areas, in: Systems Oriented Research in Agriculture and Rural Development, International Sympo-sium Montpellier, France, 599-602.

Uttarakhand Seva Nidhi Payavaran Shiksha Sansthan (USNPSS). 2005. Beyond Practical Gender Needs: Women in North-Easter and Hill States: Uttaranchal, 'National Research Programme on Growth and Human Development. UNDP-Planning commission, Government of India (Mimeo).

Pages: 56-64

AGRO-BIODIVERSITY: *CONSERVATION AND SUSTAINABLE DEVELOPMENT*
Edited by: Dr. Pankaj Sharma; Dr. Narayan Singh & Dr. Pawan Kumar 'Bharti'
ISBN: 978-93-5056-782-1
Edition: 2016
Published by: Discovery Publishing House Pvt. Ltd., New Delhi (India)

Screening of pea (*Pisum sativum L.*) Cultivars for Promoting their Cultivation in Kullu Valley, Northwestern Indian Himalaya

4

Rashmi Raghuvanshi; Rajesh Kumar Sharma* and **Rosy Kundra**

ABSTRACT

Eight cultivars of pea (*Pisum sativum* L. cv. Early Giant, Lincoln, GS-10, Saloni, Ruchi, CM-Avtar, Anmol, Prachi) were screened for promoting their cultivation in Kullu Valley, Himachal Pradesh. Economic yields and antioxidant properties of green seeds of eight cultivars of *P. sativum* plants were studied. The results showed that economic yields of test cultivars of *P. sativum* ranged between 0.21 - 0.05g/cm^2 and were found maximum for Early Giant and minimum for Anmol. Total phenolics contents was found maximum in green seeds of Early Giant (34.98 mg GAE/100g fw) and minimum in Prachi (8.36 mg GAE/100g fw), whereas total flavonoids contents were found maximum in green seeds of Lincoln (17.34 mg QE/ 100g fw) and minimum in Saloni (5.15 mg QE/100g fw). The study further revealed that antioxidant activities of extracts of green seeds, evaluated in terms of 1, 1-Dipheny l-2-picrylhydrazyl (DPPH assay), 2, 2′-azinobis-3-ethyl benzothiazoline-6-disulphonic acid (ABTS assay) and ferric reducing antioxidant power (FRAP assay). All three assays were found maximum in Early Giant, (76.62 mM AAE/100g fw, 58.08 mM AAE/100g fw and 0.09 µg Fe II/100g fw, respectively) and minimum in Ruchi, CM-Avtar and

G.B. Pant Institute of Himalayan Environment and Development, Himachal Unit, Mohal - Kullu - 175 126, Himachal Pradesh, India.

Anmol (28.73 mM AAE/100g fw, 12.10 mM AAE/100g fw and 0.02 µg Fe II/g fw, respectively). From the present study, it is concluded that cultivars Early Giant and Lincoln of *P. sativum* among the test cultivars possess higher economic yield and antioxidants and their cultivation in Kullu Valley of northwestern Indian Himalaya should be promoted for improving economic status of local poor farmers.

Keywords: *Pisum sativum* L; Cultivars; Antioxidants; Economic yield; Kullu Valley

INTRODUCTION

Food and Agriculture Organization (FAO) defined pulses as legumes harvested solely their seeds which are consumed directly for health benefits. Pulses including peas have long been important components of the human diet due to the presence of sufficient amounts of starch, protein, and other nutrients. More recently, the health benefits and other than nutrition associated with pulse consumption have attracted much interest of the scientific community (Dahl *et al.* 2012; Jaarsveld *et al.* 2014). Pea (*Pisum sativum* L.) commonly known as garden or field pea is one of the most important and popular legume vegetable crops belongs to family Fabaceae widely grown in different parts of Indian and many countries all over the world for human and animal consumption. The global production of the pea, one of the eleven primary pulses in 2009 was above ten million tons (FAO, 1994; Dahl *et al.* 2012). The green seeds of pea plants have many nutritional values such as: high contents of protein, carbohydrates, phosphorus, iron, calcium and vitamin A and B (Watt and Merrill, 1963; Hassan, 1997).

Increasing the production of pea green pod and dry seeds with high quality is considered as an important aim of today and such aim could be achieved through identification of potential cultivars of a growing region. India is one of top producers of the pea in the world (FAO, 2011). Therefore, the present study was carried out to identify the potential cultivar among the locally grown cultivars of pea (*P. sativum* L.) plants for promoting their cultivation and consumption in Kullu Valley of northwestern Indian Himalaya, Himachal Pradesh.

Material and Methods

Pea (*P. sativum* L.) cultivars such as: Lincoln and Early Giant were procured from Indian Agriculture Research Institute, Regional Station, Katrain, Kullu, whereas cultivars such as: GS-10, Saloni, Ruchi, CM-Avtar, Prachi and Anmol were procured from local seeds store, Kullu. Ten healthy seeds of pea plants were hand sown in pots (706.5 cm2) containing soil and farmyard manure in the ratios of 3:1 at G.B. Pant Institute of Himalayan Environment and Development (GBPIHED), Himachal Unit, Mohal, Kullu, Himachal Pradesh located at 31.8763^{0}N, 7.1541^{0}E and 1155m above mean sea level during October 2013 – February 2014. During the experimental period, rainfall, average maximum and minimum temperature were recorded as 276.9 mm, 17.04 °C and 9.46 °C, respectively. The pots were watered as and when required with the equal volume of water to maintain the moisture of the soil. Weeding was also performed during the course of the experiment as and when required.

Samples of plants were collected in triplicates randomly from each cultivar at the time of harvest. Economic yield *i.e.,* fresh weight of green pods was measured and presented as kg/ha. The plants were washed under running tap water and separated into roots, shoots without pods and pods. These parts were kept separately in hot air oven at 80 °C till a constant weight was achieved. Harvest index (HI) for each cultivar was calculated by dividing dry weights of green pods to that of above ground parts and represented as g/g. The contents of antioxidants in 1g of fresh green seeds of pea were extracted in 1ml of 80 per cent (v/v) methanol. Total flavonoids and total phenolics contents in methanol extracts of green seeds of each cultivar of pea were quantified using the methods of Ordon-Ez *et al.* (2006) and Wolfe *et al.* (2003), and were expressed as mg quercetin equivalents (QE)/100g fw and mg gallic acid equivalents (GAE)/100g fw, respectively. The antioxidant activities in methanol extracts of green seeds were evaluated using in-vitro assay namely: 1, 1-Diphenyl-2-picrylhydrazyl (DPPH), 2, 2′-azinobis -3-ethylbenzothiazoline-6-disulphonic acid (ABTS) and ferric reducing antioxidant power (FRAP, expressed as µg Fe II/g fw) using the methods as described by Re *et al.* (1999), Liyana-Pathirama *et al.* (2005) and Benzine and strain (1996), respectively. The DPPH and ABTS activities in methanol extracts of green seeds of pea plants were quantified in ascorbic acid equivalents (AAE) and were expressed as mM AAE/100g fw.

All the measurements were repeated three times and results were expressed as mean ± SE. A significant difference between treatments means were separated using Duncan Multiple Range Test and were considered significant at $P < 0.05$. All the statistical analyses were performed by using SPSS software (version 16).

Results and Discussion

The data corresponding to economic yield and harvest index of eight cultivars of pea (*P. sativum*) plants were presented in Fig. 4.1. Economic yield of eight cultivars of pea plants varied significantly ($p<0.05$) and ranged between 0.21-0.06 g/cm^2 with maximum in cultivar Early Giant (0.21 g cm-^{2}) and minimum in Anmol (0.06 g/cm^2). Khan *et al.* (2013) also reported the economic yields of different cultivars such as: Fallon, Shareen, DMR-4, DMR-20, PS-40, 10599, 10694, 10679, 10696, PS-810240, 94610191, 2001-55 and FS-21-87 of pea plants, ranged between 60.40 - 14.25 pods/ plant.. Oelke *et al.* (2014) also reported the economic yields of eleven cultivars of pea (cv. Belevue, Helka, Impala, Kimo, Miranda, Procon, Renata, Solara, Tipu, Titan and Trapper) ranges from minimum to maximum as 1161 kg/ha to 2697 kg/ha. The higher economic yield of Early Giant followed by Lincoln in the present study indicated that these cultivars are suitable for cultivation in Kullu valley of Himachal Pradesh. Harvest index of test cultivars of pea plants varied from 0.24g/g to 0.96 g/g and were found maximum to minimum in order: Early Giant > Lincoln > Saloni > Ruchi > GS-10 > Prachi > Anmol > CM-Avtar (Fig. 4.1). Bozoglu *et al.* (2007) reported the yield and harvest index of different cultivars of pea plants varied with seasons. Khan *et al.* (2013) reported that pod yield varied significantly among different genotypes. Ranalli *et al.* (1992) have further reported that different cultivars of *P. sativum* differed in their yield capability.

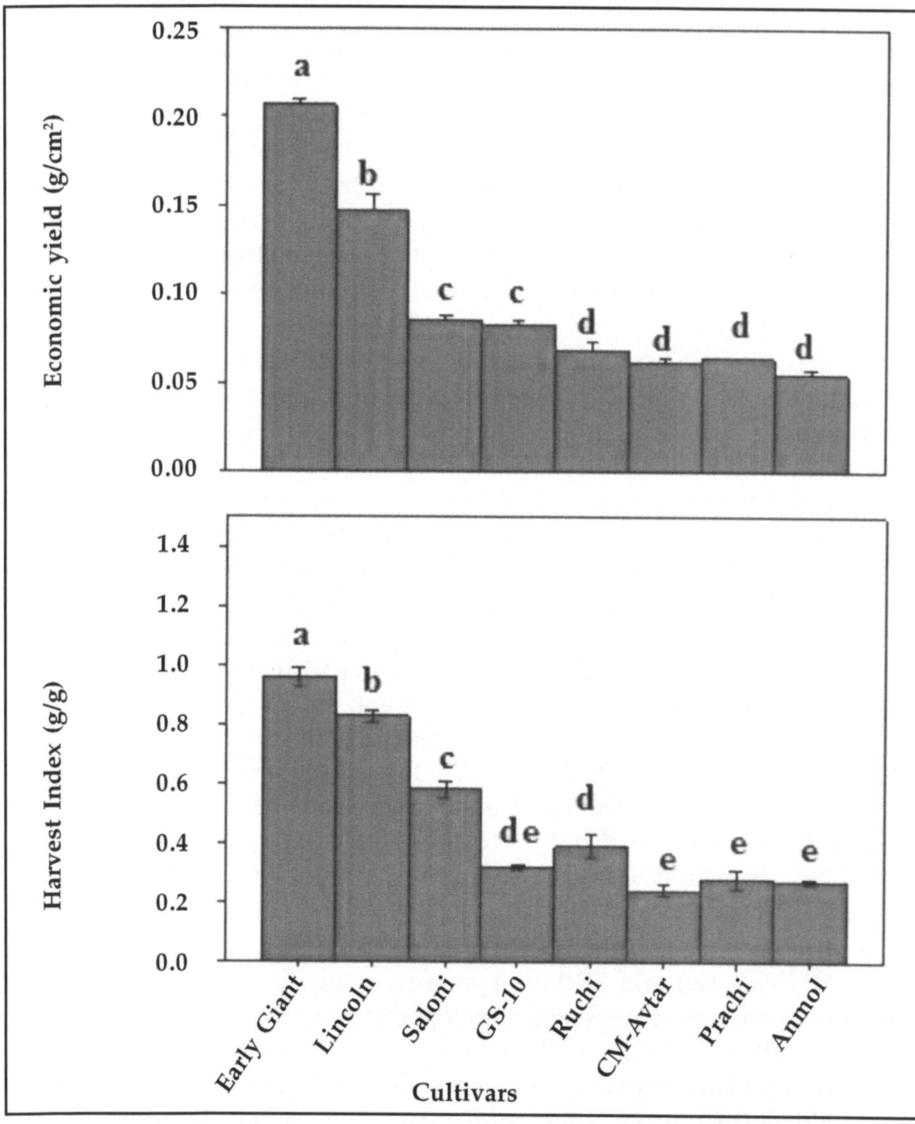

Fig.4.1: **Economic yield and harvest index of eight cultivars of *P. sativum* commonly grown in Kullu Valley, Himachal Pradesh**

Total phenolics and total flavonoids contents in methanol extracts of green seeds of pea plants were shown in Fig. 4.2. Total phenolics and flavonoids contents in different test cultivars of pea plants varied significantly ($p<0.05$) and ranged between 8.36mg GAE/100g fw - 34.98 mgGAE/100g fw and 5.15mgQE/100g fw - 17.34mg QE/100g fw, respectively. The order of variations of total phenolics and flavonoids contents in different test cultivars of pea plants from maximum to minimum were found as Early Giant > Lincoln > GS-10 > Saloni > Ruchi > CM-Avtar > Anmol > Prachi and Lincoln > Early Giant > CM-Avtar > Prachi > GS-10 > Ruchi > Anmol > lowest > Saloni (Fig. 4.2). From this study, it is clear that Early Giant and Lincoln had highest contents of total phenolics and flavonoids contents (34.98mg GAE/100g fw, and 14.14mg QE/100g fw; 29.18mg GAE/100g fw, 17.34mg QE/100g fw, respectively) as compared to others cultivars. Palazuelos *et al*. (2013) reported the total phenolics contents and antioxidant activity of different cultivars of chickpea (*Cicer aritinum* L.). Early Giant and Lincoln may be considered as a source of many bioactive compounds. In the present study, wide variations in total phenolics contents among different cultivars of *P. sativum* were also observed (Fig. 4.2).

Total polyphenol content, total flavonoid content and their relation with antioxidant capacity in 17 chickpea lines having colored seed coats (black, red, brown, green, rubiginous, gray, yellow, cream, or beige) were also reported by Segev *et al*. (2010). The seed coat usually contains more than 95 per cent of these compounds. In this study, both total phenolics and total flavonoid contents varied significantly among different lines and were highly correlated to antioxidant activity. The observed differences in total phenolics contents could be attributed to genetic background, grain physical properties and particularly to the seed coat color since the seed coat color is the structure richer in phenolic compounds. Palazuelos *et al*. (2013) also reported the total phenolics content, total flavonoids contents and antioxidant potential of five cultivars of chickpea (Red ICC5383, Red IC13124, Black ICC3761, Black ICC4418 and Black ICC6306). Yao *et al*. (2011) also reported the total phenolics contents, flavonoids contents and antioxidant potential in sixteen legumes such as: lima bean, broad bean, common bean, pea, jack bean, goa bean, adzuki bean, hyacinth bean, chicking vetch, garbanzo bean, dral, cow bean, rice bean, mung bean and soybean.

In present study, antioxidant potential *i.e.* DPPH, ABTS (expressed as mM AAE/100g fw) and FRAP (expressed as µg Fe II/g fw) activities in methanol extracts of green seeds of pea plants ranged between 28.73 - 70.62, 12.08 - 58.88 and 0.023 - 0.093, respectively among the test cultivars (Fig. 4.3). DPPH activity was found maximum in green seed extracts of Early Giant followed by Lincoln, Saloni, CM-Avtar, GS-10, Anmol, Prachi and lowest in Ruchi. Similarly, ABTS activity was maximum in Early Giant followed by

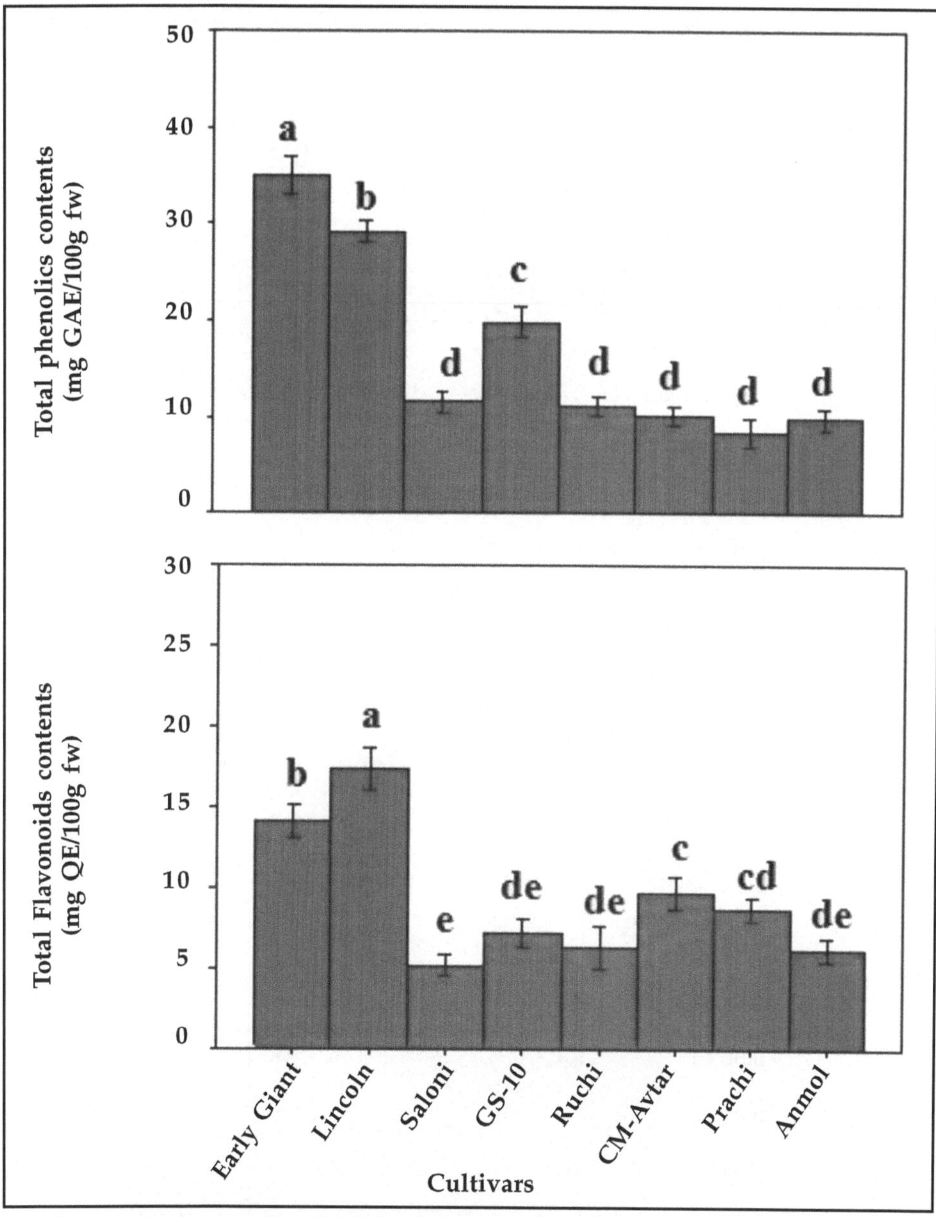

Fig. 4.2: **Total phenolic and total flavonoid contents in methanol extracts of seeds of eight cultivars of *P. sativum* commonly grown in Kullu Valley, Himachal Pradesh**

Lincoln, Saloni, Prachi, GS-10, Anmol Ruchi and lowest in CM-Avtar. FRAP activity was found maximum in Early Giant followed by Lincoln, Saloni, Prachi, GS-10, CM-Avtar, Ruchi and lowest in Anmol. In the present study, total phenolics contents were found in methanol extracts of green seeds of

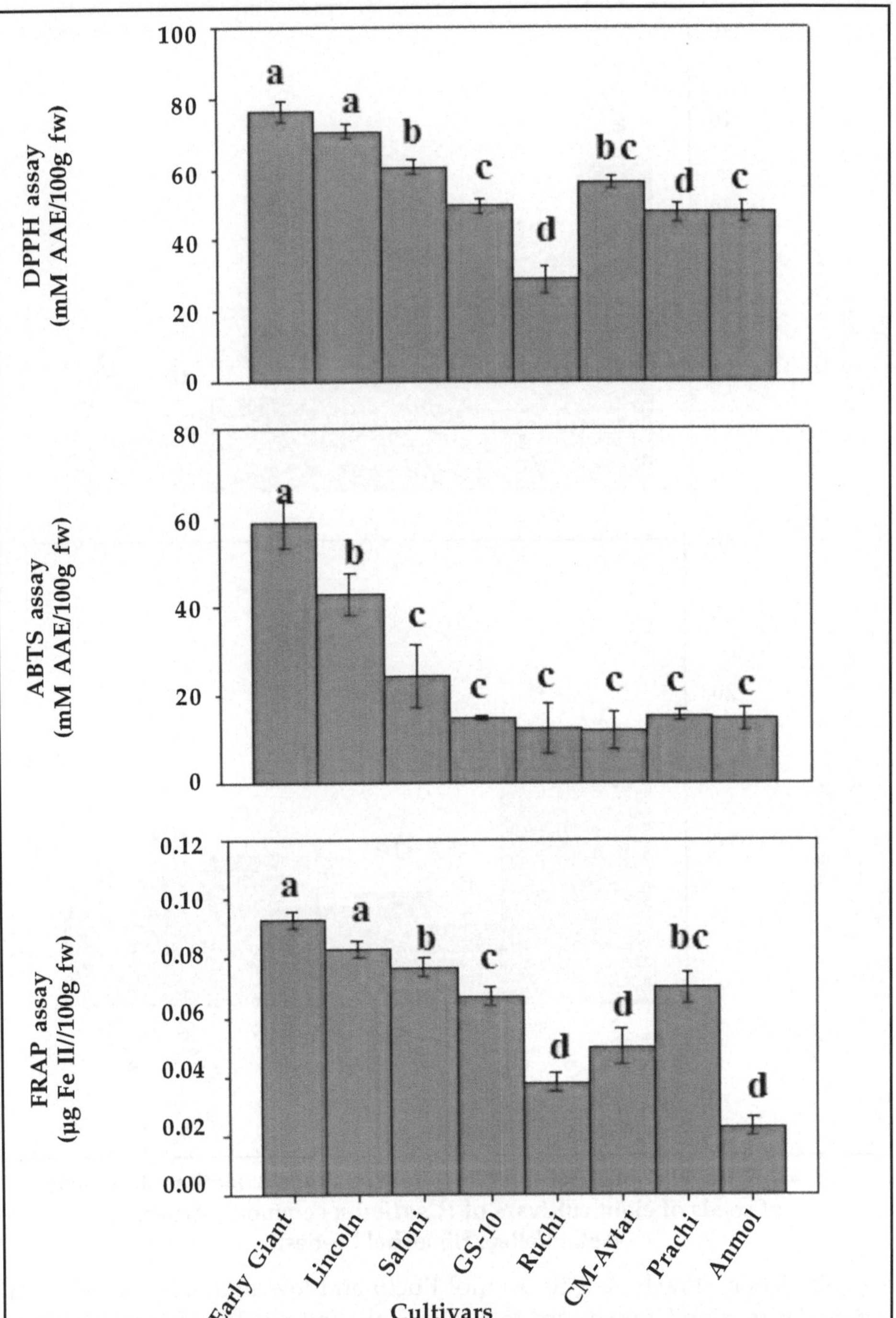

Fig. 4.3: **Antioxidant activity of methanol extracts of seeds of eight cultivars of *P. sativum* commonly grown in Kullu Valley, Himachal Pradesh**

Early Gaint, which also possess higher antioxidant activities. Many researchers have reported a positive correlation between antioxidant activity and total phenolics contents (Cao and Prior, 1998; Xu and Chang, 2007; Xu *et al.* 2007; Han and Baik, 2008; Segev *et al.* 2010; Yao *et al.* 2010, 2011). Thus, the study showed that cultivar Early Gaint and Lincoln have high contents of total phenolics and flavonoids contents and also possesses potential antioxidant activities as compared to other test cultivars.

Conclusion

The results of the present study showed that the eight cultivars of pea plants that were investigated were economically diverse and contained significant amounts of total phenolics, flavonoids and antioxidant potential. Out of eight cultivars investigated here, Early Giant and Lincoln showed higher economic yield, total phenolics and flavonoid contents and possesses higher antioxidant potential as compared to other test cultivars. For this reason, their cultivation and consumption should be promoted in Kullu Valley of northwestern Indian Himalaya. Further more research on location specific response of cultivars Early Giant and Lincoln of pea plants with a view to optimizing their nutraceutical potential is recommended.

REFERENCES

Benzine F.F. and Strain J.J. (1996). Ferric Reducing the Ability of Plasma (FRAP) as a Measure of Antioxidant Power: The FRAP assay. *Analytical Biochemistry*, 239: 70-76.

Bozoglu H., Peksen E.A., Peksen A. and Gulumser A. (2007). Determination of the Yield Performance and Harvesting Periods of Fifteen pea (*Pisum sativum* L.) Cultivars sown in autumn and spring. *Pakistan Journal of Botany*, 39: 2017-2025.

Cao G.H. and Prio R.L. (1998). Measurement of Oxygen Radical Absorbance Capacity in Biological Samples. *Methods in Enzymology*, 299: 50-62.

Dahl W.J., Lauren M., Foster L.M., Robert T. and Tyler R.T. (2012). Review of the Health Benefits of Peas (*Pisum sativum* L.). *British Journal Nutrition*, 108: S3-S10.

Food and Agriculture Organization (FAO) (2011). FAOSTAT. http:/ / faostat.fao.org (accessed in July 2011).

Food and Agriculture Organization (FAO). (1994). Definition and Classification of Commodities: Pulses and Derived Products.

Han H. and Baik B.K. (2008). Antioxidant Activity and phenolic Content of lentils (*Lens culinaris*), chickpeas (*Cicer arietinum* L), peas (*Pisum sativum* L) and soybeans (*Glycine max*), and their Quantitative Changes during Processing. *International Journal of Food Science and Technology*, 43: 1971-78.

Hassan A.A. (1997). Vegetable Fruits. Al-Dar Al-Arabia Publications and Distribution, Cairo Egypt. pp. 241.

http:/ / www.fao.org/ es/ faodef/ fdef04e.htm (accessed October in 2011).

Jaarsveld P.V., Faber M., Heerden I.V., Wenhold F., Rensburg W.J.V. and Averbeke W.V. (2014). Nutrient Content of Eight African leafy vegetables and their Potential Contribution to Dietary Reference Intake. *Journal Food Composition and Analysis*, 33: 77-84.

Khan T.N., Ramzan A., Jillani G. and Mehmood T. (2013). Morphological Performance of Peas (Pisum sativum) genotypes under rainfed conditions of potowar regions. *Journal of Agricultural Research*, 51(1): 51-60.

Liyana-Pathiranan C.M., Shahidi F. (2005). Antioxidant Activity of Commercial Soft and Hard Wheat (Triticum aestivum L.) as Affected by gastric pH conditions. *Journal of Agriculture and Food Chemistry*, 53: 2433-2440.

Oelke E.A., Oplinger E.S., Hanson C.V., Davis D.W., Putnam D.H., Fuller D.H. and Rosen C.J. (2014). Dry Field pea. Alternative Field Crops Manual pp. 51-59.

Ordon-Ez A.A.L., Gomez J.D., Vattuone M.A., Isla M.I. (2006). Antioxidant Activities of Sechium edule (Jacq.) Swart Extracts. Food Chemistry, 97: 452-458.

Palazuelos M.J.H., Lugo M.I.O., Dorado R.G., Valenzuela J.A.L., Rochin S.M., Carrilo J.M., Tiznado J.A.G. and Moreno C.R. (2013). Technological Properties, Antioxidant Activity and Total phenolic and flavonoid Content of pigmented chickpea (*Cicer arietinum* L.) cultivars. *International Journal of Food Science and Technology*, 64(1): 69-76.

Ranalli P.I., Giordano U., Ziliotto G.M., Lomabrcho V., Pirami E., Lahoz V., Bcuonaccorso P., Talluri P., Bottozzi G., Lucque D., Rosoe G., Ruaro B. and Casrini P.D. (1992). Yield Potential of pea for dry Seed in Different Italian Environments. Sementi-Elette, 38(2): 15-43.

Re R., Pellegrini N., Proteggente A., Pannala A., Yang M., Rice E.C. (1999). Antioxidant Activity Applying an Improved ABTS Radical cation decolorization assay. Free Radical Biology and Medicine, 26: 1231-1237.

Segev A., Badan H., Kapulnik Y., Shomer I., Oren-Shamir M. and Galili S. (2010). Determination of polyphenols, flavonoids, and antioxidant capacity in colored chickpea (*Cicer arietinum* L.). *Journal of Food Science*, 75: S115-S119.

Watt B.K. and Merrill A.L. (1963). Composition of Foods. U.S. Department of Agriculture, Agricultural Research Service, USDA Hand Book, 8: 190.

Wolfe K., Wu X. and Liu R.H. (2003). Antioxidant Activity of Apple Peels. *Journal of Agriculture and Food Chemistry*, 51: 609-614.

Xu B.J. and Chang S.K.C. (2007). A Comparative Study on phenolic Profiles and Antioxidant Activities of legumes as Affected by Extraction solvents. *Journal of Food Science*, 72: S159-S166.

Xu B.J., Yuan S.H. and Chang S.K.C. (2007). Comparative Analyses of phenolic composition, Antioxidant Capacity and Color of Cool Season legumes and other selected food legumes. *Journal of Food Science*, 72: S167-S177.

Yao Y., Cheng X., Wang L., Wang S. and Ren G. (2011). The Biological Potential of Sixteen Legumes in China. *International Journal of Molecular Science*, 12: 7048-7058.

Yao Y., Sang W., Zhou M. and Ren G. (2010). Antioxidant and glucosidase inhibition of colored grains in China. *Journal of Agriculture and Food Chemistry*, 58: 770-774.

Pages: 65-88

AGRO-BIODIVERSITY: ***CONSERVATION AND SUSTAINABLE DEVELOPMENT***
Edited by: **Dr. Pankaj Sharma; Dr. Narayan Singh & Dr. Pawan Kumar 'Bharti'**
ISBN: 978-93-5056-782-1
Edition: **2016**
Published by: **Discovery Publishing House Pvt. Ltd., New Delhi (India)**

5

Medicinal Plants and Potential Anticancer Activity

Showkat Ahmad Bhat[1*]; Manzoor R Mir[1];
Hilal Ahmad Wani[2] and **Sabhiya Majid[2]**

ABSTRACT

Cancer is a major public health burden in both developed and developing countries. Anticancer activity is the effect of natural and synthetic or biological and chemical agents to reverse, suppress or prevent carcinogenic progression. Several synthetic agents are used to cure the disease but they have their toxicity and hence the research is going onto investigate the plant derived chemotherapeutic agents. India is the largest producer of medicinal plants and is rightly called the 'Botanical garden of the World'. The medicinal plants, besides having natural therapeutic values against various diseases, also provide high quality of food and raw materials for livelihood. Considerable works have been done on these plants to treat cancer, and some plant products have been marketed as anticancer drugs, based on the traditional uses and scientific reports. These plants may promote host resistance against infection by re-stabilizing body equilibrium and conditioning the body tissues. Several reports describe that the anticancer activity of medicinal plants is due to the presence of antioxidants in them. In fact, the medicinal plants are easily available, cheaper and

1. Division of Veterinary Biochemistry, F.V.Sc., and AH, SKUAST-K, Shuhama, Alustang - 190 006, India.
2. Department of Biochemistry, Government Medical College, Karan-Nagar, Srinagar, Jammu and Kashmir - 190 010, India.

possess no toxicity as compared to the modern (allopathic) drugs. Thus, the various combinations of the active components of these plants after isolation and identification can be made and have to be further assessed for their synergistic effects. Preparation of standardized dose and dosage regimen may play a critical role in the remedy of cancer. The rate with which cancer is progressing, it seems to have an urgent and effective effort for making good health of humans as well as animals. There is abroad scope to derive the potent anticancer agents from medicinal plants, which need thorough research.

Keywords: Anticancer activity, medicinal plants, Indian Medicinal Plants

INTRODUCTION

For a long times plants have been provide essential nutritional values, medicinal properties and notable physiological effect to life and are a good source of food. Traditional medicine (TM) refers to the application, approach, knowledge, and belief in incorporating plant or animal based properties in remedies, singularly or in combination, for the purpose of treating or preventing disease as well as to maintain the well-being of an individual. Population rise, inadequate supply of drugs, prohibitive cost of treatments, side effects of several allopathic drugs and development of resistance to currently used drugs for infectious diseases have led to increased emphasis on the use of plant materials as a source of medicines for a wide variety of human ailments. As such herbal remedies have been used to cure a variety of disorders or conditions such as: diabetes, cardiovascular problems, weight control, dermal infirmities, sexual malfunction, and of course cancer (Dalziel, 1973).

According to the World Health Organization, more than 70 per cent of the world's population uses TM in order to fulfill their health. Plants used in traditional medicine have stood up to the test of time and contributed many novel compounds for preventive and curative medicine to modern science. India is sitting on a gold mine of well recorded and traditionally well practiced knowledge of herbal medicine. Specially, plants growing at high altitude in Himalayan pastures are time-honored sources of health and general well-being of local inhabitants. As of today, Himalayan plants are a major contributor to the herbal pharmaceutical industry both of India and other countries (Dharmani *et al*. 2004). Plants growing at higher altitudes are subjected to an assault of diverse test ingsituations including higher doses of mutagenic UV-radiation, physiological drought, desiccation and strong winds.

Plants interact with stressful environments by physiological adaptation and altering the biochemical profile of plant tissues and producing a spectrum of secondary metabolites. Secondary metabolites are of special interest to scientists because of the unique pharmacophores and medicinal properties. Secondary metabolites like: polyphenols, terpenes and alkaloids have been reported to possess antimutagenic and anticancer properties in many studies. The fundamental aspiration of the current review is to divulge the antimutagenic/anticancer potential of five alpine plants used as food or medicine by the populations living at high altitudes India is the largest producer of medicinal plants and is rightly called the 'Botanical garden of the World'.

The medicinal plants, besides having natural therapeutic values against various diseases, also provide high quality of food and raw materials for livelihood. Considerable works have been done on these plants to treat cancer, and some plant products have been marketed as anticancer drugs, based on the traditional uses and scientific reports. These plants may promote host resistance against infection by re-stabilizing body equilibrium and conditioning the body tissues. Several reports describe that the anticancer activity of medicinal plants is due to the presence of antioxidants in them. In fact, the medicinal plants are easily available, cheaper and possess no toxicity as compared to the modern (allopathic) drugs. Hence, this review article contains 66 medicinal plants, which are the natural sources of anticancer agents. Cancer (malignant tumour) is an abnormal growth and proliferation of cells.

It is a frightful disease because the patient suffers pain, disfigurement and loss of many physiological processes. Cancer may begun controllable and incurable, and may occurat any time at any age in any part of the body. It is caused by a complex, poorly understood interplay of genetic and environmental factors. It continues to represent the largest cause of mortality in the world and claims over 6 million. Cancer kills annually about 3500 per million population around the world. A large number of chemopreventive agents are used to cure various cancers, but they produce side effects that prevent their extensive usage. Although more than 1500 anticancer drugs are in active development with over 500 of the drugs under clinical trials, there is an urgent need to develop much effective and less toxic drugs the plant kingdom plays an important role in the life of humans and animals. India is the largest producer of medicinal plants and is rightly called the 'Botanical garden of the World'. Medicinal plants have been stated (Garg *et al*. 1993; Hakim, 1995; Goeland Sairam, 2002; Gupta and Tandon, 2004) to comprise about 8000 species and account for approximately 50 per cent of all the higher flowering plant species of India. In other words, there are about 400 families of the flowering plants; at least 315 are represented by India.

Medicinal properties of few such plants have been reported but a good number of plants still used by local folklore are yet to be explored. Ayurveda, Siddha and Unani systems of medicine provide good base for scientific exploration of medicinally important molecules from nature. The rediscovery of Ayurveda is a sense of redefining it is modern medicines. Emerging concept of combining Ayurveda with advanced drug discovery programme is globally acceptable. Traditional medicine has a long history of serving peoples all over the world. The ethnobotany provides a rich resource for natural drug research and development. In recent years, the use of traditional medicine in formation on plant research has again received considerable interest. The Westernuse of such information has also come under increasing scrutiny and the national and indigenous rights on these resources have become acknowledged by most academic and industrial researchers.

According to the World Health Organization (WHO), about three quarters of the world's population currently use herbs and other forms of traditional medicines to treat diseases. Traditional medicines are widely used in India. Even in USA, use of plants and phytomedicines has increased dramatically in the last two decades (Keen and Deacon, 1994; Joy *et al.* 2001). It has been also reported that more than 50 per cent of all modern drugs in clinical use are of natural products, many of which have been recognized to have the ability to include apoptosis in various cancer cells of human origin (Kokate *et al.* 2007). Natural Products have long been a fertile source of cure for cancer, which is projected to become the major causes of death in this century. However, there is a continuing need for development of new anticancer drugs, drug combinations and chemotherapy strategies, by methodical and scientific exploration of enormous pool of synthetic, biological and natural products. There are at least 250,000 species of plants out of which more than one thousand plants have been found to possess significant anticancer properties.

While many molecules obtained from nature have shown wonders, there are a huge number of molecules that still either remains to be trapped or studied in details by the medicinal chemists. The article reviews many such structures and their related chemistry along with the recent advances in understanding mechanism of action and structure-function relationships of nature derived anticancer agents at the molecular, cellular and physiological levels. Taxol, one of the most outstanding agents, has been found beneficial in treatment of refractory ovarian, breast and other cancers. Another prominent molecule includes: Podophyllotoxin. Synthetic modification of this molecule led to the development of Etoposide, known to be effective for small cell cancers of the lungs and testes. Camptothecin isolated from Camptothecaacuminata also have been extensively studied.

Other important molecules discussed include: Vincristine, Vinblastine, Colchicine, Ellipticine and Lepachol along with Flavopiridol, a semi-synthetic analogue of the chromone alkaloid Rohitukine from India, a pyridoindole alkaloid from leaves of Ochrosia species and many more. There view also deals with the lesser-known plants of sub-Himalayan region (Rao *et al.* 200; Mahendran and Vanisree, 2002; Sairam *et al.* 2002; Goel, 2003; Manish *et al.* 2008).

Plants Used for Cancer Treatment

Cancer is often deadly and affects a considerable number of people worldwide. Ongoing research is being done throughout the world to seek out effective treatments for cancer, including the use of plants to relieve and treat cancer patients. This treatment makes use of the compounds naturally present in plants that are known to inhibit or kill carcinogenic cells. An alternative to chemotherapy, which is the most common means by which doctors and specialists treat cancer, organically based treatments may not have the severe side effects that radial treatments and chemotherapy has. The harshside effects of cancer treatments is one motivating factor to finding alternative methods.

The use of botanical when treating cancer patients is considered a natural alternative, because some plants may contain properties that naturally have the ability to prevent the spread or risk of developing various forms of cancer. As in all medical testing, careful precautions and considerations are taken when studying the different compounds present in plants that are known to treat cancer. Some examples of plants that may be used for cancer treatment are discussed below with their respective advancements. Some side effects are still expected, and it is important that any patient interested in exploring botanical treatment seek the advice of a licensed medical professional.

There are around 460 species of plants that can be used as herb forremedy, including plant healer various types of cancer. Various types of anticancer plant are Zedoary (*Curcuma zedoaria*), Rodent Tuber (*Typhoniumflagelliforme*), God's Crown (*Phaleriamacrocarpa*), Madagaskar Periwinkle (*Catharanthusrosens*), Artocarpus Integer (*Selaginellacorymbosa*), Bamboo Grass (*LoathatreumGràcies*), handsome (*Taraxacummongolicum*), fruitmakasar (*Bruccajavanica*), Garlic (*Alliumsativum*), Echo China (*Smilax china*), Sunflower (*Helianthus annus*), Leunca (*Solanumnigrum*), Job's Tears (*Coixlachryma*-Jobi), Bamboo Rope (*Asparaguscochinchinensis*), and others.

Anticancer Herbs

Anticancer herbs, there are many different anticancer herbs that have been used by different cultures throughout time for medicinal purposes. In fact, much of modern medicine owes itself to plants and herbs. With such a wide variety of herbs in the world it's no surprise that there are quite a few anticancer herbs that can really help with cancer prevention. There are also many other anticancer herbs which will help to alleviate the symptoms if you already suffer from cancer treatments. One of the many anticancer herbs is Alfalfa. Considered one of the most nutritious foods available, Alfalfa has very important uses for counteracting the effects of chemotherapy.

Alfalfa contains antibacterial and anti-fungal properties that make it a great body cleanser and infection fighter. It works to increase the production of white blood cells and replace those lost during treatments. The large amount of nutrients in these anticancer herbs makes them invaluable in restoring healthy levels of vitamins in the blood stream. Alfalfa has been researched and found to help lower cholesterol levels and neutralize cancer. Another anticancer herb is Andrographis: It is an ancient medicinal herb and is an annual plant that grows in the wastelands and forests of Asia. There have been many conclusive studies of its use against cancer, AIDS and both bacterial and viral infections. This herb has been shown to have a dramatic effect in maturing cancer cells, a process which seems to stop the cancer cells growing out of control. In addition, extracts from Andrographis leaves have been recorded as being able to kill cancer cells.

Research done in Japan has reportedly found that Andrographis reduced the likelihood of cancer cells in the stomach multiplying. Many independent studies have also discovered impressive results with other cancers including prostate and breast cancer. Anticancer herbs come in many forms one of which is a type of thistle plant. Blessed thistle has a hugely positive effect on the eduction in size of tumors due to its main component cnicin. This has the effect of reducing fluid around the tumor, cooling any inflammation in the body as well as fighting off bacteria. Not only this but the anti-inflammatory properties help rejuvenate the body and speed up recovery one of the more well-known anticancer herbs is Burdock. The root has been used in natural medicine for centuries. Although it was originally used for liver function, joint pain and skin health burdock root has been discovered to have anti-tumor effects along side its detoxifying qualities.

This has been shown in animal studies where it was discovered that this anticancer herbs inhibits mutationsin cells that are exposed to mutation causing chemicals that can lead to cancer. Mushrooms, although not really an herb, are still a very natural cure. As a fungus there are many qualities that certain types of mushrooms possess that aren't found in herbs. For example the Maitake mushroom has excellent healing properties. Extracts of the mushroom are most effective when used as Maitake D-fraction and is available incapsule or tablet form. Maitake is a proven cancer fighter. The FDA has recently approved clinical studies of a Maitake extract on participants with advanced breast and prostate cancer. American studies also show positive results on colorectal cancer and Chinese studies show positive results with liver, lung, stomach cancer and leukemia.

These mushrooms should be used as a complementary therapy for such conditions and not be a substitute for standard treatments. Anticancer herbs include the garden variety rosemary that is found all over the place. Rosemary is a potent antioxidant, antispasmodic and antiseptic. It is rarely respected for its powerful effect on the body. Rosemary helps to prevent cancer from ever forming in the first place. It does this by helping to prevent carcinogenic chemicals from attaching themselves to cells and causing the mutations that lead to cancer. A number of green tea blends are also anticancer herbs and act in a very similar way to rosemary. To make a tea infusion of Rosemary, pour 1 cup boiling water over 1 teaspoon of rosemary leaves and steep for 15 minutes. Strain and drink. Half a teaspoon of cinnamon spice is also known to aid the fight against cancer.

These anticancer herbs are just a small percentage of the plants that can benefit the body through healing. These herbs can be a preventative measure to ensure the body has everything it needs to stop mutations from occurring in the firstplace. They can also be used to lessen the horrible side effects when taken along side chemotherapy treatments. But most importantly they have been shown to reduce the effects of cancerous cells and even reduce the size of tumors. With all the benefits these anticancer herbs can provide you may want to start growing some in your own garden (Mahendran and Vanisree, 2002; Manish *et al.* 2008; Sairam *et al.* 2002 and 2003; Wadker *et al.* 2008).

Birch

Species Name – *Betulaalba,* Common Name – Birch The Birch or *Betulaalba* plant has a variety of different uses. Its medicinal use include diuretic, anti-inflammatory, and a generalpain reliever. There are currently several side effects associated with the use of the birch leaf, including chest pains, tightness in the chest or that may cause breathing problems, and skin irritation. The Birch has sixty species throughout the world, ten of which are native to Canada and the northern part of the United States. Compound – Betulinic Acid The effects of Betulinic Acid, as studied by Dr. Brij Saxena of Weill Cornell Medical College, has been known to kill cancerous cells, and has been especially effective in the treatment of prostate cancer patients. This compound does not cause side effects, in typical patients. However the compound is being researched further for its compatibility with patients suffering from HIV.

Autumn Crocus

Species Name – *Colchicum autumnale,* Common Names – Naked Ladies, Colchicum, and Meadow Saffron the Autumn Crocus, of the Lily Family (Liliaceae), is a plant with small flowers of varying colors. This plant is indigenous to Europe, Northern African, and Asian continents. Being a plant with a history of medicinal use, records have shown that it had been used in Ancient Greece, India, and Egypt with records being stored in the oldest medical text, known as the Ebers Papyrus. At present, it is used to treat inflammatory disorders. The Autumn Crocus is alsovalued for its' chemotherapeutic properties. Compound – Colchicine Otherwise known as the alkaloid colchicine, its medicinal use was in the treating gout, a painful disease that is the result of the joints being inflamed. The other major use of colchicine is in its effect on the mitosis of animal and plant cells; it works by interrupting the process altogether, especially in the division of cancerous cells. Some common reactions to using cochicineare diarrhea and reversible malabsorption syndrome.

Lapacho Tree

Species Names – *Tabebuiaimpetiginosa, T. avellanedae* Common Names – Lapacho, Pau D'Arco, Taheebo, and Ipe Roxo Found in the rain forests of South America, especially in Argentina, Paraguay, and Brazil, the Lapacho Tree is an ever green with blossoms that may be red or purple. It has proven to be medically useful, even since the time of the Incas. Locals still use the tree for many diseases, including: the common cold, flue, herpes, psoriasis, as well as other discomforts that cancer patients are more susceptible to due to their decreased immune system. Compound – Beta-Lapachone, Lapachol Beta-lapachone has anticancer properties that are being researched with focus on pancreatic cancer. Dr. David Boothman of the Harold C. Simmons Comprehensive Cancer Center, and other colleagues, have conducted study on the properties that betalapachone harnesses and they have discovered that it reacts with NQ01, anenyzme present in lung cancer and solid tumors. The interaction between the betalapachone and the NQ01 form a bond that extinguishes the tumor cells that the NQ01 catalyzes.

Camptotheca

Species Name – *Camptothecaacuminata* Common Names – Xi Shu, Happy Tree The Camptotheca, otherwise known as the Happy Tree, is a fern-like deciduous tree with a variety of medicinal uses. From its scientific name, *Camptothecaacuminata*, its genus 'Camptotheca' is Greek for 'curved sheath' which resembles the pods that are formed in a curve found in the plant. Although its used medically, Camptotheca is very unstable. It isn't soluble in water and can be highly toxic, so special care should be taken to observe any dangerous side effects and a patient's health should be carefully monitored by a medical professional. Although Camptotheca has been used medically, it has since been discontinued by many professionals due to the development of treatments with less severe side effects. The side effects of Camptotheca are attributed to its compounds. Compound – Camptothecia, Topotecan, CPT-11, 9-Aminocamptothecin Extracted from the Camptotheca Acuminataplant, CPT-11 is a compound administered in patients with brain tumors through the drug Irinotecan. It contains antineoplastic, used to prevent the mutation of cells intocancerous cells with the possibility of preventing or reducing the disease into one that is benign. Some common side effects of this compound include: diarrhea, alopecia or hair loss, vomiting, weakness, and lowering of white and red blood cells. Species Name – Taxus Baccata Common Name – Yew The English Yew is an ever green tree that flowers from March to April. Not self fertile, the yew is known for attraction of wildlife. This plant can grow in almost any soil, but it is most prominent in groups. This tree has known to be used in wood furniture, especially cabinets. English Yew can also be used medicinally to treat chest pains. English Yew is also valued for it's 'taxol' that has been found to effectively been used as treatment for ovarian cancer, as well as less serious ailments. Compound – Docetaxel, Taxol although toxic, the occasional use of the docetaxel in medicine has shown potential in being an anticancer drug, especially in breast cancer cases. The toxicity of the compound requires proper management to avoid the worsening of the situation. Other treatments that are possible are cystitis, heart and kidney problems, and others. Common side effects of docetaxel are constipation, dizziness, diarrhea, hair loss, loss of appetite, joint pain, as well as weakness indifferent parts of the body. When these side effects persist, medical attention should besought right away.

Hemp

Species Name – *Cannabis sativa,* Common Names – Marijuana, Bhang, Ganja, and Hashish. The Hemp is an annual herb that may reach 5 meters in height with leaves that form a fan-like structure with jagged edges. This plant is native to central Asia and as a result of importation, has expanded toward Europeand the Americas. This plant has many uses, some of which are furnishing fiber, oil, in medicine, and narcotics. Commonly referred to as Cannabis, Hemp is a very versatile material and is frequently used to relieve cancer pain, treat depression, and hypothermia, it also works as an appetite suppressant. A controversial plant in the field of medicine, it has been up for the debate of its use being an abused or medically prosperous drug.

Compound – Delta-9-Tetrahydrocannabinol Research has shown that the administering of smoked marijuana helped treated thenausea that was caused by cancer chemotherapy, thereby being an aid to the cancer treatment process. Side effects of this compound are not often seen in the physical aspect, rather in the mental or cognitive domain such as: inability to distinguish space distances and time intervals, vigilance, and memory processes.

Mayapple

Species Name – *Podophyllumpeltatum,* Common Names – Devil's Apple, Hog Apple, Indian Apple, Umbrella Plant, Wild Lemon Known to be a perennial native herb, it is native in Eastern North America. This plant resembles a fan-like structure with wide leaves that is edible and medicinal. The medicinal property of this plant has been used by the Native Americans. Although the plant is edible, its seeds and rind are not and they have been known to be poisonous. May apple has been used to treat snakebites and as a laxative. Recently, May apple has been used in the United States to treat bothlung and testicular cancer. Compound – Podophyllotoxin, Etoposide,

Podophyllinic Acid, and Teniposide with the other forms of the compound, medicinally in the removal of genital wartswhich was first used in 1942 with out standing success. The Etoposide compound form is useful in anticancer drugs which kill the cancerous cells through the process of enzyme-mediated DNA scission. This blocks the action of the cell on the DNA of the cancer cells that will prevent their development, thereby killing them.

Some side effects of Etoposide are loss of appetite, back pain, skin discoloration, hair loss, diarrhea, and increased sweating.

Nothapodytes Tree

Species Name – *Nothapodytesfoetida,* Common Name – Nothapodytes Tree The Nothapodytes Tree has its medicinal use whose wood-extract is used in treating diseases. This tree is found in western Ghats, India, which have become important because of it being an anti-cancerous compound containing plant with medicinal properties similar to the camptothecin plant, due to their remarkably similar chemical makeup. Compound – Acetylcamptothecin, Camptothecin, Scopolectin Camptothecin found in the Nothapodytes Tree is an inhibitor of the DNA topoisomerase found in cancerous cells. This halts the process of mutation and development of the cancer cells that render them useless and as a result, they die. This means of cancer curation makes use of the property of inhibition that the camptothecin compound has with the DNA of the cancerous cells. Some side effects in using this compound include: diarrhea and anemia.

Periwinkle

Species Name – *Catharanthusroseus,* Common Names – Madagascar Periwinkle, Periwinkle The Periwinkle plant is located in the southern portion of North America. Its fruith as an ellipsoid structure with pink or purple shaded petals in its flower. Being an annual plant, this plant has medicinal properties, such as: being hypoglycemic to lower the blood glucose, especially for diabetics. Other than that, research has shown that Periwinkle has anticancer properties that have shown promise. Compound – Vinblastine, Vincristine, Vindesine, Vinorelbine Vinblastine, being an anti-cancer drug extracted from the periwinkle plant has shown to be effective in slowing down the effect of tumors. This is due that the compound has been studied to have an inhibiting property that slows down microtubule formation in cancer cells. This then disrupts the assembling of mitoticspindles in tumor cells which halt the development of the cancer. Vinblastine cancause side effects including: bone pain, depression, dizzines, constipation, hair loss, stomach pain, and loss of appetite.

Pacific Yew

Species Name – *Taxusbrevifolia*, Common Name – Yew The Pacific Vew, otherwise known as the Western Yew, is a tree with many specialuses. Its bark contains valuable properties that are effective in treating various forms of cancer. Native to Southeast Alaska, this coniferous tree commonly exists in the western part of the United States as well. A plant of many uses; its medicinal uses are integral in cancer treatment, especially refractory ovarian cancer. Compound – Paclitaxel Taxol, or a variant of which being Paclitaxel, has been studied to have anticancer properties as identified by the National Cancer Institute to be a very likely candidate in the cancer treatment process. The compound works in the way that it binds with cancer cells thus stopping their division. This method of cancer treatment limits the spread of the disease on to other parts of the body, thereby allowing further chemotherapy to deal with the now bounded cells. Side effects include: anemia, neutropenia, and hair loss.

Herbs and Anti-oxidants that Fight Cancer

A number of studies from all over the world are pointing to culinary herbs as sources of anti-oxidants and other substances that have anticancer characteristics. The scientists found that these herbs help reduce cancer risk and some can even modify tumor behaviour. Some of these cancer preventing herbs are discussed here.

Basil

Basil is well known for its medicinal value. Apart from having anti inflammatory, blood pressure lowering, and nervous system stimulating properties, this popular herb has been found to have chemoprotective potential for colon cancer. In fact, a study found that basil played a significant role in reducing colon tumors in experimental animals. However, no human clinical trials have been conducted to confirm this experiment.

Oregano

Amongst the dried herbs, oregano has perhaps the highest anti-oxidant levels. Rosmarinic acid is the compound inoregano that has the strong anti-oxidant activity. An Indian study reported that oregano supplementation of 40 mg per kg., of body weight had a modulatory role on tissue lipid peroxidation in colon cancer-bearing experimental rodents. The dosage for human beings has not yet been determined, butthen, how much of oregano would you need to flavor your dish. 2.2 Thyme: Thyme is sweeter and milder than oregano. Thyme as a dried herb contains very high levels of anti-oxidants in the form of rosmarinic acid and phenolic compounds such as: thymol and carvacrol. ATurkish study supported by Hacettepe University Research Foundation suggested that these phenolic compounds atconcentrations below 0.2 mM and 0.1 mM respectively can significantly reduce the oxidative DNA damage and thus prevent the development of any type of cancer.

Cilantro

Cilantro or, more commonly, coriander is another potent herb that has anticancer properties. The prevalent anti-oxidants in cilantro are beta-carotene, quercetin and rutin. This herb, normally used in chelation therapy for people suffering from lead poisoning, helps remove free radicals by getting rid of the heavy metals in your body. Dr. Yoshiaki Omurafrom the Heart Disease Research Foundation, New York, NY, USA, has actually found that fresh cilantro removes heavy metals – and with it the free radicalstoo – from the body in less than 2 weeks.

Garlic

The National Cancer Institute (affiliated to the NIH) recognizes garlic to have potential anticancer properties. The sulphydryl compounds in garlic have the ability to block the formation of cancer – causing substances. Several population studies have shown an association between increased garlic consumption and reduced risk of cancers of the stomach, colon, esophagus, pancreas, and also breast cancer. A study has found that garlic intake of 10 g per day could reduce the risk of prostate cancer by 50 per cent.

Green tea

Polyphenols in green tea and sometimes black tea, help kill cancerous cells and stop their progression. Mayo Clinic studies have revealed that a substance called epigallocatechin gallate (EGCG) in green tea reduces the number of leukemia cells inpatients with CLL (chronic lymphocytic leukemia), a form of blood cancer. Similarly, another study found that women who drank powdered green tea were less likely to develop bladder cancer. Again, men who drank the most green tea were 37 per cent less likely to develop pancreatic cancer. A large Chinese clinical study found that the risk of prostate cancer declined with increasing frequency and quantity of green tea consumption. However, scientists found that green tea could reduce the chances of recurrence of breast cancer but it could not prevent or improve breast cancer.

Maitake

Mushroom: Maitake is anedible mushroom native to the mountains of northeast Japan. Its active ingredient is a polysaccharide called beta glucan. Maitakemushroom extract is said to limit or even reverse tumor growth. It also enhances the benefits of chemotherapy and lessens the side effects of anticancer drugs. It acts by activating certain cells and proteins that attack cancer, T-cells and interleukin-1 and interleukin-2. The daily dose of driedmushroom is between 3 to 7 g. Maitake may not be suitable for those on hypoglycemic medication.

Ginger

Some pungent substances present in ginger rhizome have anti-oxidant and anti-inflammatory activities. The anticancer properties of ginger are attributed tophenolic substances such as: 6-gingerol and 6-paradol and other constituents such as: shogaols and zingerone. A study publishedin the journal Biochemical and Biophysical Research Communications reported that 6-gingerol can reduce viability of gastric cancer cells and limit the spread of cancer.

Turmeric

Although turmeric is promoted mainly as anti-inflammatory herbal remedy, some scientists believe that the anti-oxidant curcumin present inturmeric may prevent or slow the growth of many cancers including: tumor of esophagus, stomach and intestine, breast cancer and also skin cancer in experimental animals. However, clinical research is needed to determine its efficacy in cancer prevention and treatment in human beings. But, the laboratory studies have confirmed the cucumin interferes with several molecular pathways involved in cancer development, growth and spread. Further, a study found that ethanolic extract of turmeric producesre markable symptomatic relief in patients with external cancerous lesions. There was a reduction in smell in 90 per cent of cases and reduction in itching in almost all cases.

Cinnamon Bark

Cinnamon has antioxidant properties that can significantly decrease lipid peroxidation that lead to cancer. Further, cinnamon bark oil has been found by researchers to be one of the most effective inhibitors of bacteria, such as: Helicobacter pylori, that facilitate the invasion and progression of cancer. However, high amount of coumarin presentin cinnamon can damage liver tissues. Although there are no reports of coumarinrelated tumor formation, high levels of coumarin did trigger cancer in experimental rodents.

Anticancer

Potential Herbs in India As we can see, herbs and other anti-oxidants are not only very helpful inpreventing cancer and in some cases inhibiting progression of cancer, they also help with overall wellness by improving the immune system. But be sure to consult your doctor before taking any of these herbs for preventing or treating cancer.

Alpiniagalanga

Acetoxy-chavicol-acetate (ACA), isolated from Alpiniagalanga, possesses significant anticancer activity against cancers of breast, lung, stomach, colon, prostate, multiple myeloma and leukaemia. Pinocembrinisolated from Alpiniagalanga inhibits growth and spread in colon cancer by arresting cell proliferation and inducing apoptosis. Galangin, a flavonoid isolated from

Alpiniagalanga, possesses strong anticancer, antioxidant, antimutagenic and anti-inflammatory properties. Galanginprotects against breast and prostate cancers.

Amoorarohituka

Amooranin (a triterpene acid), isolated from *Amoorarohituka* inhibits growth and spread of breast and cervical cancers by arresting G2/M phase of the cell cycle and by inducing apoptosis. Amooranin and its derivatives are effective in both chemotherapy-sensitive and chemotherapy resistant cancers. Amooranin has the ability to overcome (reverse) multi drug resistance in breast cancer, colon cancer and leukaemia.

Aegle marmelos

Lupeol, isolated from *Aegle marmelos*, possesses strong anticancer activity against breast cancer, malignant lymphoma, malignant melanoma, malignant ascites and leukaemia. Aegle marmelos possesses significant antioxidant activity and reduces side effects of chemotherapy and radiotherapy.

Aloe Vera

Acemannan (a polysaccharide), isolated from *Aloe vera*, stimulates the immune system, accelerates wound healing and possess significant anticancer property. Emodin and Lectins isolated from *Aloe vera* exhibit strong anticancer and immunoenhancing activities. Aloe-emodininhibits growth and spread of stomach cancer and various sarcomas by inducing apoptosis. Aloe-emodin has selective anticancer activity against neuroectodermal tumours (PNET). Alexin B isolated from *Aloe vera* possesses strong anticancer activity against leukaemia. Polysaccharides isolated from *Aloe vera* have strong immune enhancing and anticancer properties. *Aloe vera* contains 'super carbohydrates' that protect against many cancers, particularly the liver cancer. *Aloe vera* prevents genesis of cancer, regresses growth of cancer and prevents metastasis of cancer. *Aloe vera* stimulates immune system response of the body by activate ingmacrophages and releasing cytokines such as: interferon, interleukin and tumour necrosis factor. *Aloe vera* has an extraordinary antioxidant profile and reduces side effects of chemotherapy and radiotherapy.

Andrographispaniculata

Andrographolide, active diterpinecomponent, isolated from Andrographis-paniculata, has immunoenhancing and strong anticancer activity against cancers of breast, ovary, stomach, colon, prostate, kidney, nasopharynx malignant melanoma and leukaemia. Andrographolide exerts direct anticancer activity on cancer cells by arresting G0/G1 phase of cell-cycle and inducing apoptosis. Dichloromethanefraction of methanolic extract of Andrographis-paniculata has strong anticancer activity against coloncancer. Andrographis-paniculata possesses anticancer, immunostimulant, antioxidant, anti-HIV and anti-inflammatory properties. Andrographispaniculata enhances the activity of protective liver enzymes and reduces side effects of chemotherapy and radiotherapy.

Azadirachtaindica

Azadirachtaindica contains about 40 different active principles, known asliminoids, which exhibit immune enhancing, anti-inflammatory, antiulcer, antifungal, antiviral, antioxidant, hepatoprotective, antimutagenic, anticancer and antimetastatic properties. Liminoids regress growth and spread of various cancers such as: cancers of breast, lung, stomach, prostate and skin.

Nimbolide, a natural triterpenoid, isolated from *Azadirachtaindica* leaves and flowersinhibits growth and spread of various cancers including colon cancer, malignant lymphoma, malignant melanoma and leukaemia by inducing apoptosis (programmed cell death), a process that directs the body's immune cells to identify and destroy cancer cells. Nimbolide also prevents metastasis of cancer. Ethanolic extract of *Azadirachtaindica* inhibits growth and spread of prostate cancer by inducing apoptosis and its antiandrogenic effect. *Azadirachtaindica* reduces side effects of chemotherapy and radiotherapy.

Catharanthusroseus

Catharanthus roseus (*Vincarosea*, Madagascar periwinkle) contains more than 70 alkaloids, known as vinca alkaloids such as: Vinblastine, Vincristine and their derivatives. Vinca alkaloids arrest cancer cell proliferation by binding to tubulin in themitotic spindle. Vinca alkaloids also induceapoptosis (programmed cell death) and inhibit angiogenesis (formation of newblood vessels). Vinca alkaloids inhibit growth and spread of various cancers including: that of breast, ovary, cervix, lung, colon, rectum, testis, neuroblastoma, Hodgkin's disease, malignant lymphoma, multiple myeloma, various sarcomas, rhabdomyosarcoma and leukaemia.

Curcuma Longa

Curcumin (Di-feruloyl-methane) and curcuminoids isolated from *Curcuma longa* suppress cancer at every step, *i.e.*, initiation, growth and metastasis. Curcuminarrests the cancer cells proliferation in G2/Sphase and induces apoptosis (programmed cell death). It inhibits angiogenesis, a crucial step in the growth and metastasis of cancer. Curcumin and Genistein (isolated from Glycine max) act synergistically to inhibit growth and spread of oestrogen-positive breast cancer. Curcumin works even in multi-drug-resistant breast cancers. Curcumin suppresses adhesion of cancer cells, thus preventing metastasis. Curcumin inhibits growth and spread of various cancers including that of breast, lung, oesophagus, liver, colon, prostate, head and neck and skin. Curcumin is particularly effective in radiotherapy-resistant prostate cancer. Curcumin is effective even in advanced stages of cancer. Curcumin also protects from stomach cancer and coloncancer. Curcuma longa also possesses antimutagenic, antioxidant, immunostimulant, anti-inflammatory, hepatoprotective and radio protective properties.

Bauhinia Variegata

Cyanidin glucoside, malvidin glucoside, peonidin glucoside and kaempferol galactoside isolated from Bauhiniavariegata inhibit growth and spread of various cancers such as: cancers of breast, lung, liver, oral cavity, larynx and malignantascites. Bauhinia variegata also possesses significant hepatoprotective activity.

Berberis Vulgaris

Berberis vulgaris root contains berberine, berbamine, chelidonic acid, citric acid, columbamine, hydrastine, isotetrandrine, jacaranone, magnoflorine, oxycanthine and palmatine. Berberine (an isoquinoline alkaloid), possesses anticancer, immunoenhancing, antioxidant and anti-inflammatory properties. Berberine arrests cancer cell cycle in G1-phase and induces apoptosis. Berberine possesses strong anticancer activity against prostate cancer, liver cancer and leukaemia. Berberine interferes with P-glycoprotein inchemotherapy-resistant cancers. Berberinealso increases the penetration of some chemotherapy drugs through the blood-brainbarrier, thereby enhancing their effect onintracranial tumours. Berberis vulgaris rootbark contains three phenolic compounds, tyramine, cannabisin-G and lyoniresinol. Cannabisin-G and lyoniresinol exhibit strong antioxidant activity. Cannabisin-Gprotects against breast cancer. *Berberis vulgaris* also inhibits growth of stomach and oral cavity cancers.

Emblicaofficinalis

Emblicaofficinalis contains ellagic acid, gallic acid, quercetin, kaempferol, emblicanin, flavonoids, glycosides and proanthocyanidins. Emblicaofficinalis is valued for its unique tannins and flavanoids, which possess powerful antioxidant and anticancer properties. Ellagic acid isolated from *Emblicaofficinalis* is a powerful anti-oxidant and has the ability to inhibitmutations in genes. Ellagic acid also repairs chromosomal abnormalities. Quercetin, isolated from *Emblicaofficinalis* has hepatoprotective effect. Emblicanin A&B (tannins) possess strong antioxidant and anticancer properties. Emblicaofficinalis inhibits growth and spread of various cancers including that of the breast, uterus, pancreas, stomach, liver and malignant ascites. Emblicaofficinalis is an excellent rejuvenator and antioxidant herb. It is highly nutritious and an important source of Vitamin C, minerals and aminoacids. Emblicaofficinalis protects against much cancer particularly the liver cancer. Emblicaofficinalis reduces side effects of chemotherapy and radiotherapy.

Ginkgo Biloba

Ginkgetin and Ginkgolides (A & B), isolated from Ginkgo biloba inhibits growth and spread of various aggressive cancers such as: invasive oestrogen-receptor negative breast cancer, glioblastoma multiforme, hepatocellular carcinoma and cancers of ovary, colon, prostate and liver by inducing apoptosis. Ginkgobiloba extract is well-known for its antioxidant activity. Ginkgobiloba also reduces side effects of chemotherapy and radiotherapy.

Glycine Max

Isoflavones (such as: genistein & daidzein) and saponins isolated from Glycinemax inhibit growth and spread of various cancers such as: cancers of the breast, uterus, cervix, ovary, lung, stomach, colon, pancreas, liver, kidney, urinary bladder, prostate, testis, oral cavity, larynx, and thyroid. Glycine max is also effective in nasopharyngeal carcinoma, skin cancer, malignant lymphoma, rhabdomyosarcoma, neuroblastoma, malignant brain tumours and leukaemia. Isoflavones and saponins isolated from Glycine maxpossess wide ranginganti cancer properties such as: inhibition of cancer cell proliferation, promotion of cell differentiation and induction of apoptosis. Genistein works by blocking angiogenesis (formation of new blood vessel), acting as atyrosine kinase inhibitor (the mechanism of action of many new cancer drugs) and inducing apoptosis. Genistein is an excellent intracellular antioxidant. Genistein also blocks the supply of oxygen and nutrients to cancer cells, thus killing them by starving. Genistein and quercetin have synergistic anticancer effect against ovarian carcinoma. Saponins isolated from Glycinemax decrease invasiveness of the glioblastoma cells. Anthocyanins isolated from Glycine max induce apoptosis inleukaemic cells. Glycine max protects against many cancers including that of the colon, lung and ovary.

Morindacitrifolia

Damnacanthol, NB10 and NB11 isolated from *Morindacitrifolia* possess strong anticancer activity against various cancers particularly lung cancer and sarcomas. Morindacitrifolia, possesses strong antioxidant, hepatoprotective and immunoe nhancing properties.

Nigella Sativa

Thymoquinone and dithymoquinone isolated from Nigella sativa have strong anticancer activity against various cancers including: cancers of the colon, prostate, pancreas, uterus, malignant ascites, malignant lymphoma, malignant melanoma, sarcomas and leukaemia. Thymoquinone is effective in both hormone-sensitive and hormone refractory prostate cancer. Nigellasativa kills cancer cells by binding to the asialofetuin (lectin) on the surface of cancerous cells, causing their aggregation and clumping. Nigella sativa also possesses immuno enhancing and anti-inflammatory properties.

It protects against liver cancer. Nigella sativa enhances immune function of the body and reduces side effects of chemotherapy and radiotherapy.

Ocimum Sanctum

Ocimum sanctum contains eugenol, eugenolderivatives, linolenic acid, rosmarinic acid and flavonoids such as: orientin, vicenin, cirsilineol, cirsimaritin, isothymusin, isothymonin and apigenein. Eugenol, orientin and vicenin inhibits growth and spread of various cancers such as: breast cancer, liver cancer and sarcomas particularly fibrosarcoma by blocking supply of oxygen and nutrients to the cancer cells and killing them by starving. Ursolic acid isolated from Ocimum sanctum has immune enhancing and tissue-protective properties. Polysaccharides isolated from Ocimum sanctum have antioxidant and radioprotective properties. Ocimumsanctum protects against various cancers particularly the breast cancer and reduces side effects of chemotherapy and radiotherapy.

Glycyrrhizaglabra

Flavonoids (flavones, flavonals, isoflavones, chalcones, licochalcones and bihydrochalcones), derived from *Glycyrrhizaglabra* possess strong anticancer, antioxidant, antimutagenic, antiulcer, anti-HIV and hepatoprotective properties. Licochalcone-A isolated from *Glycyrrhizaglabra,* inhibits growth and spread of various cancers particularly the androgen-refractory prostate cancer by inducing apoptosis and arresting cancer cells division. Licoagrochalcone, possesses strong anticancer activity against cancers of breast, lung, stomach, colon, liver, kidney and leukaemia. Glycyrrhizin isolated from *Glycyrrhizaglabra* inhibits growth and spread of lung cancer and fibrosarcomas. Glycyrrhizic acid isolated from Glycyrrhiza glabra protects against aflatoxins (powerful fungal carcinogens of the liver). *Glycyrrhizaglabra* stimulates immune system response of the body and protects against coloncancer and oestrogen-positive breast cancer.

Gossypiumhirsutum

Gossypol isolated from *Gossypiumhirsutum* inhibits growth and spread of various cancers such as: cancers of the breast, oesophagus, stomach, colon, liver, pancreas, adrenal gland, prostate, urinary bladder, malignant lymphoma, malignantascites, brain tumours, sarcomas and leukaemia by inducing apoptosis and arresting cancer cell division in G0/G1phase. The negative isomer of gossypol, (-)gossypol, inhibits growth and spread of chemotherapy and radiotherapy-resistant cancers of prostate, breast, ovary, lung, pancreas, head and neck and brain by inducing apoptosis. Gossypolone, oxidativemetabolite of gossypol, inhibits growth and spread of various cancers including that of the breast, cervix, lung, malignantmelanoma and leukaemia.

Oldenlandiadiffusa

Oldenlandiadiffusa (Bai Hua She She Cao) contains oldenlandosides, stigmasterol, ursolic acid, oleanolic acid, beta-sitosterol, p-coumaric acid and flavonoid glycosides. Ursolic acid inhibits growth and spread of various cancers such as: cancers of lung, ovary, uterus, stomach, liver, colon, rectum, brain, malignant melanoma, malignantascites, lymphosarcoma and leukaemia. Ursolic acid works by a typical cytotoxic effect on cancer cells and by inducing apoptosis.

Panax Ginseng

Ginsenosides (panaxadiol and panaxatriolsaponins) isolated from *Panaxginseng* inhibits growth and spread of various cancers such as: cancers of breast, ovary, lung, prostate, colon, renal cell carcinoma, malignant melanoma, malignant lymphoma and leukaemia. Panaxadiol ginsenosides (Rb1, Rb2, Rc, Rd, Rg3, Rh2) and Panaxatriols ginsenosides (Re, Rf, Rg1, Rg2, Rhi) have both preventive and therapeutic role in cancer treatment. Ginsenosides possess strong anticancer activity against lung cancer and also prevent lung metastasis by blocking angiogenesis. Compound K (a metabolite of ginsenosides) inhibits growth and spread of chemo-resistantlung cancer. Ginsenosides Rc, Rd, Rg1 and Re overcome (reverse) P-glycoproteinmediated multi-drug resistance to chemotherapy. Ginsenoside Rf helps inreducing doses of morphine in terminally ill cancer patients. Polysaccharides of *Panaxginseng* possess strong immunoenhancing and anticancer activities against many cancers, particularly lung cancer. Thes epolysaccharides also reduce side effects of chemotherapy and radiotherapy. Panaxginseng also possesses antistress, hepatoprotective, haemopoietic, immunoenhancing, antioxidant, radioprotective, chemoprotective, and anti-inflammatory properties. Panaxginseng inhibits proliferation and seeding (metastases) in various cancers by inducing cell differentiation and apoptosis. Panaxginseng is effective in both hormone responsive and hormone-refractory prostate and breast cancers.

Prunella Vulgaris

Ursolic acid and oleanolic acid, isolatedfrom *Prunella vulgaris* (Xia-ku-cao/Selfheal), inhibit growth and spread of various cancers such as: cancers of the breast, cervix, lung, oral cavity, oesophagus, stomach, colon, thyroid, malignant lymphoma, intracranial tumours and leukaemia. *Prunella vulgaris*, is traditionally used in China to treat sores in mouth and throat. Prunella vulgaris also possesses immune enhancing, hepatoprotective, antioxidant, anti-HIV and anti-Herpes properties. Prunella vulgaris has normoblastic effect on the bone marrow.

Psoraleacorylifolia

Bavachinin, corylfolinin and psoralenisolated from *Psoraleacorylifolia* (Bu GuZhi), possess strong anticancer activity against lung cancer, liver cancer, osteosarcoma, fibrosarcoma, ascites and leukaemia. Psoralen enhances immunity of the body by stimulating natural killer cell activity. Psoralidin isolated from *Psoraleacorylifolia* inhibits growth and spread of stomach and prostate cancers by inhibiting G2/M phase of cell cycle. Psoralidin induces apoptosis in bothandrogen-responsive and androgen refractory prostate cancers. *Psoraleacorylifolia* also possesses strong antioxidant, immunomo enhancing and hepatoprotective properties.

Rubiacordifolia

Rubidianin, rubiadin, RA-7, RA-700 and RC-18 isolated from *Rubiacordifolia* inhibit growth and spread in cancers of breast, ovary, cervix, colon, lung, malignant ascites, malignant lymphoma, malignant melanomasarcoma and leukaemia. Rubiadin also possesses hepatoprotective activity.

Saussurealappa

Sesquiterpenes and costunolide dehydrocostus lactone, isolated from *Saussurealappa* inhibit growth and spread of breast cancer. Cynaropicrin, isolated from Saussurealappa possesses strong anticancer activity against malignant lymphoma and leukaemia. Costunolide, isolated from *Saussurealappa* inhibits growth and spread of intestinal cancer. Mokkolactone isolated from *Saussurealappa* induces apoptosis in leukaemic cells. Shikokiols isolated from *Saussurealappa* exhibit anticancer activity against cancers of the ovary, lung, colon and central nervous system. *Saussurealappa* inhibits growth and spread of cancers by arresting cancer cell division in G2 phase and inducing apoptosis.

Solanumnigrum

Solamargine and solasonine, isolated from *Solanumnigrum* (Lo-ing-kue) inhibit growth and spread of various cancers including: that of the breast, liver and lung. Steroidal glycosides (spirostane, furostane, spirosolane and pregnane), isolated from *Solanumnigrum* inhibit growth and spread of colon cancer and pheochromocytoma. Glycoproteins isolatedfrom *Solanumnigrum* have antiproliferative and apoptotic effects on colon and breast cancers. Polysaccharides isolatedfrom *Solanumnigrum* have significant inhibitory effect on growth of cervical cancer. *Solanumnigrum* inhibits growth and spread of liver cancer by two distinct anticancer activities, *i.e.,* apoptosis (programmed cell death) and autophagy (autophagocytosis). Higher doses of *Solanumnigrum* induce apoptotic cell death while lower doses lead to autophagocytic death of cancer cells. Lunasin, isolated from *Solanumnigrum* is a cancer-preventive peptide. *Solanumnigrum* and *Solanumlyrati* (Shu-yang-quan) inhibit growth and spread of stomach cancer, sarcomas, malignant ascites and leukaemia.

Plumbagozeylanica

Plumbagin isolated from *Plumbagozeylanica* inhibits growth and spread of breast cancer, liver cancer, fibrosarcoma, malignant ascites and leukaemia by inhibiting cancer cell proliferation. *Plumbagozeylanica* also possesses strong antioxidant, hepatoprotective, neuroprotective and immunoenhancing properties.

Podophyllum Hexandrum

Podophyllotoxin and podophyllin (lignans) isolated from *Podophyllum hexandrum* (Himalayan May Apple) inhibit growth and spread of various cancers including that of the breast, ovary, lung, liver, urinary bladder, testis, brain, neuroblastoma, Hodgkin's disease, non-Hodgkin's lymphoma and leukaemia. Podophyllotoxin is the most active amongall the natural anticancer compounds. *Podophyllum hexandrum* also possesses potent radioprotective and haemopoietic properties.

Tinosporacordifolia

Sesquiterpenes and diterpenes isolated from *Tinosporacordifolia* inhibit growth and spread of various cancers including: cancers of lung, cervix, throat and malignant ascites. Polysaccharide fraction isolated from *Tinosporacordifolia* inhibits lung metastasis. Arabinogalactan, syringine, cordiol, cordioside, cordifoliosides (A&B) isolated from Tinosporacordifolia possesses significant immunoenhancing activity. *Tinosporacordifolia* also possessesneuro protective, hepatoprotective, antistress, antiulcer and antipyreticproperties. *Tinosporacordifolia* reduces side effects of radiotherapy and chemotherapy.

Viscum Album

Lectins (such as: viscumin), polypeptides (viscotoxins) and phenolic compounds (such as: digallic acid) isolated from Viscum album inhibit growth and spread of various cancers including that of the breast, cervix, ovary, lung, stomach, colon, rectum, kidney, urinary bladder, testis, malignant melanoma, sarcomas, fibrosarcoma, malignant ascites, lung metastasis and leukaemia by inducing apoptosis and anti-angiogenesis activity. Lectins isolated from Viscum album possess both anticancer and immunostimulating activities. Viscumin, responsible for most of the biological activities of Viscum album, works by bringing together immune system effector cells and cancer cells. Lectin-IIinduces apoptosis in cancer cells via activation of caspase cascades.

Withaniasomnifera

Withanolides isolated from *Withaniasomnifera*, are similar to ginsenosides (the active principles of *Panax ginseng*) in both structure and activity. Withanolides (including: Withaferin A, Sitoindoside IX, Physagulin D, Withanoside IV and Viscosalactone B) inhibit growth and spread of various cancers such as: cancers of the breast, lung, colon and central nervous system due to their antiproliferative and antiangiogenic properties. Withaferin-A (the most important withanolides) inhibit growth and spread of various cancers including that of the breast, cervix, colon, prostate, nasopharynx, larynx, malignant ascites and sarcomas by inducing apoptosis. Withaferin A is effective in both androgen-responsive and androgen-refractory prostate cancers.

Sitoindosides VII-X and Withaferin A have strong antioxidant, antistress, immunomodulatory, anti-inflammatory and anti-aging properties. Withanolide D inhibitsthe metastatic colony formation in the lungsby malignant melanoma. Ashwagandhanolide, a new dimeric withanolide, isolated from *Withaniasomnifera*, inhibits growth and spread in cancers of breast, stomach, colon, lung and central nervous system. *Withaniasomnifera* also possesses immunoenhancing, haemopoietic and neuroprotective properties and reduces side effects of radiotherapy and chemotherapy.

Table 5.1: List of plants has Anticancer activity

S. No.	Common Name	Botanical Name	Part Used	Family	Uses
1.	Kalmegh	*Androgarphispaniculata*	Dried leaves	Acanthacae	Anticancer
2.	Vinca	*Catharanthusroseus*	Whole plant	Apocynacae	Anticancer
3.	May Apple	*Podophyllumpeltatum*	Dried Rhizome	Berberidacae	Anticancer
4.	Arjuna Bark	*Terminalia arjuna*	Bark	Combertacae	Anticancer
5.	Ginger	*Zingiberofficinalis*	Rhizome	Zingibaracae	Anticancer
6.	deerberry	*Vacciniumstamineum*	fruit	Ericaceae	Anticancer
7.	Indianmulberry	*Morindacitrifolia*	fruit	Rubiaceae	Anticancer
8.	Ochrosia	*Ochrosiaelliptica*	Trunk Bark	Apocynacae	Anticancer
9.	Turmeric	*Curcuma longa*	Rhizome	Zingibaracae	Anticancer
10.	Bhilwa	*Semecarpusanacardium*	fruit	Anacardiaceae	Anticancer
11.	Madar	*Calotrophisgigantea*	Whole plant	Asclepiadaceae	Anticancer
12.	Arhar Dal	*Cajanuscajan*	Leaves	Fabaceae	Anticancer
13.	Palash	*Butea monosperma*	Bark	Fabaceae	Anticancer
14.	Orchid Tree	*Bauhinia variegata*	Root	Caesalpinaceae	Anticancer
15.	Onion	*Aliumcepa*	Bulb	Liliaceae	Anticancer
16.	Indian Aloe	*Aloe barbadensis*	Leaves	Liliaceae	Anticancer
17.	Tarwar	*Cassia auriculata*	Root	Caesalpinaceae	Anticancer
18.	Senna	*Cassia senna*	Leaves	Caesalpinaceae	Anticancer
19.	Lemon	*Citrus medica*	Root	Rutaceae	Anticancer
20.	Carrot	*Daucuscarota*	Root	Apiaceae	Anticancer
21.	Danti	*Jatropha curcas*	Leaves, seed, oils	Euphorbiaceae	Anticancer
22.	Mint	*Mimosa pudica*	Whole plant	Mimosaceae	Anticancer
23.	Tobacco	*Nicotianatabacum*	Leaves	Solanaceae	Anticancer
24.	Indian Ipecac	*Tyloporaindica*	Root, Leaf	Asclepiadaceae	Anticancer
25.	Nichinda	*Vitextrifolia*	Leaf	Verbanaceae	Anticancer

Zingiberofficinale

Gingerols isolated from *Zingiberofficinale* inhibit growth and spread of various cancers including that of the ovary, cervix, colon, rectum, liver, urinary bladder, oral cavity, neuroblastoma and leukaemia by inducing apoptosis. The most active individual component, 6-shogaol, isolatedfrom *Zingiberofficinale*, inhibit growth and spread of many cancers particularly the ovarian cancer by blocking formation of new blood vessels and by inducing apoptosis and autophagy. It is effective even inchemotherapy resistant ovarian cancer. *Zingiberofficinale* also possesses anti-oxidant, antimutagenic and anti-inflammatory properties and reduces side effects of chemotherapy and radiotherapy.

Conclusion

We have tried to explore the discovered plants components with proved anticancer activity both in vitro and in vivo. Cancer is a major public health burden in both developed and developing countries. Cancer is an abnormal malignant growth of body tissue or cell. A cancerous growth is called a malignant tumor or malignancy. A noncancerous growth is called benign tumor. The process of cancer metastasis is consisting of series of sequential inter-related steps, each of which is ratelimiting. Plants with loaded with chemical with chemo protective activities of some of them are undergoing clinical trial. Inhibition of angiogenesis is a novel process of cancer therapy. The selected and careful use of medicinal plant and herbs may definitely in cancer management. India is one of the most promising regions for discovering novel biologically-active substances from its flora. More efforts are needed to explore potent anticancer plants from the mother earth and save humans around the world from cancer.

REFERENCES

Dalziel T.M. (1973). The Useful Plants of West Tropical Africa. 3rd ed. Bradford and London: Watmought Ltd., Idle; pp. 526-530.

Dharmani P., Kuchibhotla V.K., Maurya R., Srivastava S., Sharma S. and Palit G. (2004). Evaluation of Anti-ulcerogenic andulcer Healing Properties of Ocimumsanctum Linn. *J Ethnopharmacol*. 93:197-206.

Garg G.P., Nigam S.S. and Ogle C.W. (1993). The Gastric Antiulcer Effects of the Leaves of the Neem Tree. *Planta Medica*. 59:215-7.

Goel R.K. and Sairam K. (2002). Anti-ulcer Drugs from Indigenous Sources with Emphasis on Musa sapientum, Tamrabhasma, Asparagus racemosus and Zingiberofficinale. *Indian J Pharmacol*. 34:100-10.

Gupta A.K. and Tandon N. (2004). Reviews on Indian Medicinal Plants. Vol. 2. New Delhi: Indian Council of Medical Research.

Hakim Z.S. (1995). Potential Antidiabetic Agents from Plant Sources; Pharmacological Aspects. *Indian J Natural Product*. 11(1):3.

Joy P.P., Thomas J., Mathew S., Jose G. and Joseph J. (2001). Medicinal Plants. In: Bose T.K., Kabir J., Das P., Joy P.P. Editors. Tropical Horticulture Vol. 2. Calcutta: Naya Prokash. pp. 449-632.

Keen R.W. and Deacon A.C. (1994). Indian Herbal Remedies for Diabetes as a cause of lead Poisoning. *Postgrad Med J*. 70:113 -114.

Kokate C.K., Purohit A.P. and Gokhale S.B. (2007). Pharmacognosy. 13th ed. Pune: Nirali Prakashan Publisher. p. 35.

Mahendran P. and Vanisree A.J. (2002). Theantiulcer Activity of Gacinia cambogia extract against indomethacin inducedgastric ulcer in rats. *Phytotherapy Research*. 16:80-83.

Manish A. R. and Sunita M. Jain. (2008). Gastroprotective Effect of Benincasahispida Fruit Extract. *Indian Journal of Pharmacology*. 40(6):129-36.

Muralidharan P. and Srikanth J. (2009). Antiulcer Activity of *Morindacitrifolia* Linn Fruit Extract. *J Sci Res*.1(2): 345-352.

Rao C.V., Sairam K. and Goel R.K. (2000). Experimental Evaluation of Bacopamonniera on rat gastric ulceration and secretion. *Indian J Physiol Pharmacol*. 44:435.

Sairam K., Priyambada S., Aryya N.C. and Goel R.K. (2003). Gastroduodenal ulcer protective activity of Asparagus racemosus: An Experimental, Biochemical and Histological Study. *J. Ethnopharmacol*. 86:1-10.

Sairam K., Rao C.V., Babu M.D., Kumar V.K., Agarwal V.K. and Goel R.K. (2002). Antiulcerogenic Effect of ethanolic extract of Emblicaofficinalis: An Experimental Study. *J Ethnopharmacol*. 82:1-9.

Wadker K.A. and Magdum C.S. (2008). Antdiabetic Potential and Indian Medicinal Plant. *Journal of Herbal Medicine and Toxicology*. 2(1):45-50.

Pages: 89-100

AGRO-BIODIVERSITY: *CONSERVATION AND SUSTAINABLE DEVELOPMENT*
Edited by: **Dr. Pankaj Sharma; Dr. Narayan Singh & Dr. Pawan Kumar 'Bharti'**
ISBN: 978-93-5056-782-1
Edition: **2016**
Published by: **Discovery Publishing House Pvt. Ltd., New Delhi (India)**

6

A Socio-pecuniary Citation for Geographical Indications Awareness in India

M. Baunthiyal[1]; A. K. Bhandari[2]*; V.K. Bisht[2] and Narayan Singh[3]

ABSTRACT

A geographical indication (GIs) is a name or sign used on certain products which corresponds to a specific geographical location or origin of the region or vicinity. The purpose of a GIs may act as a certification that the product possesses certain qualities, or to take pleasure in a certain status, essentially attributable to their geographical origin. It is mainly used to identify the agricultural, handicraft, manufacturing goods. The geographical indication is generally possessed by a community which belongs to that particular location. A Geographical Indications Registry with all India jurisdictions operates, as per the Geographical Indication of Goods (Registration and Protection) Act 1999. As a public policy instrument, GIs have potentially positive implications towards the protection of indigenous knowledge and as a means for generating livelihood and income. However, this potential is constrained by a number of factors related to the limitations of GIs. For example the misappropriation of knowledge, otherwise termed biopiracy, embedded in an indication will not be protected against. As such, GIs

1. Department of Biotechnology, G.B. Pant Engineering Collage, Ghurdauri, Uttarakhand, India.
2. Herbal Research and Development Institute, Mandal, Gopeshwar - Chamoli - 246 401, Uttarakhand, India.
3. The Energy and Resources Institute (TERI), New Delhi, India.

should be considered part of a wider set of policies directed at these aims. In India the GIs registrations started from 2004 under the Act 1999 (Registration and Protection). In India till 235 GIs was registered in different orbs such as: Handicraft, Agriculture, Manufactured, Textile, Food staff etc.

Keywords: Geographical Indications (GIs), Trade Related Aspects of Intellectual Property Rights (TRIPS), Intellectual Property Rights (IPRs), World Trade Organization (WTO)

INTRODUCTION

The security of Geographical Indications (GIs) has, quite a few years, come out as one of the most debatable intellectual property rights (IPRs) issues in the dominion of the Agreement on Trade Related Aspects of Intellectual Property Rights (TRIPS) of the World Trade Organization (WTO). TRIPS describe that the GI as any indication which identifies a good as originating from a particular place, where a given quality, reputation or other characteristics of the good are essentially attributable to its geographical origin. GIs, as defined by TRIPS, need not always be geographical names (such as: name of a town, region or country) to designate the origin of the goods to which they are associated, but may consist of symbols as well, if such symbols are capable of indicating the origin of the goods concerned without literally naming the place of their origins. One such indication is 'Basmati' for particular varieties of fragrant rice produced in certain regions of India and Pakistan. 'Basmati' is not a geographical name. But if it is perceived as an indication of rice originating from those particular geographical regions of India and Pakistan, then 'Basmati' can very well qualify as a GI [1].

India has put in place a *sui generis* system of protection for GI with enactment of a law exclusively dealing with protection of GIs. The legislations which deals with protection of GI's in India are 'The Geographical Indications of Goods (Registration & Protection) Act, 1999' (GI Act), and the 'Geographical Indications of Goods (Registration and Protection) Rules, 2002 (GI Rules). India enacted its GI legislations for the country to put in place national intellectual property laws in compliance with India's obligations under TRIPS. Under the purview of the GI Act, which came into action, along with the GI Rules, with effect from 15 September 2003, the central government has established the Geographical Indications Registry with all-India jurisdiction, at Chennai, where right-holders can apply and register their GI. First Indian GI was registered in 2004, 172 GIs have been registered with the GI Registry of India. Handicrafts sector registered more than half (64%), more than one fourth (26%) are agricultural products, and the remaining are food and manufacturing products [1-4].

Geographical indications can be understood by consumers to denote the origin and the quality of products. Maximum number of them has acquired valuable reputations which, if not adequately protected, may be misrepresented by dishonest commercial operators. Counterfeit use of geographical indications by illegal practices of parties is detrimental to consumers and legitimate producers [5].

Registration Process for GIs in India

In the Section 11(2) of the GI Act specifies the documentation requirements for applying for a GI in India. Section 32(1) of the GI Rules replicates these provisions and in addition stipulates a few more documentation requirements that include, among other things, the following: [6].

- A proclamation as to how the GI serves to designate the goods as originating from the concerned geographical territory in respect of certain quality, status or other characteristics that are due exclusively or essentially to the geographical environment, with its natural genetics inherent and human factors; and the production, processing or preparation of which takes place in such geographical location.
- The geographical map of the region concerned.
- The particulars regarding the appearance of the GI as to whether it is comprised of the words or figurative elements or both.
- An affidavit as to how the applicant claims to represent the interest of the association of persons or producers or any organization or authority established by or under any law.
- The standards benchmark for the use of the GI or the industry standard as regards the production, exploitation, making or manufacture of the goods having specific quality, reputation, or other characteristic of such goods that is essentially attributable to its geographical origin with the detailed description of the human creativity involved, if any, or other characteristic from the definite geographical territory.
- The particulars of the mechanism to ensure that the standards, quality, integrity and consistency or other special characteristic in respect of the goods to which the GI relates, which are maintained by the producers, makers or manufacturers of the goods, as the case may be; The particulars of special human skill involved or the uniqueness of the geographical environment or other inherent characteristics associated with the GI to which the application relates.
- The particulars of the inspection structure, if any, to regulate the use of the GI in respect of the goods for which application is made in the definite territory, region or locality mentioned in the application.

Registration Status of GIs in India

Around 1500 products from India have reportedly been identified as having the potential to get registered as GIs (Natarajan, 2008). Till March 2015, 235 GIs got registered (Table 6.1) with the GIs Registry [7].

Table 6.1: State-wise registration details of Geographical Indication (GI) applications 15th september, 2003 – march 2015

S. No.	Application No.	Geographical Indications (GIs)	Goods (As per Sec 2 (f) of GI Act 1999)	State
1	2	3	4	5
		From April 2004 – March 2005		
1.	1 and 2	Darjeeling Tea (word & logo)	Agricultural	West Bengal
2.	3	Aranmula Kannadi	Handicraft	Kerala
3.	4	Pochampalli Ikat	Handicraft	Andhra Pradesh
		From April 2005 – March 2006		
4.	5	Salem Fabric	Handicraft	Tamil Nadu
5.	7	Chanderi Fabric	Handicraft	Madhya Pradesh
6.	8	Solapur Chaddar	Handicraft	Maharashtra
7.	9	Solapur Terry Towel	Handicraft	Maharashtra
8.	10	Kotpad Handloom fabric	Handicraft	Odisha
9.	11	Mysore Silk	Handicraft	Karnataka
10.	12	Kota Doria	Handicraft	Rajasthan
11.	13 and 18	Mysore Agarbathi	Manufactured	Karnataka
12.	15	Kancheepuram Silk	Handicraft	Tamil Nadu
13.	16	Bhavani Jamakkalam	Handicraft	Tamil Nadu
14.	19	Kullu Shawl	Handicraft	Himachal Pradesh
15.	20	Bidriware	Handicraft	Karnataka
16.	21	Madurai Sungudi	Handicraft	Tamil Nadu
17.	22	Orissa Ikat	Handicraft	Odisha
18.	23	Channapatna Toys and Dolls	Handicraft	Karnataka
19.	24	Mysore Rosewood Inlay	Handicraft	Karnataka
20.	25	Kangra Tea	Agricultural	Himachal Pradesh
21.	26	Coimbatore Wet Grinder	Manufactured	Tamil Nadu
22.	28	Srikalahasthi Kalamkari	Handicraft	Andhra Pradesh
23.	29	Mysore Sandalwood Oil	Manufactured	Karnataka
24.	30	Mysore Sandal Soap	Manufactured	Karnataka
25.	31	Kasuti Embroidery	Handicraft	Karnataka

Contd...

1	2	3	4	5
26.	32	Mysore Traditional Paintings	Handicraft	Karnataka
27.	33	Coorg Orange	Agricultural	Karnataka
From April 2006 – March 2007				
28.	34	Mysore Betel Leaf	Agricultural	Karnataka
29.	35	Nanjanagud Banana	Agricultural	Karnataka
30.	37	Madhubani Paintings	Handicraft	Bihar
From April 2007 – March 2008				
31.	44	Kondapalli Bommallu	Handicraft	Andhra Pradesh
32.	47	Thanjavur Paintings	Handicraft	Tamil Nadu
33.	53	Silver Filigree of Karimnagar	Handicraft	Telangana
34.	54	Alleppey Coir	Handicraft	Kerala
35.	55	Muga Silk	Handicraft	Assam
36.	65	Temple Jewellery of Nagercoil	Handicraft	Tamil Nadu
37.	69	Mysore Jasmine	Agricultural	Karnataka
38.	70	Udupi Jasmine	Agricultural	Karnataka
39.	71	Hadagali Jasmine	Agricultural	Karnataka
40.	17	Navara Rice	Agricultural	Kerala
41.	36	Palakkadan Matta Rice	Agricultural	Kerala
42.	63	Thanjavur Art Plate	Handicraft	Tamil Nadu
43.	76	Ilkal Sarees	Handicraft	Karnataka
44.	73	Applique – Khatwa Patch Work of Bihar	Handicraft	Bihar
45.	74	Sujini Embroidery Work of Bihar	Handicraft	Bihar
46.	75	Sikki Grass Work of Bihar	Handicraft	Bihar
47.	49 and 56	Malabar Pepper	Agricultural	Kerala
48.	50	Allahabad Surkha	Agricultural	Uttar Pradesh
49.	52	Nakshi Kantha	Handicraft	West Bengal
50.	60	Ganjifa Cards of Mysore (Karnataka)	Handicraft	Karnataka
51.	61	Navalgund Durries	Handicraft	Karnataka
52.	62	Karnataka Bronze Ware	Handicraft	Karnataka
53.	77	Molakalmuru Sarees	Handicraft	Karnataka
54.	85	Monsooned Malabar Arabica Coffee	Agricultural	Karnataka
55.	114	Monsooned Malabar Robusta Coffee	Agricultural	Karnataka
56.	72	Spices – Alleppey Green Cardamom	Agricultural	Kerala
57.	78	Coorg Green Cardamom	Agricultural	Karnataka

Contd...

1	2	3	4	5
58.	95	E. I. Leather	Manufactured	Tamil Nadu
59.	94	Salem Silk known as Salem Venpattu	Handicraft	Tamil Nadu
60.	93	Kovai Cora Cotton	Handicraft	Tamil Nadu
61.	92	Arani Silk	Handicraft	Tamil Nadu
From April 2008 – March 2009				
62.	83	Bastar Dhokra	Handicraft	Chattisgarh
63.	84	Bastar Wooden Craft	Handicraft	Chattisgarh
64.	91	Nirmal Toys and Craft	Handicraft	Telangana
65.	59	Maddalam of Palakkad	Handicraft	Kerala
66.	58	Screw Pine Craft of Kerala	Handicraft	Kerala
67.	64	Swamimalai Bronze Icons	Handicraft	Tamil Nadu
68.	82	Bastar Iron Craft	Handicraft	Chattisgarh
69.	87	Konark Stone Carving	Handicraft	Odisha
70.	88	Orissa Pattachitra	Handicraft	Odisha
71.	90	Machilipatnam Kalamkari	Handicraft	Andhra Pradesh
72.	110	Eathomozhy Tall Coconut	Agricultural	Tamil Nadu
73.	57	Brass Broidered Coconut Shell Crafts of Kerala	Handicraft	Kerala
74.	66	Blue Pottery of Jaipur	Handicraft	Rajasthan
75.	67	Molela Clay Work	Handicraft	Rajasthan
76.	68	Kathputlis of Rajasthan	Handicraft	Rajasthan
77.	97	Leather Toys of Indore	Handicraft	Madhya Pradesh
78.	98	Bagh Prints of Madhya Pradesh	Handicraft	Madhya Pradesh
79.	100	Sankheda Furniture	Handicraft	Gujarat
80.	101	Agates of Cambay	Handicraft	Gujarat
81.	102	Bell Metal Ware of Datia	Handicraft	Madhya Pradesh
		and Tikamgarh		
82.	103	Kutch Embroidery	Handicraft	Gujarat
83.	51	Kani Shawl	Handicraft	Jammu & Kashmir
84.	79	Chamba Rumal	Handicraft	Himachal Pradesh
85.	80	Dharwad Pedha	Foodstuff	Karnataka
86.	81	Pokkali Rice	Agricultural	Kerala
87.	86 and 108	Pipli Applique Work	Handicraft	Odisha
89.	96	Thanjavur Doll	Handicraft	Tamil Nadu
90.	104	Santiniketan Leather Goods	Handicraft	West Bengal

Contd...

1	2	3	4	5
91.	105	Nirmal Furniture	Handicraft	Telangana
92.	106	Nirmal Paintings	Handicraft	Telangana
93.	107	Andhra Pradesh Leather Puppetry	Handicraft	Andhra Pradesh
94.	111	Laxman Bhog Mango	Agricultural	West Bengal
95.	112	Khirsapati (Himsagar) Mango	Agricultural	West Bengal
96.	113	Fazli Mango grown in the district of Malda	Agricultural	West Bengal
97.	46	Kashmir Pashmina	Handicraft	Jammu & Kashmir
98.	48	Kashmir Sozani Craft	Handicraft	Jammu & Kashmir
99.	109	Naga Mircha	Agricultural	Nagaland
100.	116 and 117	Nilgiri (Orthodox) Logo	Agricultural	Tamil Nadu
101.	115 and 118	Assam (Orthodox) Logo	Agricultural	Assam
102.	119	Lucknow Chikan Craft	Handicraft	Uttar Pradesh
103.	124	Virupakshi Hill Banana	Agricultural	Tamil Nadu
104.	126	Sirumalai Hill Banana	Agricultural	Tamil Nadu
105.	120	Feni	Manufactured	Goa
106.	122	Uppada Jamdani Sarees	Handicraft	Andhra Pradesh
		From April 2009 – March 2010		
107.	121	Tirupathi Laddu	Food Stuff	Andhra Pradesh
108.	125	Mango Malihabadi Dusseheri	Agricultural	Uttar Pradesh
109.	128	Puneri Pagadi	Handicraft	Maharashtra
110.	99	Banaras Brocades and Sarees	Handicraft	Uttar Pradesh
111.	127	Tangaliya Shawl	Handicraft	Gujarat
112.	130 and 141	Vazhakulam Pineapple	Agricultural	Kerala
113.	131	Devanahalli Pomello	Agricultural	Karnataka
114.	132	Appemidi Mango	Agricultural	Karnataka
115.	133	Kamalapur Red Banana	Agricultural	Karnataka
116.	138	Santipore Saree	Handicraft	West Bengal
117.	144	Cannanore Home Furnishings	Handicraft	Kerala
118.	43	Peruvian Pisco	Manufactured	Peru
119.	147	Sanganeri Hand Block Printing	Handicraft	Rajasthan
120.	152	Balaramapuram Sarees and Fine Cotton Fabrics	Handicraft	Kerala
		From April 2010 – March 2011		
121.	142	Bikaneri Bhujia	Agricultural	Rajasthan

Contd...

1	2	3	4	5
122.	143	Guntur Sannam Chilli	Agricultural	Andhra Pradesh
123.	123	Nashik Valley Wine	Manufactured	Maharashtra
123.	137	Gadwal Sarees	Handicraft	Telangana
125.	149	Kinnauri Shawl	Handicraft	Himachal Pradesh
126.	170	Kasaragod Sarees	Handicraft	Kerala
127.	179	Kuthampully Sarees	Handicraft	Kerala
128.	134	Sandur Lambani Embroidery	Handicraft	Karnataka
129.	148	Handmade Carpet of Bhadohi	Handicraft	Uttar Pradesh
130.	150 and 153	Paithani Sarees and Fabrics	Handicraft	Maharashtra
131.	154	Mahabaleshwar Strawberry	Agricultural	Maharashtra
132.	193	Hyderabad Haleem	Food Stuff	Telangana
133.	140	Champagne	Manufactured	France
134.	146	Napa Valley	Manufactured	USA
135.	163	Central Travancore Jaggery	Agricultural	Kerala
136.	172	Champa Silk Saree and Fabrics	Handicraft	Chhattisgarh
137.	186	Wayanad Jeerakasala Rice	Agricultural	Kerala
138.	187	Wayanad Gandhakasala Rice	Agricultural	Kerala
139.	191	Kota Doria (Logo)	Handicraft	Rajasthan
140.	165	Nashik Grapes	Agricultural	Maharashtra
141.	171	Surat Zari Craft	Handicraft	Gujarat
142.	190	Cheriyal Paintings	Handicraft	Telangana
143.	194	Pembarthi Metal Craft	Handicraft	Telangana
144.	6	Payyannur Pavithra Ring	Handicraft	Kerala
145.	27	Phulkari	Handicraft	Punjab, Haryana and Rajasthan
146.	136	Khandua Saree and Fabrics	Handicraft	Odisha
147.	129	Byadagi Chilli	Agricultural	Karnataka
148.	151	Scotch Whisky	Manufactured	United Kingdom
149.	164	Prosciutto di Parma	Food Stuff	Italy
From April 2011 – March 2012				
150.	192	Bagru Hand Block Print	Handicraft	Rajasthan
151.	189	Venkatagiri Sarees	Handicraft	Andhra Pradesh
152.	185	Gir Kesar Mango	Agricultural	Gujarat
153.	192	Bhalia Wheat	Agricultural	Gujarat
154.	201	Villianur Terracotta Works	Handicraft	Pondicherry

Contd...

1	2	3	4	5
155.	202	Tirukanur Papier Mache Craft	Handicraft	Pondicherry
156.	230	Cognac	Manufactured	France
157.	174	France	Handicraft	Gujarat
158.	199	Udupi Mattu Gulla Brinjal	Agricultural	Karnataka
159.	173	Baluchari Saree	Handicraft	West Bengal
160.	1.76	Dhaniakhali Saree	Handicraft	West Bengal
161.	181	Kashmir Paper Machie	Handicraft	Kashmir
162.	182	Kashmir Walnut Wood Carving	Handicraft	Kashmir
163.	203	Bobbile Veena	Handicraft	Andhra Pradesh
164.	204	Khatamband	Handicraft	Kashmir
165.	213	Kinhal Toys	Handicraft	Karnataka
166.	225	Chendamangalam Dhoties and Set Mundu	Handicraft	Kerala
167.	216	Porto	Manufactured	Portugal
168.	227	Douro	Manufactured	Portugal
169.	167	Gopalpur Tussar Fabrics	Handicraft	Odisha
170.	188	Siddipet Gollabama	Handicraft	Telangana
171.	228	Ganjam Kewda Rooh	Agricultural	Odisha
172.	229	Ganjam Kewda Flower	Agricultural	Odisha
From April 2012 – March 2013				
173.	197	Maheshwar Sarees and Fabrics	Handicraft	Madhya Pradesh
174.	207	Dhalapathar Parda and Fabrics	Handicraft	Odisha
175.	208	Sambalpuri Bandha Saree and Fabrics	Handicraft	Odisha
176.	217	Bomkai Saree and Fabrics	Handicraft	Odisha
177.	219	Habaspuri Saree and Fabrics	Handicraft	Odisha
178.	220	Berhampur Patta (Phoda Kumbha) Saree and Joda	Handicraft	Odisha
179.	180	Bhagalpur Silk	Handicraft	Bihar
180.	190	Mangalagiri Sarees and Fabrics	Handicraft	Andhra Pradesh
181.	238	Madurai Malli	Agricultural	Tamil Nadu
182.	243	Tequila	Manufactured	Mexico
183.	195	"Pattamadai Pai ('Pattamadai Mat')"	Handicraft	Tamil Nadu
184.	196	"Nachiarkoil Kuthuvilakku ('Nachiarkoil Lamp')"	Handicraft	Tamil Nadu
185.	200	Chettinad Kottan	Handicraft	Tamil Nadu

Contd...

1	2	3	4	5
186.	214	Narayanpet Handloom Sarees	Handicraft	Telangana
187.	135	Toda Embroidery	Handicraft	Tamil Nadu
188.	209	Thanjavur Veenai	Handicraft	Tamil Nadu
189.	211	Bangalore Blue Grapes	Agricultural	Karnataka
190.	233	Agra Durrie	Handicraft	Uttar Pradesh
191.	234	Farrukhabad Prints	Handicraft	Uttar Pradesh
192.	236	Lucknow Zardozi	Handicraft	Uttar Pradesh
193.	237	Banaras Brocades and Sarees (Logo)	Handicraft	Uttar Pradesh
From April 2013 – March 2014				
194.	205	Kalanamak Rice	Agricultural	Uttar Pradesh
195.	232	Patan Patola	Handicraft	Gujarat
196.	386	Orissa Pattachitra (Logo)	Textile	Odisha
197.	387	Bastar Dhokra (Logo)	Handicraft	Chhattisgarh
198.	388	Bell Metal Ware of Datia and Tikamgarh (Logo)	Handicraft	Madhya Pradesh
199.	242	Kaipad Rice	Agricultural	Kerala
200.	383	Kullu ShawL (Logo)	Textile	Himachal Pradesh
201.	384	Muga Silk of Assam (Logo)	Handicraft	Assam
202.	155	Firozabad Glass	Handicraft	Uttar Pradesh
203.	157	Kannauj Perfume	Manufactured	Uttar Pradesh
204.	159	Kanpur Saddlery	Manufactured	Uttar Pradesh
205.	161	Moradabad Metal Craft	Handicraft	Uttar Pradesh
206.	184	Saharanpur Wood Craft	Handicraft	Uttar Pradesh
207.	215	Dharmavaram Handloom Pattu Sarees and Paavadas	Textile	Andhra Pradesh
208.	239	Warli Painting	Handicraft	Maharashtra
209.	240	Kolhapur Jaggery	Agricultural	Maharashtra
210.	244	Thewa Art Work	Handicraft	Rajasthan
211.	371	Shaphee Lanphee	Textile	Manipur
212.	372	Wangkhei Phee	Textile	Manipur
213.	373	Moirang Phee	Textile	Manipur
214.	381	Kangra Paintings	Handicraft	Himachal Pradesh
215.	385	Nagpur Orange	Agricultural	Maharashtra
From April 2014 – March 2015				
216.	399	Leather Toys of Indore (Logo)	Handicraft	Madhya Pradesh

Contd...

1	2	3	4	5
217.	212	Bangalore Rose Onion	Agricultural	Karnataka
218.	389	Meerut Scissors	Manufactured	Uttar Pradesh
219.	178	Khurja Pottery	Handicraft	Uttar Pradesh
220.	374	Naga Tree Tomato	Agricultural	Nagaland
221.	375	Arunachal Orange	Agricultural	Arunachal Pradesh
222.	376	Sikkim Large Cardamom	Agricultural	Sikkim
223.	377	Mizo Chilli	Agricultural	Mizoram
224.	382	Joynagar Moa	Food Stuff	West Bengal
225.	397	Banaras Gulabi Meenakari Craft	Handicraft	Uttar Pradesh
226.	435	Assam Karbi Anglong Ginger	Agricultural	Assam
227.	436	Tripura Queen Pineapple	Agricultural	Tripura
228.	479	Chengalikodan Nendran Banana	Agricultural	Kerala
229.	434	Ratlami Sev	Food Stuff	Madhya Pradesh
230.	438	Tezpur Litchi	Agricultural	Assam
231.	465	Khasi Mandarin	Agricultural	Meghalaya
232.	466	Kachai Lemon	Agricultural	Manipur
233.	405	Makrana Marble	Natural Goods	Rajasthan
234.	457	Varanasi Wooden Lacquerware and Toys	Handicraft	Uttar Pradesh
235.	458	Mirzapur Handmade Dari	Handicraft	Uttar Pradesh

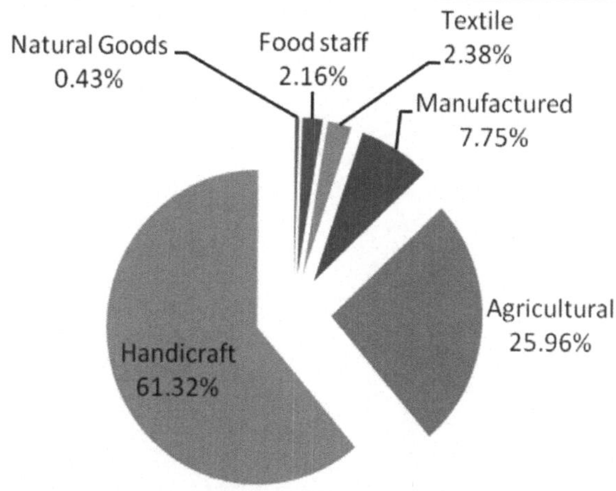

G.I. from Sep.2003 to March 2015

Fig. 6.1:

In India till 235 G.Is was registered up to the March 2015 the most attention were found in the sector of Handicraft followed by Agriculture, Manufactured, Textile, Food staff although very not as much of in Natural Goods since Sep. 2003 to March 20015. The state wise awareness Karnataka registered the maximum G.Is than Kerala, Uttar Pradesh, Tamil Nadu, Odisha, West Bengal, Maharashtra, Andhra Pradesh, and Rajasthan. Large number of state did not aware that much for the identity of their Geographical indication; Southern state of India has much attention for their geographical-rights.

REFERENCES

1. Das, Kasturi (2009). 'Prospects and Challenges of Geographical Indications in India', *Journal of World Intellectual Property*, Blackwell Publishing Ltd., forthcoming.
2. The Geographical Indications of Goods (Registration and Protection) Act, 1999 - Section 22.
3. The Geographical Indications of Goods (Registration and protection) Act, 1999 - Section 2 (e).
4. The Geographical Indications of Goods (Registration and Protection) Act, 1999 - Section 11(3).
5. The Geographical Indications of Goods (Registration and Protection) Act, 1999 - Section 18 (1).
6. Rangnekar, D. (2003). Geographical Indications: A Review of Proposals at the TRIPs Council, Extending Article 23 to Products other than Wines and Spirits.. UNCTAD-ICTSD Capacity Building Project on IPRs and Sustainable Development, Geneva.
7. www. http://ipindia.nic.in/girindia/.

Pages: 101-118

AGRO-BIODIVERSITY: *CONSERVATION AND SUSTAINABLE DEVELOPMENT*
Edited by: Dr. Pankaj Sharma; Dr. Narayan Singh & Dr. Pawan Kumar 'Bharti'
ISBN: 978-93-5056-782-1
Edition: 2016
Published by: Discovery Publishing House Pvt. Ltd., New Delhi (India)

7 Formulation of Insect Pest Management Modules and its Effect in Cauliflower Crop in Kullu Valley, Himachal Pradesh

Sarla Shashni[1*] and **J.K. Sharma**[2]

ABSTRACT

The use of pesticides enhances the economic potential of crops in terms of increased production and amelioration of vector borne diseases, but also results in serious health implication to the mankind and environment. Therefore, there is an urgent need of lowering the effect of these pesticides on the crops in order to maintain the health of soil, human and environment as a whole in sustained manner. In the present study, insect pest management modules of different chemical, bio pesticides and insecticides were formulated to check its effects on the insect, pest, disease incidence and yield attributes of cauliflower crop in Kullu Valley, Himachal Pradesh.

The study was carried out in field condition of *rabi* season, 2011 with five modules *viz.* M_1, M_2, M_3, M_4 and M_5 (control). Further yield in q/ha, net additional return and net return per rupee invested was analyzed statically using appropriate transformation. Incidence of insect-pest and diseases were also recorded to check the effect of different modules on the crop. Result shows the effectiveness of these modules in controlling the insect-pest and disease infestation of cauliflower crop in greater extent.

1. G.B. Pant Institute of Himalayan Environment and Development, Himachal Unit, Mohal-Kullu -175 126, Distt. Kullu, Himachal Pradesh, India.
2. Associate Director (Retd.), CSK Himachal Pradesh Krishi Vishwavidhyalaya, Regional Agriculture Research Station, Bajaura-Kullu -175 126, Himachal Pradesh, India.

It also shows the good economic return to the farmer through better yield and less pesticides application which further lowers its negative impact to the environment and human health.

Keywords: IPM, modules, insecticide and bio-pesticides

INTRODUCTION

Agriculture is the corner stone of hill economy as it forms the major sector of livelihood and employment to a large chunk of working population. However, the increasing population exposed by WTO reforms as in other parts of the country, are also the major concerns in hill agriculture. The staggeringly high rural population, unless it finds its small and medium holdings more productive and remunerative, and farming operations more dignified, will become more discontented. As the major population of our country is engaged in farming the supply of pesticides is also increasing to prevent the crop from getting damaged and fulfilling the demand. The use of pesticides enhances the economic potential of crops in terms of increased production and amelioration of vector borne diseases, but also results in serious health implication to the men and environment (Aktar *et al.* 2009). Now there is an overwhelming evidence of some of the chemicals do pose a potential risk to humans and other life forms and unwanted side effects to the environment (Forget, 1993; Igbedioh, 1991). According to WHO, 1999 there is no population segment in the world that is completely protected against exposure to pesticides and potentially serious health problem? Due to pesticide poisoning worldwide death reaches about 1 million per year (Environew Forum, 1999). Despite its benefit in controlling the insect pest of the crop it also had proved harmful because of the non-biodegradable chemical which do not breaks into smaller compound and remains in soil, air and water for long time. There is now increasing awareness and concern on sustainability of agriculture to meet the expanding needs of the future generations without disturbing the quality of ecosystem. Integrated pest management, the use of multiple approaches to control pests, is becoming widespread. With the increasing awareness it is recognizing as an alternative approach for the excessive use of chemical pesticides.

Cruciferous vegetables are the important source of vitamin and fiber used in Indian diet. It is one of the important vegetable crops of India cultivated in 0.35 hectare with 6.5 million tons of production (Ahuja *et al.* 2012) and worldwide it ranks number one or two in production of cauliflower (FAOSTAT, 2005).) Cabbage and cauliflower are some of the important vegetable crops in Kullu valley of Himachal Pradesh. Cauliflower (*Brassica oleracea*) is an annual plant that is grown in fields of Kullu valley. Cauliflower is grown on many different types of soil but does best in a rich, well drained soil with high moisture-holding capacities which provide better aeration and water penetration. Cauliflower grows best on a neutral or slightly acid soil (pH 6.0 to 6.5) (Girish *et al.* 2010) or green manure is supplied in the soil if it is low in organic matter. This cruciferous vegetable contains higher concentrations of vitamin C, minerals, and dietary fiber. Vegetable crops are attacked in every season by number of fungal disease, bacteria, virus, insects and pests caused high damage to the production.

Insects and pests generally attacked because of their liking and to complete their life cycle. They damage and used every parts of the plant and ultimate causes high economic loss to the farmers. Pest is an organism that effect vegetable crop. Most of the insects considered common vegetable pests undergo a developmental process known as metamorphosis, which simply means that the insect changes form during its life. Metamorphosis may be complete or incomplete. Complete metamorphosis consists of four stages – *(i)* egg; *(ii)* larva; *(iii)* pupa and *(iv)* adult. Worldwide, major constraints upon production of cruciferous vegetables are insect pests (Capinera, 2001). Increasing international trade and tourism have led to an increase in the introduction of exotic pests that pose a considerable economic threat to the agro-ecosystems. Thousand types of insects can affect vegetables (Mohammed *et al.* 2011).

Insect pest management mostly relies on synthetic insecticides, and indiscriminate use of pesticides among the farmers in all the developing countries (FAO, 2005). Among insect pests which are affecting cruciferous vegetables, the caterpillar has been the most difficult insect pest to control (Loganathan, 2002; Rao *et al.* 2003; Monobrullah *et al.* 2007) with diamond back moth, pieris, semilooper, alternaria leaf spot (Kohl *et al.* 2010) and damping off (Bhagat and Pan, 2008) are considered to be the most destructive throughout the world in cauliflower crop (Talekar, 1992). Due to this farmers are applying 10-12 pesticide application in the crops for the management of these insect-pest and diseases (Weinberger and Srinivasan, 2009; Ahuja *et al.* 2012). These higher pesticidal application increases the limit value (Shah *et al.* 2000; Kole *et al.* 2002; Cesnik *et al.* 2009; Islam *et al.* 2009). This is not only due to the pest infestation but also due to the resistance development of these pest against the pesticides (Sudhakar and Dhingra, 2002; Kranthi *et al.* 2002; Ashwinder Kaur *et al.* 2006).

The main objective of the current study was to formulate and validate the insect pest management modules among the farmers of Kullu valley which further reduce the application of pesticides and its long time effect on human and environment. This study was also aimed to validate this insect pest management module appropriateness and its acceptance among farmers after suitable refinement of these management modules.

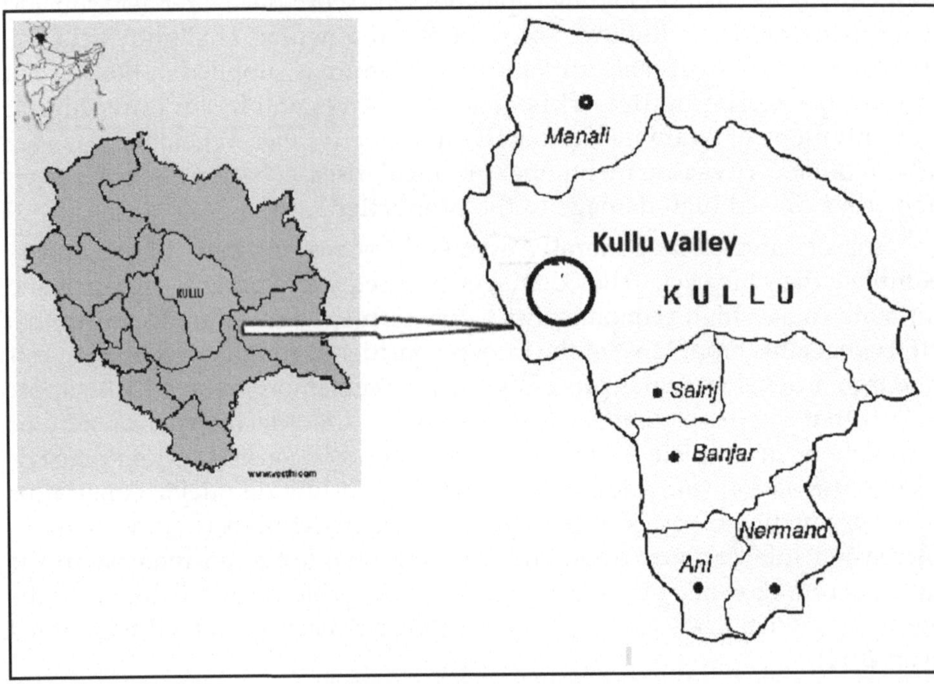

Map Showing Study Site

Material and Methodology

Present study was conducted in the field condition during the Rabi season of 2011. The study was conducted in the different locations at farmer's field to check the effect of IPM modules on the insect pests and yield in cauliflower crop. For this study, 3 farmers were selected for the trial of cauliflower. Plot size was restricted to 3.15 x 2.70 m for each trials and the spacing during transplantation was taken 45 x 45cm. The cauliflower crop variety used was hybrid S-626. The study was carried out with 5 different modules each with three replicates.

1. *Nursery and Seed Treatment*: Nursery treatment was done with formaldehyde @ 1:7 and covered with polyethylene sheet for 10 days for proper fumigation. After 10 days of removing polythene, sowing was done. Seed treatment in hot water at 52°C for 30 minutes followed by treatment with streptocycline @ 200 mg/litre of water for 30 minutes was given before sowing to the nursery bed.
2. *Nursery Management:* To control the disease incidence during nursery raising following treatments were given:
   (a) dipping seedlings in a mixture of Streptocycline (0.2g) + Carbendazim (1g) per litre of water for 30 min before transplanting;

(*b*) drenched nursery beds with Companion @ 0.25 per cent after 7 days and 14 days of seedling/plant emergence with the appearance of damping off;

(*c*) sprayed with Ridomil M Z @ 0.25 per cent after 25 days of plant emergence for the control of downy mildew.

3. *Transplanting*: Seedlings were dipped before transplanting in a mixture of streptocycline (0.2g) + carbendazim (1g) per litre of water for 30 min.
4. *Crop Duration:* Transplanting was done on the last week of March, 2011 and the crop was harvested by the last week of June and July first week.
5. *Modules:*

M1

(*a*) lambda-cyhalothrin @ 0.004 per cent (Bravo 5%) after 45 days of transplanting;

(*b*) mixture of Lambda-cyhalothrin @ 0.004 per cent (Bravo 5%) and Difenconazol @ 0.02 per cent (Score 25 EC) after 15 days of 1st spray;

M2

(*a*) azadirachtin @ 5ml/L (Neembaan 0.15%) after 45 days of transplanting;

(*b*) mixture of Azedarachtin @ (Neembaan 0.15%) and Difenconazol @ 0.02% (Score 25 EC) after 15 days of 1st spray;

(*c*) mechanical destruction of infested leaves for egg clusters/young larvae of butterfly at frequent intervals;

M3

(*a*) lambda-cyhalothrin @ 0.004 per cent (Bravo 5%) after 45 days of transplanting;

(*b*) mixture of Malathion (0.05%) and Dithane Z 78 @ 0.25% (Dithane 75 WP) after 15 days of 1st spray;

M4

(*a*) azadirachtin @ 5ml/L (Neembaan 0.15%) after 45 days of transplanting;

(*b*) mixture of Btk (15g/10 L) and Dithane Z - 78 @ 0.25% (Dithane 75 WP) after 15 days of 1st spray;

(*c*) mechanical destruction of infested leaves for egg clusters/young larvae of butterfly at frequent intervals;

M5. Control.

6. *Integrated Pest Management Method:* Experiments on the formulation and validation of integrated pest management for cauliflower were carried out at different sites of farmer's field in Kullu. Two sprays of each pest

management modules were spread on all the sites. Among the insects, larvae of *Pieris brassicae*, *Spodoptera* larvae, larvae of diamond back moth, and fruit borer are some of the major pests in farmers' fields. Data on the incidence of lepidopterous larvae, black rot and Alternaria blight were recorded on 10 plants per plot. Pre-treatment data on the incidence of lepidopterous larvae, Black rot and *Alternaria* blight was recorded 1-day before and post-treatment data after 7 - days and 14 - days of each spray were recorded. Data were recorded on the plant stand (%), plants (%) that formed curds, plants (%) that did not form the curds, marketable curds and unmarketable curds due to insect/disease attack. Yield was recorded plot wise and converted to q/ha.

7. *Monitoring of Insect-Pests*:

   (i) *population monitoring through light trap:* light trap studies were carried out at CSKHPKV, HAREC, Bajaura (1100 m amsl) Distt. Kullu (H.P.) during IV-week of March to last week of August, 2011 to monitor the population of insect-pests. A light trap made of galvanized tin sheet fitted with 160 watts mercury bulb, as alight source, was installed near to experimental field at about 2.50 m height from the ground on a iron pole. Observations were recorded daily except on rainy days. Data showed (Table 7.1) that beetles of the white grubs were most predominant constituting 31.10 per cent of the total insects caught. It was followed by fruit borer, *Helicoverpa armigera* (28.41% of the total insects caught), *Agrotis* spp. (12.08% of the total insects) and diamond back moth (10.29% of total insects caught). Moths of cabbage semi-looper and Spodoptera constituted 8.24 and 9.84 per cent, respectively of the total insects caught in the light trap. Period of maximum catches was April 4th week to May 2nd week for moths of cut worms and April 4th week to May 4th week for *Helicoverpa armigera*. Moths of cabbage semi-looper were active from April 1st week to May 1st week. Adults of diamond back moth were caught in the light trap from first week of April to 2nd week of August.

   (ii) *population monitoring through pheromone traps:* funnel trap and delta (sticky) trap were installed at Jhiri farm on last week of April to monitor the population of *Helicoverpa armigera, Spodoptera* and diamond back moth. Tubes/septa containing the lures were replaced after 3 weeks. Data were recorded after every two days on the number of insects trapped. Data showed (Table 7.2) that moths of DBM were caught in the trap for first three weeks only after that these were not trapped in the delta - sticky trap. Catches of the moths of *H. armigera* and *Spodoptera* was from 4th week of April to 2nd week of August with peak period of the moth catches between 3rd week of May and 1st week of June

for *H. armigera* and those of *Spodoptera* between 4th week of May to 3rd week of June. Comparatively more numbers of moths of *Spodoptera* were captured in the pheromone traps than in the light trap and vice-a-versa for *H. armigera*. Moths of both the species were first captured in the pheromone traps on 24th April, 2011 while those of DBM on 22nd April, 2011.

Table 7.1: Catches of insect - pests in the light trap at CSKHPKV, HAREC, Bajaura, Distt. Kullu during 2011

Period/Month		Number of Insects Trapped Per Week							
		Agro.	DBM	Ha	CSL	*Sp*	White Grub beetles	Total	% of Total
March	IV - wk	0	0	4	0	4	9	17	3.28
April	I - wk	0	2	13	4	9	12	40	7.72
	II - wk	0	1	2	0	5	7	15	2.90
	III - wk	7	2	9	3	7	4	32	6.18
	IV- wk	15	7	27	8	4	17	78	15.06
May	I - wk	8	4	13	5	7	18	55	10.62
	II - wk	9	0	6	3	2	4	24	4.63
	III - wk	7	9	12	3	0	4	35	6.76
	IV - wk	2	7	17	4	4	12	46	8.87
June	I - wk	0	3	7	1	0	14	25	4.83
	II - wk	1	5	4	2	0	7	19	3.67
	III - wk	4	2	6	2	0	8	22	4.25
	IV - wk	0	1	4	1	0	13	19	3.67
July	I - wk	1	3	3	1	2	10	20	3.86
Total		54	46	127	37	44	139	447	
% of Total		**12.08**	**10.29**	**28.41**	**8.28**	**9.84**	**31.10**		

Agro = *Agrotis* spp., DBM = Diamond back moth, Ha = *Helicoverpa armigera*, CSL = Cabbage Semi Looper, Sp = Spodoptera

8. *Economics of Crop Yield*: Economics of different pest management modules was calculated on the basis of market price of cauliflower (Rs. 1,000/ha); insecticides/fungicides *viz*: Lambda-cyhalothrin (Bravo 5%) @ Rs. 520/L, azadirechtin (Neembaan 0.15%) @ Rs. 320/L, difenconazol (Score 25 EC) @ Rs. 3,000/L, malathion (Malathion 50 EC) @ Rs. 320/L, streptocycline @ Rs. 5,500/kg, Companion (Carbedazim 12% + Mancozeb 63%) @ Rs. 560/kg, *Bacillus thuringiensis var kurstaki* (Lipel SP) @ Rs. 1,500/kg, Dithane Z - 78 @ Rs 320/kg, Ridomil MZ @ 1,300/kg, and labour

charges for pesticide application (Rs. 1,200/ha @ Rs. 120/day: total 10 man days/ha). Net additional return (Rs/ha) of each module was calculated by subtracting the total cost (Rs/ha) of pesticide application from net return (Rs/ha) in the pesticidal treatments over the control. Net returns per rupee invested was calculated by dividing the net additional return (Rs/ha) with the cost of pesticide application. Data were analyzed statistically after appropriate transformation using significant difference at 5 per cent probability using CPCS-1 data analysis package.

Table 7.2: Catches of insects in the pheromone traps CSKHPKV, HAREC, Bajaura, Distt. Kullu during 2011

Month/Period		No. of Insects Trapped Per Week in		
		Delta Sticky Trap (DBM Lure)	Funnel Trap (Heli lure)	Funnel Trap (Spodo lure)
April	IV - wk	8 (1st moth caught on 22.04.11)	1 (1st moth caught on 24.04.11)	2 (1st moth caught on 24.04.11)
May	I - wk	3	2	13
	II - wk	5	2	9
	III - wk	6	6	13
	IV - wk	0	4	18
June	I - wk	0	7	22
	II - wk	0	2	16
	III - wk	0	2	17
	IV - wk	0	5	14
July	I - wk	0	3	12
Total		**14**	**33**	**134**

Results

Data presented in Tables 7.1 to 7.9 showed that Modules M_3 and M_1 have also been found most effective and economical for the management of insects and diseases on cauliflower. In the M_3 and M_1 modules, average net additional returns were Rs. 1,09,894/- and Rs. 89,230/-. Net returns per rupee invested in the respective modules were Rs. 26.49/- and Rs. 25.12/- per rupee invested. It was also observed that in larval incidence reduced to 0 per cent in M_3 and 3.33 per cent in M_1 as compared to 18.89 per cent in control. Whereas, alternaria blight and black rot incidence also reduced to 13.71 per cent and 11.90 per cent in M_3; and 12.50 per cent and 13.19 per cent in in M_1 respectively as compared to 45.70 per cent and 37.94 per cent in control. Application of pesticides also reduced to 50-60 per cent by only two sprays as compared to the 4-5 time spray earlier. It was also found that the bio pesticides based formulation M_2 and M_4 were also found effective in controlling the insect pest. Average net additional return in M_4 was Rs. 87,443/- as compared to M_2 where it was Rs. 73,124/- with net return per rupee invested Rs. 17.34/- and Rs. 12.34/-. Larval incidence was also reduced to 0 per cent in M_4 and 5.56 per cent in M_2 as compared to 18.89 per cent in control. While alternaria blight and black rot incidence was reduced to 13.09 per cent; 13.84 per cent in M_4 and 13.77 per cent and 16.92 per cent in M_2 as that of 45.70 per cent and 37.94 per cent in control. Monitoring of insect pest through light trap and different pheromone traps (DBM lure, Heli lure and Spodo lure) were also found effective in monitoring and controlling the insect pest at great extent.

Fig. 7.1: **(a & b) Cauliflower trial at farmers field (c) Harvested cauliflower curds**

Conclusion

IPM modules implementation in the fields resulted reduction in the number of sprays by 40-50 per cent as well as the replacement of the highly toxic pesticides with biopesticides like Neem (*Azadirachta indica*) based formulation. As a result there was reinforcement of sustainable and stable pest control warranting less pesticide application with good economic gain. Farmers were educated about the proper time of application, proper doses and about the right choice of pesticides with good profit. Farmers could

Table 7.3: Effect of different pest management modules on the yield attributes and Economics of Cauliflower in Site I

Modules	Plant Stand (%)	Curds Formation (%)	Plant (%) that did not Formed the Curds	Marketable Curds (%)	Un-marketable Curds (%) Due to		Average Marketable Yield (q/ha)	Net Additional Return (Rs/ha)	Net Return per Rs. Invested
					Insect Attack	Disease Incidence			
M_1	97.78 (9.34)	93.22 (9.71)	6.77 (2.78)	90.28 (9.55)	5.47 (2.53)	3.63 (2.15)	388.34	121644.33	29.32
M_2	97.78 (9.34)	95.47 (9.82)	4.52 (2.33)	86.94 (9.38)	7.70 (2.93)	5.35 (2.50)	348.42	79945.00	13.49
M_3	97.77 (9.93)	96.59 (9.88)	3.39 (2.07)	91.18 (9.60)	5.64 (2.52)	3.54 (2.52)	361.59	95491.33	26.88
M_4	97.22 (9.91)	92.59 (9.67)	7.98 (2.98)	85.85 (9.32)	8.58 (9.32)	5.56 (2.56)	395.20	127602.67	25.30
M_5	96.67 (9.88)	89.07 (9.49)	10.93 (9.49)	70.15 (8.43)	20.07 (8.43)	9.01 (3.16)	262.55	0.00	0
CD (5%)	**NS**	**0.21**	**0.66**	**0.43**	**0.99**	**0.43**	**37.16**		

Figures with in the parentheses are: * $\sqrt{n+1}$ transformation.

Table 7.4: Incidence of lepidopterous larvae and diseases on cauliflower in Site I

Modules	Pre - Treatment larval Incidence		Post - Treatment larval Incidence after						Disease Incidence after 14 days of 1st Spray	
			7 - days of 1st Spray		14 - days of 1st Spray		7 - days of 2nd Spray			
	No. of larvae/10 plants)*	Plant Infestation** (%)	No. of larvae/10 plants)*	Plant Infestation** (%)	No. of larvae/10 plants)*	Plant Infestation** (%)	No. of larvae/10 plants*	Plant Infestation** (%)	Alternaria Blight* Severity (%)	Black Rot* Incidence (%)
M_1	48.66 (7.04)	40.00 (39.13)	0.00 (1.00)	0.00 (0.00)	21.00 (4.68)	20.00 (4.68)	0.00 (1.00)	0.00 (0.00)	11.11 (19.03)	14.44 (22.16)
M_2	45.33 (6.75)	40.00 (39.11)	3.33 (1.77)	6.67 (8.85)	24.67 (5.03)	23.33 (28.77)	0.00 (28.77)	6.67 (8.45)	14.12 (20.96)	16.11 (23.57)
M_3	49.33 (7.02)	43.33 (41.05)	2.67 (1.67)	3.33 (6.14)	23.00 (4.81)	23.33 (28.79)	0.00 (1.00)	0.00 (0.00)	12.85 (20.81)	14.54 (21.95)
M_4	59.00 (7.72)	53..33 (46.90)	3.00 (1.72)	6.67 (8.25)	24.00 (4.95)	16.67 (23.84)	0.00 (1.00)	0.00 (0.00)	9.44 (17.78)	10.55 (18.23)
M_5	56.67 (7.56)	46.90 (46.10)	32.67 (5.75)	26.67 (30.98)	33.00 (5.81)	26.67 (30.98)	17.67 (4.31)	16.68 (14.74)	40.33 (39.34)	37.56 (37.72)
CD (5%)	**NS**	**NS**	**2.19**	**NS**	**NS**	**NS**	**0.32**	**14.71**	**9.25**	**10.07**

Figures within the parentheses are: * $\sqrt{n+1}$ transformation and ** arc sine transformation.

Table 7.5: Effect of different pest management modules on the yield attributes and Economics of Cauliflower in Site II

Modules	Plant Stand (%)	Curds Formation (%)	Plant (%) that did not Formed the Curds	Marketable Curds (%)	Un-marketable Curds (%) Due to		Average Marketable Yield (q/ha)	Net Additional Return (Rs/ha)	Net Return per Rs. invested
					Insect Attack	Disease Incidence			
M_1	97.62 (9.93)	98.39 (9.97)	1.60 (1.56)	79.64 (8.98)	13.83 (3.84)	6.53 (2.73)	322.95	98921.00	23.84
M_2	98.41 (9.96)	97.58 (9.92)	2.42 (1.75)	78.17 (8.90)	16.15 (4.12)	5.67 (2.53)	280.81	55011.67	9.28
M_3	98.41 (9.96)	97.62 (9.93)	2.38 (1.74)	85.39 (9.29)	8.13 (2.97)	6.47 (2.72)	310.60	87174.67	24.54
M_4	96.83 (9.89)	95.89 (9.84)	4.10 (2.24)	85.29 (9.28)	9.82 (3.27)	3.27 (2.05)	296.89	71966.00	14.27
M_5	96.03 (9.85)	96.69 (9.88)	3.31 (2.05)	69.43 (8.39)	22.30 (4.82)	8.27 (3.03)	219.88	0.00	0.00
CD (5%)	**NS**	**NS**	**NS**	**(0.37)**	**(0.74)**	**NS**	**50.47**		

Figures with in the parentheses are: * $\sqrt{n+1}$ transformation.

Table 7.6: Incidence of lepidopterous larvae and diseases on Cauliflower in Site II

Modules	Pre - Treatment larval Incidence		Post - Treatment larval Incidence after						Disease Incidence after 14 days of 1st Spray	
			7 - days of 1st Spray		14 - days of 1st Spray		7 - days of 2nd Spray			
	No.of larvae/10 plants)*	Plant Infestation** (%)	No.of larvae/10 plants)*	Plant Infestation** (%)	No.of larvae/10 plants)*	Plant Infestation** (%)	No.of larvae/10 plants*	Plant Infestation** (%)	Alternaria Blight* Severity (%)	Black Rot* Incidence (%)
M1	48.33 (6.99)	46.67 (43.06)	0.00 (1.00)	0.00 (0.00)	24.67 (4.44)	16.67 (19.92)	0.00 (1.00)	0.00 (0.00)	16.86 (14.11)	15.19 (22.53)
M2	38.67 (22.53)	33.33 (34.91)	0.00 (1.00)	0.00 (0.00)	23.00 (4.87)	23.33 (28.77)	0.00 (1.00)	0.00 (0.00)	15.04 (22.54)	19.84 (21.19)
M3	37.67 (6.18)	36.67 (37.21)	0.00 (1.00)	0.00 (0.00)	27.33 (5.29)	30.00 (33.20)	0.00 (1.00)	0.00 (0.00)	15.07 (22.74)	9.52 (17.87)
M4	47.00 (6.87)	46.67 (43.06)	0.00 (1.00)	0.00 (0.00)	25.00 (4.39)	23.33 (23.85)	0.00 (1.00)	0.00 (0.00)	15.55 (23.16)	12.99 (21.01)
M5	43.33 (6.64)	40.00 (39.13)	21.33 (4.72)	23.33 (28.77)	32.67 (5.79)	33.33 (35.20)	27.00 (5.25)	30.00 (32.99)	47.76 (43.69)	43.62 (41.29)
CD (5%)	NS	NS	**(0.22)**	**(3.23)**	NS	NS	**(0.61)**	**(5.33)**	**(6.69)**	**(4.41)**

Figures with in the parentheses are: * $\sqrt{n+1}$ transformation and ** arc sine transformation.

Table 7.7: Effect of different Pest management modules on the yield attributes and Economics of Cauliflower in Site III

Modules	Plant Stand (%)	Curds Formation (%)	Plant (%) that did not Formed the Curds	Marketable Curds (%)	Un-marketable Curds (%) Due to		Average Marketable Yield (q/ha)	Net Additional Return (Rs/ha)	Net Return per Rs. Invested
					Insect Attack	Disease Incidence			
M1	95.24 (9.81)	98.33 (9.97)	1.67 (1.58)	85.57 (9.30)	9.34 (3.20)	5.19 (2.48)	320.99	109117.67	26.30
M2	97.62 (9.93)	92.60 (9.67)	3.23 (2.04)	83.18 (9.17)	12.63 (3.67)	4.18 (2.26)	300.02	84415.00	14.25
M3	98.41 (9.96)	96.82 (9.89)	3.17 (1.93)	87.50 (9.40)	6.67 (2.76)	5.83 (2.60)	298.26	85024.67	23.94
M4	96.03 (9.84)	95.89 (9.84)	4.10 (2.24)	82.76 (9.15)	11.23 (3.49)	6.00 (2.63)	277.48	62759.33	12.44
M5	92.86 (9.68)	94.04 (9.74)	6.84 (2.79)	69.27 (8.31)	19.07 (4.47)	11.01 (3.31)	209.68	0.00	0.00
CD (5%)	**NS**	**NS**	**NS**	**(0.47)**	**0.52**	**(0.46)**	**48.28**		

Figures within the parentheses are: $\sqrt{n+1}$ transformation.

Table 7.8: Incidence of lepidopterous larvae and diseases on Cauliflower in Site III

Modules	Pre -Treatment larval Incidence		Post - Treatment larval Incidence after						Disease Incidence after 14 days of 1st Spray	
			7 - days of 1st Spray		14 - days of 1st Spray		7 - days of 2nd Spray			
	No.of larvae/10 plants)*	Plant Infestation** (%)	No.of larvae/10 plants)*	Plant Infestation** (%)	No.of larvae/10 plants)*	Plant Infestation** (%)	No.of larvae/10 plants*	Plant Infestation** (%)	Alternaria Blight* Severity (%)	Black Rot* Incidence (%)
M1	48.33 (6.91)	46.67 (43.06)	0.00 (1.00)	0.00 (0.00)	29.00 (5.42)	33.33 (35.10)	4.00 (2.05)	10.00 (15.00)	9.52 (17.47)	9.95 (18.30)
M2	51.00 (7.19)	43.33 (41.05)	0.00 (1.00)	0.00 (0.00)	26.33 (4.53)	30.00 (27.98)	3.67 (2.03)	10.00 (15.00)	12.16 (20.08)	14.81 (22.52)
M3	46.67 (6.71)	40.00 (39.13)	0.00 (1.00)	0.00 (0.00)	30.67 (5.62)	33.33 (35.20)	0.00 (1.00)	0.00 (0.00)	13.22 (21.20)	11.64 (19.87)
M4	56.00 (7.45)	50.00 (44.98)	0.00 (1.00)	0.00 (0.00)	33.00 (5.80)	40.00 (39.13)	0.00 (1.00)	0.00 (0.00)	14.28 (22.13)	17.99 (25.08)
M5	54.67 (7.42)	46.67 (43.06)	36.67 (5.94)	43.33 (41.14)	54.67 (7.42)	46.67 (43.06)	26.67 (5.18)	10.00 (15.00)	49.00 (32.56)	32.64 (34.77)
CD (5%)	**NS**	**NS**	**(0.68)**	**(2.80)**	**NS**	**NS**	**(1.55)**	**NS**	**(7.21)**	**(5.20)**

Figures within the parentheses are: * $\sqrt{n+1}$ transformation and ** arc sine transformation.

Table 7.9: Average net additional return, net gain per rupee invested and incidence of insect/diseases in different IPM modules on cauliflower

Modules	Net Additional Return (Rs/ha)				Net Gain (Rs)/ Rupee Invested				Average Incidence Rupee Invested		
	Site I	Site II	Site II	Average	Site I	Site II	Site II	Average	Plant Infestation (%)	Alternaria Blight (%)	Black Rot (%)
M_1	1,21,644	98,921	1,09,118	1,09,894	29.32	23.84	26.30	26.49	3.33	12.50	13.19
M_2	79,945	55,012	84,415	73,124	13.49	9.28	14.25	12.34	5.56	13.77	16.92
M_3	95,491	87,175	85,025	89,230	26.88	24.54	23.94	25.12	0.00	13.71	11.90
M_4	1,27,603	71,966	62,759	87,443	25.30	14.27	12.44	17.34	0.00	13.09	13.84
M_5	–	–	–	–	–	–	–	–	18.89	45.70	37.94

know about the pest monitoring and application of pesticides based on action threshold. Women laborer who were engaged for hoeing and weeding were educating about the management of insect pest through mechanical method *i.e.,* women were imparted training to identify the egg masses, bunches of neonate larvae and later instars of caterpillar of *S. litura* and *H. armegira.* This resulted value addition to their work and helped generating employment opportunities. Farmers were able to identify the various stages of the pest and damage cause by them and could differentiate between the symptom of damage due to insects and diseases, thereby helping to make right choice of the pesticides. The empowerment with knowledge of the producer and consumer would further propel the adoption of the IPM modules as increase in public awareness would also like to fetch a premium price for the farmers following integrated pest management strategies (Govindasamy and Italia, 1997). In order to achieve the use of these IPM modules use and educate the farmers about the pheromone traps in the field can be the other good option.

Pesticides here refer as all types of insecticides, pesticides, weedicides, etc., used to control various insects, pest and diseases in the crop. They are often considered as quick, easy and inexpensive solution for controlling the pathogens. However its use comes as a significant cost contaminated almost every part of our environment. Pesticide contamination poses significant risks to the environment and non targeting organism such as: many soil microorganisms, some friendly insects, plants and birds. We cannot neglect or stop it completely but we can educate the farmers about its usage and promoting other alternatives such as: bio pesticides for the sustainable development of the environment. Therefore, there is also a need to convey the message among farmers that prevention of adverse health effect and promotion of healthy crops are profitable investment to the sustainable development of economics. Thus there is every reason to develop heath education package based on knowledge and awareness campaign and practice to disseminate them within the community in order to minimize the effect of pesticides. Reducing the pesticide use and choosing bio pesticides further reduce the risk of these chemicals on society and the environment.

REFERENCES

Ahuja D.B., Ahuja U.R., Srinivas P., Singh R.V., Malik M., Sharma P. and Bamawala O.M. (2012). Development of Farmer-led Integrated Management of Major Pests of Cauliflower Cultivated in Rainy Season in India. *Journal of Agriculture Science,* 4 (2): 79-90.

Aktar M.W., Sengupta D. and Chawdhury A. (2009). Imapcts of Pesticide use in Agriculture: Their Benefits and Hazards. *Interdisciplinary Toxicol,* 2 (1): 1-12.

Bhagat S. and Pan S. (2008). Biological Management of Root and Collar rot of Cauliflower (*Rhizoctonia solani*) by a talc-based Formulation of *Trichoderma harzianum* Rifai. *Journal of Biological Control,* 22 (2): 483-486.

Capinera J.L. (2001). Handbook of Vegetable Pests. New York: Academic Press.

Cesnik H.B., Gregorcic A. and Bolta S.V. (2009). Plant Protection Product Residues in Apples, Cauliflower, Cereals, Grape, Lettuce, Peas, Peppers, Potatoes and Strawberries of the Slovene Origin in 2006. *Journal of Central European Agriculture,* 10 (3): 311-320.

FAO. (2005). International Code of Conduct on the Distribution and use of Pesticides. Rome, Italy: Food and Agriculture Organization of the United Nations.

FAOSTAT. (2005). Available: http://apps.fao.org. Food and Agriculture Organization of the United Nations.

Forget G. (1993). Balancing the Need for Pesticides with the Risk to Human Health. In: Forget G, Goodman T, de Villiers A, (eds.). Impact of Pesticide Use on Health in Developing Countries. IDRC, Ottawa: 2.

Govindasamy R. and Italia J. (1997). Consumer Response to Integrated Pest Management and Organic Agriculture: An Econometric Analysis. In: Consumer *Response to Integrated Pest Management and Organic Agriculture: Aneconometric Analysis.* (p. iii + 50). New Brunswick, Publisher Rutgers University Press USA.

Igbedioh S.O. (1991). Effects of Agricultural Pesticides on Humans, Animals and Higher Plants in Developing Countries. *Arch Environ Health,* 46:218.

Islam S., Nazneen A., Hossain M.S., Nilufar N., Mohammad M., Mamun and M.I.R. (2009). Analysis of Some Pesticide Residues in Cauliflower by High Performance Liquid Chromatography. *American Journal of Environmental Sciences,* 5: 325-329.

Kaur A., Kang B.K., and Singh B. (2006). Monitoring of Insecticide Resistance in *Spodoptera litura* (Fabricius) in Punjab, India. *Pesticide Research Journal,* 18: 51-53.

Kohl J., Tongeren C.A.M., Haas V.G.D., Hoof B.H., Driessen V.R. and Heijden L.V.D. (2010). Epidemiology of Dark Leaf Spot Caused by Alternaria brassicicola and Brassicae in Organic Seed Production of Cauliflower. *Plant Pathology,* 59(2): 358-367.

Kranthi K.R., Jadhav D.R., Kranthi S., Wanjari R.R., Ali S.S. and Russell D.A. (2002). Insecticide Resistance in Five Major Insect Pests of Cotton in India. *Crop Protection,* 21, (6), 449-460.

Loganathan M. (2002). Insect Pest Complex of Cauliflower in Tamil Nadu. *Insect Environment,* 8: 46-47.

Mohapatra S., Sawarkar S., Patnaik H.P. and Senapati B. (1995). Antifeedant Activity of Solvent Extracts of Neem seed Kernel against Spodoptera litura F. and their Persistency against Sunlight through Encapsulation. *International Journal of Pest Management,* 41 (3): 154-156.

Monobrullah M., Bharti P., Shankar U., Gupta R.K., Srivastava K. and Ahmad H. (2007). Trap Catches and Seasonal Incidence of Spodoptera Litura on Cauliflower and Tomato. *Annals of Plant Protection Sciences,* 15(1): 73-76.

Ram D., Pandey D.K., Devi S. and Chanu T.M. (2012). Adoption Level of IPM Practices in Cabbage and Cauliflower Growers of Manipur. *Indian Research Journal on Extension and Education,* 12(2): 34-37.

Rao J.R., Babu B.R., Krishnayya and P.V. (2003). Correlation of Weather Parameters with the Insect-pests Incidence on Cauliflower. *Crop Research (Hisar),* 25 (2): 341-346.

Sudhakar K. and Dhingra S. (2002). Effect of Combinations of Sub Lethal Concentration of Chemical and Microbial Insecticides to different Larval Instars of *Spodoptera litura* (Fab.). *Pesticide Research Journal,* 14: 32-39.

Talekar N.S. (1992). Management of Diamondback moth and other crucifer pests. In: Talekar NS, (ed). Proceedings of the Second International Workshop. Shanhua, Taiwan: Asian Vegetable Research and Development Centre.

Weinberger K. and Srinivasan R. (2009). Farmer's Management of Cabbage and Cauliflower Pests in India and their Approaches to Crop Protection. *Journal of Asia Pacific Entomology,* 12 (4): 253-259.

Pages: 119-130

AGRO-BIODIVERSITY: *CONSERVATION AND SUSTAINABLE DEVELOPMENT*
Edited by: Dr. Pankaj Sharma; Dr. Narayan Singh & Dr. Pawan Kumar 'Bharti'
ISBN: 978-93-5056-782-1
Edition: 2016
Published by: Discovery Publishing House Pvt. Ltd., New Delhi (India)

8

Farmer's Perception and Adoption of Modern Agro Technologies in Vegetable Farming
A Case Premise to the Farming Community of Solan District of Himachal Pradesh

Piyush Mehta*; Yasmin Janjhua and **Rashmi Chaudhary**

ABSTRACT

The adoption of modern agricultural production technologies amongst farmers' in the state of Himachal Pradesh has been very low over the last couple of decades. This infact has emerged as one of the main reasons for the low agricultural productivity in the state. The paper examined the key elements of modern agro technologies in the vegetable farming and also attempted to identify the significant factors that helped in easy adoption and practice of modern agro technologies among vegetable growing farm community in the state. The paper also extended to study the perceptual awareness level of farmers' towards modern agro farm technologies, resulting to identify the key problems and challenges faced by the famers' while adopting agro technologies and to seek the suggestions and recommendations from the farmers to improvise the usage capability and easy adoption of modern agro technologies in the vegetable farming. Interview Schedules were administered to 240 vegetable growing farmers at the Solan district of Himachal Pradesh, emerging as the largest quality vegetable producing region of the state. Total weightage method was computed to ascertain the elements and factors. The results showed that

Department of Business Management, College of Horticulture, Dr. Y.S. Parmar University of Horticulture and Forestry, Nauni - Solan - 173 230, Himachal Pradesh, India.

Market Information network and Farming credit management followed by agri supply chain management, warehousing and quality testing and protective farming (polyhouse and greenhouse cultivation) are the critical factors that significantly influenced technology adoption decisions of farming community in the study area. Paper concludes that farmer's agricultural technology adoption decisions depends on support of subsidies and trade discounts related financial support followed by technological awareness and training sessions. Further, it was recommended that in order to strengthen the technological awareness among farmers, government interventions policies shall be substantiated and farmers' active participation along with conducive banking schemes and financial services may positively influence farmers' adoption of modern agricultural production technologies.

Keywords: Agricultural production technologies, Farming community, Agri supply chain management, Technological awareness, Farming credit management

INTRODUCTION

Technological change is possibly the single most important factor driving globalisation and the development of world agriculture. The gap between rich and poor countries is often a technology gap, the changing relations between farmers and society are often a result of changes in technology used by farmers and New technology is increasingly at the forefront of international trade conflicts. Typically, market-driven technological progress has led to the intensification of farming systems, the use of more industrial inputs and the adoption of management methods that stress low costs and high yields. Farmers must be aware of the technological and policy changes on the horizon. Thus, developments in research need to be accompanied by training for farmers on new developments and how they should adapt. Consideration should be given to establishing regional centres where information on best practices or success stories can be accessed by farmer organizations and others (OECD, 2001). One of the key factors that influence the farmer's decision to adopt or not to adopt farming technology is the perception associated with the technology which are sometimes backed by cultural and traditional considerations (Emmanuel, 2014). Farmers' subjective preferences for characteristics of new agricultural technologies are very important determinants of adoption behaviour. Farmers are consumers of the products of agricultural research and their subjective preferences for characteristics of new agricultural technologies affect their adoption decisions (Akinwumi and Jojo, 1995).

Farmers should obtain certain levels of education that are associated with their farming activity, and have a willingness to learn new technologies. In addition, well-organized mass media and responsible bodies can play an important role via advertisement in order to embolden technology adoption among farmers. Furthermore, extension workers should update their knowledge on the new technology that will be introduced to farmers. They should also arrange suitable times for training, teach farmers by sequence, and practice technology adoption together (Abdullah and Samah, 2013). Farmer's perception of the relevance of technologies is affected by awareness of the technology; and the relevance propels adoption. But the awareness has not influenced perception because the perceived cost/benefit ratio is not sufficiently attractive. Agricultural research policy should enhance existing agricultural technologies since farmers' awareness of the technology significant affect their perception to the relevance of the agricultural technology (Mukadasi and Lusiba, 2006).

Access to credit, higher levels of education, access to extension advisory services, and members of agricultural associations are more likely to adopt new agricultural technologies (Uaiene, Arndt and Masters, 2009). The factors that influence the adoption of modern agricultural production technologies are broadly categorised into economic factors, social factors and institutional factors. The economic factors include: farm size, cost of technology or modernization, expected benefits from adoption of the technology, and off-farm activities. The social factors that influence probability of adoption of modern agricultural production technologies by farm households include age, level of education and gender and the institutional factors including access to information and extension services are the significant factors that influence the adoption of modern agricultural production technologies (Mamudu *et al*. 2012).

Research Objectives

The research's objectives have taken an overall overview and attempt to indicate the comprehensive notion pertain to farmers' perception for modern agro technologies. Largely study has focussed with the following objectives:

- To study the key elements of modern agro technologies in the vegetable farming.
- To identify the significant factors helps in easy adoption and practice of modern agro technologies among vegetable growing farm community.
- To study the perceptual awareness level of farmers' towards modern agro farm technologies.
- To identify the key problems and challenges faced by the famers' while adopting agro technologies.
- To seek the suggestions and recommendations from the farmers to improvise the usage capability and easy adoption of modern agro technologies in the vegetable farming.

Material and Methods

The concerned research has been carried to take farmer as the main research unit. Though under the given study Solan district was purposively choosen as a sample district to cover the research population of Himachal Pradesh. But considering the time and cost constraints. The cluster sampling was applied to draw the sample of 240. Wherein, the district was divided into four research zones, on the basis of four sub divisions of Solan district, north zone including Arki sub-division, 40 respondents were selected considering the convenient sampling. Further the same amount of sample was collected from the southern zone comprising Solan as the sub-division of the district, and equal number of sample was drawn from the eastern zone comprising Kandaghat sub-division and the same number of sample was also drawn from the western zone comprising Nalagarh sub-division.

The data was primarily collected with the help of self structured interview schedule comprising the information pertained to basic information related to demographic aspects of the respondents and also including the detailed information pertained to the objectives of the concerned study. Later the collected data was analysed with the suitable statistical analytical tools including Chi Square and total weightage score method. Total Weight age Score method has been computed by providing different weights according to the importance and multiply the values of the items (X) by the weights (W) as provided. Then add all the values to obtain the total weights of all the items and the one which gets highest score will get the first rank and the one which gets the lowest score will get the lowest rank.

$$TWS = W_1{*}X_{1+} W_2{*}X_{2+} W_3{*}X_3 +\text{--}\ \text{-}\ W_nX_n$$ (*Where, TWS = Total weight score; W_i = Weights, X_i = frequency*)

Results and Discussion

Demographic attributes and agro technological components and constraints perceived by farmers have been discussed and presented in the following Table 8.1 to 8.6:

Table 8.1 indicates that the demographic and economic status of the respondents. It was noted that larger number of respondents were taken from the age category of 18-35 years, larger number of respondents hold the educational qualification ranging from Senior secondary to Graduation, the farming experience of the respondents majorly lying in the range of 5-20 years, the annual income of the majority of the respondents were in the range of Rs. 3-6 Lakhs per annum, In reference to the vegetable cropping pattern it was noted that majority of respondents preferred to crop Tomatoe, capsicum, peas and cabbage largely, among majority of respondents 2-4 number of family members were actively involved in the farming business and it was also observed that majority of respondents owned farming land holding of around 6-20 bighas, though other land holders were also accessed in the research data.

Table 8.1: Socio-economic profile of the respondents

Demographic Variables	Details	No. of Respondents (%)
Age (Years)	Below 18	13.8
	18-35	43.4
	36-50	25.3
	Above 50	17.5
Educational Qualification	> = Matriculation	9.4
	10 + 2 and Graduate	64.8
	PG and Higher Education	12.5
	Professional Education and others	13.3
Farming Experience (Years)	Below 5 years	21.2
	5 - 10	39.8
	11 - 20	23.8
	Above 20	15.2
Income (Rs./Annum)	Less than Rs. 1,00,000	7.2
	Rs. 1,00,000 - Rs. 3,00,000	26.2
	Rs. 3,00,001 - Rs. 6,00,000	34.2
	Above Rs. 6,00,000	32.4
Vegetable crops using modern agro technologies	Tomatoes, Capsicum and Peas	32.5
	Cauliflower	12.7
	Cabbage	15.4
	Beans	3.2
	Cucumber, Brinjal, carrots	2.1
	Ginger	1.8
	Turnip and Radish	1.2
	Mushroom	12.4
	Potato	5.2
	Others	13.5
No. of family members involved in farming	Below 2	33.1
	2 - 4	48.8
	5 - 7	14.5
	Above 7	3.6
Farming Land holding status (Bighas)	Below 5	29.6
	6 - 20	44.7
	21 - 40	18.3
	Above 40	7.4

Source: Primary field survey, 2014-15; figures in percentage of sample respondents.

Table 8.2: Key elements of modern agro technologies in the vegetable farming

Key Elements of Modern Agro Technologies	Varied Sub-divisions			
	North Zone (Arki)	South Zone (Solan)	East Zone (Kandaghat)	West Zone (Nalagarh)
Market Information network	23.3	20.0	16.7	23.3
Supply chain Management	6.7	11.7	5.0	16.7
Integrated Pest Management	5.0	10.0	5.0	6.7
Genetically modified seeds	1.7	3.3	3.3	1.7
Warehousing and quality testing	21.7	15.0	18.3	10.0
Soil and irrigation management	6.7	13.3	6.7	8.3
Protective farming (Polyhouse and Greenhouse cultivation)	13.3	10.0	20.0	13.3
Tissue culture	3.3	6.7	8.3	5.0
Farming credit management	18.3	10.0	16.7	15.0

Source: Primary field survey, 2014-15; figures in percentage of sample respondents.

Table 8.2 indicates the percentage of farmers' stating their significance on account of the stated set of commonly used modern agro technologies in the research area. Largely market information, warehousing and quality testing, protective farming and farming credit management were perceived to be the most significant technologies being used or tend to be used among the farming community. Observing the significance of key elements of modern agro technologies in respect to the respective zones, it was observed that farmers' in the North zone (Arki) observed that Market Information network followed by Warehousing and quality testing and Farming credit management are the key elements of modern agro technologies, Where as in South Zone (Solan), Market Information network followed by Warehousing and quality testing and Soil and irrigation management were considered to be the most significant elements of modern agro technologies. Further, East Zone (Kullu, Mandi and Una) observed that Warehousing and quality testing followed by Market Information network and Farming credit management are the key elements of modern agro technologies and West Zone (Hamirpur, Bilaspur and Kangra) observed that Market Information network followed by Supply chain Management and Farming credit management are the key elements of modern agro technologies.

Table 8.3: Perceptual awareness level of farmers towards modern agro farm technologies

Key Elements of Modern Agro Technologies Perceptional Level Across Varied Zones	Total Weightage Score (TWS) and Rank in Parantheses of Varied Zones			
	North Zone (Arki)	South Zone (Solan)	East Zone (Kandaghat)	West Zone (Nalagarh)
Market Information network	29 (I)	36 (I)	30 (I)	23 (II)
Supply chain Management	19 (III)	24 (II)	21 (III)	17 (IV)
Integrated Pest Management	17 (IV)	14 (VI)	9 (VII)	15 (V)
Genetically modified seeds	12 (V)	9 (VIII)	8 (VIII)	9 (VIII)
Warehousing and quality testing	19 (III)	15 (V)	17 (V)	17 (IV)
Soil and irrigation management	23 (II)	11 (VII)	12 (VI)	14 (VI)
Protective farming (Polyhouse and Greenhouse cultivation)	29 (I)	23 (III)	25 (II)	19 (III)
Tissue culture	11 (VI)	10 (VIII)	6 (IX)	10 (VII)
Farming credit management	29 (I)	20 (IV)	20 (IV)	25 (I)

Table 8.3 indicating the perceptual awareness level of farmers towards modern agro farm technologies has been analysed with total weighatge score method applied on the varied zones of the research area. It was observed that Market Information network has been considered as the primary element of modern agro technology as perceived by the farming community. Followed by Protective farming cultivation through polyhouse and Greenhouse has also been highly perceived as the agro technology among the North zone and with low perception level at other zones, whereas farming credit management has also been perceived as the emerging concept of adopting modern agro-technologies among the farming systems. Whereas, rest of the core modern agro technologies including soil and irrigation management, Tissue culture, Genetically modified seeds, Integrated pest management and warehousing and quality testing have been observed to be least perceived among majority of the farming respondents. Thus, it is highly demanded that a massive awareness programmes and movements are required to be initiated to mitigate the knowledge gaps of most emerging and useful modern agro technologies with its most requisite beneficiaries, so that it may be highly used and accepted and totally adopted in the farming culture.

Table 8.4: Significant factors for easy adoption and practice of modern agro technologies among vegetable growing farm community

Factors for Easy Adoption and Practice of Modern Agro Technologies	Level of Significance			Total Weightage Score (TWS)	Rank
	Highly Significant	Moderately Significant	Least Significant		
Technological Awareness	12	8	3	55	III
Educational Background	8	8	2	42	V
Practical initiation	5	7	3	32	VII
Acceptability to new Technologies	5	5	2	27	IX
Subsidies and Discounts	16	8	1	65	I
Working proficiency	6	3	3	27	IX
Field trials	12	6	2	50	IV
Training sessions	8	5	4	38	VI
Community support	6	4	2	28	VIII
Financial support	15	9	1	64	II
Miscellaneous factors	4	2	1	17	X

In order to analyse the impact and inclination of significant factors for the comprehensive adoption and practice of modern agro technologies among vegetable growing farm community, Table 8.4 indicates the observations computed by applying Total Weightage score method on the overall zoneal data collected from the research area. It was observed that factors including Subsidies and Discounts, closely followed by Financial support, Technological Awareness and Field trials were perceived to be the most considerable factors by the farmers' for the comprehensive acceptance and usage of modern agro technologies. Whereas, on the contrary Working proficiency, Acceptability to new Technologies followed by Community support and Practical initiation were least considered by the farmer's to bring know how and positive outlook for the agro technologies in the farming system. Thus, considering the similar factoral inclination, it must be considered that financial support and technological mass awareness is essentially required to be attached with the larger acceptance of agro technologies.

Table 8.5: Problems and issues faced by farmers' in context to the adoption and practice modern agro technologies

Farmers' Problems Associated to Modern Agro Technologies	Frequency of Occurrence			Total Weightage Score (TWS)	Rank
	Highly Occurred	Moderately Occurred	Least Occurred		
Lack of Information	18	7	4	72	II
Lack of awareness programmes	14	8	2	60	IV
Minimal efforts and support at Local self government Level (Panchayats)	14	8	2	60	IV
Low or least Subsidies and Discounts	17	11	4	77	I
High risk of success rate	9	5	2	39	VII
Mishandling	11	8	3	52	VI
Complex process of usage	14	8	2	60	IV
Highly cost sensitive	16	9	3	69	III
Lack of usage inclination	7	3	1	28	IX
Weak financial support	12	8	1	53	V
Miscellaneous issues	8	3	2	32	VIII

As far as the problems and issues faced by farmer's in context to the adoption and practice modern agro technologies is concerned, Table 8.5 has analysed the cumulative data collected from the farmers' located at the four blocks nominated as four zones of the districts. The data was further analysed with the help of Total Weightage Score method, providing the inclination of respondents towards various problems coming across the adoption of agro technologies. Largely, it was observed that lack of adequate subsidies and discounts on available technologies, followed by Lack of Information regarding the availability, usefulness and real practice of the agro technologies and incurring high cost on farming business are some of the key problems highlighted by the farmers, which in fact are needed to be addressed on the priority basis, if agro technologies truly required to be adopted and accepted among the farming community. However, some of the key problems mainly Risk and usage inclination or interest among the farmers' and the minimal efforts and support at Local self government level (Panchayats) along with the minimal efforts and support at local self government Level) were responded to be less perceived problems.

Table 8.6: Farmers suggestions to improvise the extent of usage of modern agro technologies in the vegetable farming

Farmers' Suggestion to Improvise the usage of Modern Agro Technologies	Frequency of Occurrence			Total Weightage Score (TWS)	Rank
	Highly Occurred	Moderately Occurred	Least Occurred		
Extension Support Services	11	6	3	48	VII
Government Interventions	14	11	5	69	III
Technological Networking Establishments	11	7	3	50	V
Technological Awareness and Empowerment	19	15	4	91	I
Conducive Banking Schemes and Financial Services	15	13	3	74	II
Farm community recognition and participation	11	7	2	49	VI
Public Partnership Projects in Technological area	13	7	3	56	IV
Infrastructural Development	16	9	3	69	III
Miscellaneous	7	4	4	33	VIII

While anlysing the farmers suggestions to improvise the extent of usage of modern agro technologies in the vegetable farming, Total Weightage Score was used as stated in the above Table 8.6. It clearly signifies that Technological Awareness and Empowerment and Conducive Banking Schemes and Financial Services followed by Infrastructural Development and Public Partnership Projects in Technological area were perceived to be the key suggestions of the farming community. On the contrary, suggestions comprised of Extension Support Services and Farm community recognition and participation followed by Technological Networking Establishments were least suggested recommendations. Thus, it may have been noted that farmers' intend to build up a sound technological know how and also inclined to learn the real usage of the adequate agro technologies before it may have been fully adopted and implemented in the agriculture business.

Conclusion

It is evident that modern agro technologies is the need of an hour for the farming community especially for the vegetable growing farmers, since there has been a large volatility of market demand and prices related to vegetables in the country. But the optimum adoption of rightful agro technologies has enabled the farmers to gain lucrative margins and sustain a developmental agricultural system. The research study revealed that market information network, farming credit management, Warehousing and quality testing, Protective farming and Supply chain Management are the key components of modern agro technologies, largely preferred among the farming community engaging in the vegetable production. As far as the perceptual awareness is concerned, it was noted that Market Information networking system, Protective Farming and farm credit management oriented techniques were highly perceived to be useful and beneficial by the farmers. Whereas, the core techniques of modern agro farm practices including tissue culture, soil and irrigation management and integrated pest management were least aware, thus perceived to be of low utility to actual farm practices. Subsidies and discounts provided by the companies providing the agro technologies and the financial support back up by the banking institutions and government agencies and technological awareness among the farming community through extension agencies and non government organizations were the key highlighted factors perceived by the farmers for the easy adoption and practice of modern agro technologies. It was noted that least Subsidies and Discounts initiatives at the procurement level of agro technologies followed by lack of information regarding the rightful and most adequate technique required for the farming and high cost associated with the usage of agro technologies were the substantive problems raised by the farming in context to the application of modern agro technologies. It was asserted by the farmers' that technological awareness and empowerment, supported by conducive banking schemes and financial services, government interventions and Public Partnership Projects in Technological area can substantially improvise the extent of usage of modern agro technologies in the vegetable farming. The results of this research strongly suggest that research, innovative credit schemes, market, and farmer involvement are significant components of an investment in a value chain through adoption of modern agro technologies.

REFERENCES

Organization for Economic Cooperation and development (OECD). 2001. *Adoption of Technologies for Sustainable Farming Systems*, Wageningen Workshop Proceedings. US.

Emmanuel, A.D. (2014). Agriculture, Forestry and Fisheries. *Farmers' Perception on Agricultural Technologies a Case of some Improved crop Varieties in Ghana*. Ghana: Science Publishing Group. 3(1): 13-16.

Akinwumi, A. A. and Jojo B.F. (1995). *Farmers' Perceptions and Adoption of New Agricultural Technology: Evidence from Analysis in Burkina Faso and Guinea, West Africa. Agricultural Economics*. Elsevier Publishing House. (13) 1-9.

Abdullah F.A. and Samah Bahaman A. (2013). *Factors Impinging Farmers' Use of Agriculture Technology*. Canadian Center of Science and Education. Asian Social Science. Vol. 9, No. 3. 120-124.

Mukadasi B. and Lusiba B. (2006). *Farmers' Perception of the Relevance of Agricultural Technologies under Plan for Modernization of Agriculture in Uganda. Journal of Agricultural Sciences.* Uganda: National Agricultural Research Organisation (NARO). Vol. 12 (2) 7-15.

Uaiene R.N., Arndt C. and Masters W.A. (2009). *Determinants of Agricultural Technology Adoption in Mozambique.* National Directorate of Studies and Policy Analysis. Republic of Mozambique: Ministry of Planning and Development Publications. pp. 1-31.

Mamudu A.A., Emelia G. and Samuel K.D. (2012). *Adoption of Modern Agricultural Production Technologies by Farm Households in Ghana: What Factors Influence their Decisions. Journal of Biology, Agriculture and Healthcare.* US: International Institute for Science, Technology and Education (IISTE). Vol 2, No. 3, 1-14.1

Pages: 131-147

AGRO-BIODIVERSITY: *CONSERVATION AND SUSTAINABLE DEVELOPMENT*
Edited by: Dr. Pankaj Sharma; Dr. Narayan Singh & Dr. Pawan Kumar 'Bharti'
ISBN: 978-93-5056-782-1
Edition: 2016
Published by: Discovery Publishing House Pvt. Ltd., New Delhi (India)

9 Impact of Climate Change on Livestock *viz-a-viz* Role of Agroforestry in Mitigation

Manoj Kumar Thakur[1]; **Rohit Bishist**[2] and **Dinesh Gupta**[3*]

ABSTRACT

The climate change represents one of the greatest environmental, social and economic threats facing the planet today. In developing countries, climate change will have a significant impact on conditions of the poor people who rely heavily on the natural resource base for their livelihoods. Livestock is a global resource or both developing and industrialized societies. They provide multiple benefits that include: food and clothing, fuel, nutrients cycling for soils, draught, a means of insurance weather risk management, income and employment. The livestock itself a major source of GHGs and largely contributes to climate change. Livestock production globally contributes about 9 per cent of total anthropogenic carbon dioxide (CO_2), 37 per cent of methane (CH_4) and 65 per cent of nitrous oxide (N_2O) emissions. The hot environment impairs the livestock production, reproductive performance, metabolic and health status, immune response. Climate change affect the pasture by affecting its

1. Department of Silviculture and Agroforestry, College of Forestry, Dr. Y.S. Parmar University of Horticulture and Forestry, Nauni, Solan - 173 230, Himachal Pradesh, India.
2. Department of Silviculture and Agroforestry, College of Forestry, Dr. Y.S. Parmar University of Horticulture and Forestry, Nauni, Solan - 173 230, Himachal Pradesh, India.
3. Himachal Pradesh State Biodiversity Board, H.P. State Council for Science, Technology and Environment, 34 SDA Complex, Kasumpti, Shimla -171 011, Himachal Pradesh, India.

productivity, quality of forage, change in spp. Composition, biodiversity loss and carrying capacity of pasture. Agroforestry and livestock-keeping both have the potential to promote anthropogenic climate change resilience. Today agroforestry play a significant role in mitigating the atmospheric accumulation of greenhouse gases (GHG), it also has a role to play in helping small-holder farmers adapt to climate change. Agroforestry is recognised as an important component in climate-smart agriculture for both its adaptation and mitigation roles. Agroforestry is an attractive and promising option for sequestering carbon on agricultural land because it can sequester significant amounts of carbon while leaving the bulk of land for agricultural production. Agroforestry has such a high potential, not because it is the land use Practice with highest carbon density but also because of such a large area is susceptible for the land use change. Agroforestry can also help to decrease pressure on natural forest and promote soil conservation and provide ecological services to livestock.

Keywords: Climate change, global greenhouse gas (GHG), livestock, Agroforestry

INTRODUCTION

The livestock sector accounts for 40 per cent of the world's agriculture Gross Domestic Product (GDP). It employs 1.3 billion people, and creates livelihoods for one billion of the world's population living in poverty (FAO, 2006). Climate change is seen as a major threat to the survival of many species, ecosystems and the sustainability of livestock production systems in many parts of the world (Moss *et al.* 2000). Whenever the causes of climate change are discussed, fossil fuels top the list. Oil, natural gas, and especially coal are indeed major sources of human-caused emissions of carbon dioxide (CO_2) and other greenhouse gases (GHGs). But we believe that the life cycle and supply chain of domesticated animals raised for food have been vastly under estimated as a source of GHGs, and in fact account for at least half of all human caused GHGs. If this argument is right, it implies that replacing livestock products with better alternatives would be the best strategy for reversing climate change.

In fact, this approach would have far more rapid effects on GHG emissions and their atmospheric concentrations and thus on the rate the climate is warming than actions to replace fossil fuels with renewable energy. Developing countries are going to bear the brunt of climate change and suffer most from its negative impacts. Global conventions are not sufficiently effective to halt the increase of atmospheric greenhouse gases (GHG) concentrations, and we now accept that the primary drivers of climate change are not going to stop. Mitigation efforts will therefore only provide a partial softening of the effects of climate change.

Local climates and terrestrial ecosystems will change, threatening biota and human livelihoods. The double potential of agroforestry to address climate change issues is Greenhouse gas mitigation strategy through carbon sequestration because of greater efficiency of integrated systems in resource (nutrients, light, and water) capture and utilization than single-species systems and another is Sustainable adjustment to changing conditions because agroforestry systems can be called perennial farming systems. They maintain and develop their root and woody biomass throughout seasons while providing food, fibre, energy and vegetative cover for soils (Nair *et al.* 2009).

Agroforestry has a role to play in helping small-holder farmers adapt to climate change. They suggest that trees in the agro-ecosystem may help buffer against both production risk and income risk (Verchot *et al.* 2007).

Livestock and Climate Change

The major global warming potential (GWP) of livestock production worldwide comes from the natural life processes of the animals. Table 9.1 describes the salient features of the three major GHGs. Methane production appears to be a major issue although it presently contributes only 18 per cent of the over all warming. It is accumulating at a faster rate, and is apparently responsible for a small proportion of the depletion of the protective ozone layer. Methane arises largely from natural anaerobic ecosystems, rice/paddy field and fermentative digestion in ruminant animals. In fact, CH_4 is considered to be the largest potential contributor to the global warming phenomenon (Johnson *et al.* 2002; Steinfeld *et al.* 2006). It is an important component of GHG in the atmosphere, and is associated with animal husbandry (Moss *et al.* 2000).

Much of the global GHG emissions currently come from enteric fermentation and manure from grazing animals and traditional small-scale mixed farming in developing countries. The development of management strategies to mitigate CH_4 emissions from ruminant livestock is possible and desirable. Not only can the enhanced utilization of dietary 'C', improve energy utilization and feed efficiency hence animal productivity, but a decrease in CH_4 emissions and also reduce the contribution of ruminant livestock to the global CH_4 inventory.

Table 9.1: Global warming potential and related data for major greenhouse gases

GHGs	Current Concentration (ppmV)*	Rate of Increase (%/yr)	Lifetime in Atmosphere (yr)	GHG Contribution (%)	Global Warming Potential
CO_2	360	0.5	5-200	55-60	1
CH_4	1.7	0.7	12	15-20	23
N_2O	0.31	0.2	114	5	310

*ppmv is parts per million by volume (IPCC, 2007).

Effect of Livestock on Climate Change

The livestock sector, which is vulnerable to climate change, is itself a large contributor to climate change through emission of methane and nitrous oxide. Livestock sector contributes about 18 per cent of the global greenhouse gas (GHG) emissions, and as much as 37 per cent of anthropogenic methane. Livestock sector contributes as much as 9 per cent of the total CO_2, 65 per cent of N_2O (296 times the GWP of CO_2) and 37 per cent of CH_4 (23 times as warming as CO_2) produced through human-related activities and which comes from mainly manure and enteric fermentation. The animal production system, which is vulnerable to climate change, is itself a large contributor to global warming through emission of methane and nitrous oxide.

There are two sources of GHG emissions from livestock:

(i) *From the Digestive Process:* Methane is produced in herbivores as a by-product of 'enteric fermentation' a digestive process by which carbohydrates are broken down by micro-organisms into simple molecules for absorption into the bloodstream.

(ii) *From Animal Wastes:* Animal wastes contain organic compounds such as: carbohydrates and proteins. During the decomposition of livestock wastes under moist, oxygen free (anaerobic) environments, the anaerobic bacteria transform the carbon to methane. Animal wastes also contain nitrogen in the form of various complex compounds. The microbial processes of nitrification and de-nitrification forms nitrous oxide, which is emitted to the atmosphere.

Enteric Emissions

Livestock farming has been found to be the most important anthropogenic activity that results in methane emissions. Recent estimation of livestock methane production using IPCC methodology indicate that the total methane emitted due to enteric fermentation and manure management of 485 million heads of livestock was 9.37 Tg/annum for the year 2003. The major contributors to methane emission were Indigenous, crossbred cattle, buffalo, sheep and goat accounting 40, 8, 40, and 10 per cent respectively. The other livestock with minor population consisting of equines (horses, ponies, mules and donkeys), pigs, yak, mithun and camels contributed only 2 per cent (0.15 Tg) of total emission from livestock sector. The ruminants, both small and large, were the main contributors (98%) to the enteric methane emission in India. Lactating animals comprising of buffaloes and cattle contributed 3.42 Tg with a major share of 2.04 Tg from lactating buffaloes (Upadhyay *et al.* 2009).

The indigenous female cattle (82.9 million) contributed 2.2 Tg and 77.53 million indigenous males emitted 1.55 Tg methane. Crossbred females though in small number compared to indigenous cattle, emitted more methane per animal (0.63 Tg methane from 19.74 million heads) indicating that crossbreds produce more methane than indigenous animals. The emission from buffalo females was also higher and 80 million females produced 3.42 Tg in 2003. The contribution of buffalo females was about 36.5 per cent to total methane emission from livestock sector. The contribution of milch buffaloes was 59.6 per cent, crossbred cows 11.4 and Indigenous cows 28.9 per cent to the total emissions from dairy animals (Upadhyay *et al.* 2009). In a study by Singh (1998) where emission factors are based on laboratory experiments, the emissions were estimated to be 9.0 Tg/annum in 1996. The estimates were later revised by author to 8.9 Tg/annum (Singh, 2001). Another study of total enteric emissions in India, based on the emission rates observed in controlled laboratory experiments, estimates methane emissions of 10.07 Tg/year in 1994 (Singhal and Madhu Mohini, 2002). The has been found that about half of the annual global emission of 75.8 Tg from enteric fermentation came from only five countries; *viz;* India (10.27 Tg), the erstwhile USSR (8.05 Tg), Brazil (7.46 Tg), the USA (6.99 Tg) and China (4.37 Tg). Species wise, cattle contributed 75 per cent, buffaloes 8 per cent, sheep 9 per cent and goats 3 per cent to the total emission from animal sources.

India emerged as the largest contributor to the livestock methane budget, simply because of its enormous livestock population, although the emission rate per animal in the country was much lower than in the developed countries. For instance, the annual methane production per animal was estimated to be 95 kg., for the dairy cows in Germany, nearly threefold higher than 35 kg., for the Indian cattle. (Crutzen *et al.* 1986).

Emissions from Manure

The total global methane emissions from livestock manure management have been estimated as 9.3 Tg/year, of which the developed countries contribute about 52 per cent. The sharply different manure management practices in India, as compared to the western countries, lead to much lower methane emissions from manure. Cattle and buffalo manure is extensively used in the country as fuel and is largely managed in dry systems. The emissions for India are estimated to be 0.905 Tg/year in 1990 (Scheehle, 2002), and about 1.27 Tg in the year 1994 (Singhal and Madhu Mohini, 2002). India's contribution to nitrous oxide emissions from manure management in 1990 is estimated to be 0.017 Tg/year, which is projected to increase to 0.022 Tg by 2020 (Scheehle, 2002).

Effect of Climate Change on Livestock

Climate change poses formidable challenges to the development of livestock sector in India. The climate change impact directly livestock production and also affects indirectly through availability of feeds, fodder and pastures. Climate also determines the type of livestock suitability and adaptation in different agro-ecological conditions and therefore the animal species or breeds that are able to sustain rural communities. Climate change is expected to affect not only livestock at the species level but also decide sustainability of a breed or a species. Benefits of temperature rise that might be realized during cooler seasons will be less than that of negative impacts during hot and hot humid conditions. Climate changes will also affect nomadic, landless and small farmers with few heads of livestock. Climate affects animal production in the following ways:

1. *Effect of Climate Change on Animal Health*: The acclimation of the animals to meet the thermal challenges results in the reduction of feed intake and alteration of many physiological functions that are linked with impaired health and the alteration of productive and reproductive efficiency (Lacetera *et al.* 2003a). Acclimation to high environmental temperatures involves responses that lead to reduce heat load. The immediate responses are the reduction of feed intake, increase in respiration rate and water intake and changes in hormonal signals that affect target tissue responsiveness to environmental stimuli (Collier and Zimbelman, 2007). The decrease in energy intake due to reduced feed intake, results in a negative energy balance (NEB), and partially explains why cows lose significant amounts of body weight and body score when subjected to heat stress (Lacetera *et al.* 1996b). If exposure to high air temperature is prolonged, lower feed intake is followed by a decline in the secretion of calorigenic hormones (growth hormone, catecholamines and glucocorticoids in particular), in thermogenic processes of digestion and metabolism, and metabolic rate (Johnson, 1980; Webster, 1991). All these events together (lower feed intake, change in endocrine status and lower metabolic rate) tend to reduce metabolic heat production (Yousef, 1987) and might be responsible for modifications of energy, lipids, protein and mineral metabolism, and liver function.
2. *Effect on Production:* Climate change, particularly global warming, may strongly affect production performances of farm animals and impact worldwide on livestock production. A thermal environment is a major factor that can negatively affect milk production in dairy cows, especially in animals of high genetic merit. The linear reduction of dry matter intake (DMI) and milk yield when THI exceeded 70. The reductions were 0.23 and 0.26 kg/day per unit of THI for DMI and milk yield, respectively.

In climatic chambers, described a decrease in milk yield of 35 per cent in mid-lactating dairy cows and of 14 per cent in early lactating dairy cows kept under heat stress conditions. The extent of milk yield decline observed in heat-stressed cows is dependent on several factors that interact with high air temperature. Themilk yield losses seem positively related with milk yield of cows found a higher average persistency decline in cows with milk yield higher than 30 kg/day (0.059%/day) compared with cows yielding less than

25 kg/day (0.019%/day). The increase in milk yield increases sensitivity of cattle to thermal stress and reduces the 'threshold temperature' at which milk losses occur. This is because metabolic heat production increases as the production level of a cow increases. For example, heat production of cows producing 18.5 and 31.6 kg/day of milk was 27.3 and 48.5 per cent higher than non-lactating cows. The stage of lactation is an important factor affecting dairy cows' responses to heat. It has been observed that the mid-lactating dairy cows were the most heat sensitive compared to their early and late lactating counterparts. In fact, mid lactating dairy cows showed a higher decline in milk production (38 %) when the animals were exposed to heat. On comparing milk production during summer and spring in a dairy herd located in central Italy we found a lower milk yield (10%), and also lower casein percentages and casein number in summer (2.18 *vs*. 2.58% and 72.4 *vs*. 77.7% respectively). Solar radiation seems to have a lesser effect on milk yield, but a greater effect on yield of casein, fat and clot firmness in the milk of Comisana ewes. Some modelling work reported by Chase (2006) using the Cornell Net Carbohydrate and Protein System (CNCPS) model indicated that the maintenance energy requirement of a dairy cow weighing 635 kg., and yielding 36 kg., of milk per day is increased by 22 per cent at 32°C compared with the energy requirement at 16°C; for the same temperature increase, predicted dry matter intake decreases by 18 per cent and milk yield decreases by 32 per cent.

3. *Effect on Reproduction:* The rise in temperature due to global warming will negatively impact growth and time to attain puberty of livestock species. In addition to this the reproductive efficiency of livestock is also negatively influenced by high ambient temperatures.

Effect on Male Reproduction

- Inverse correlation between environmental ozone and sperm conc.
- Decrease sperm mortality.
- Increased no. of dead sperms.
- Increased abnormal morphology of sperm. *e.g.*, abnormal acrosome.
- Decreased total protein and albumin conc.
- Decreased level of testosterone.

Effect on Female Reproduction

- Reduction in duration of estrous.
- Reduced diameter and volume of developing follicle.
- Uterine blood flow decrease 20-30 per cent in ewe with 1°C increase in core temp.
- Conception rates declines in *Bos taurus* (bovine) cattle for temperatures above 23.4°C and at high values of thermal humidity index (THI).

- Heat stress between 8-16 days after insemination increase fertility failure.
- Inverse relationship between Temp. and Pregnancy Rate.
- Retarded fetal growth.
- A rise in 1.5°C in core body temperature cause death of embryo.

4. *Impact on Physiological Functions:* Physiological functions of livestock species exhibit diurnal variations and are affected by ambient temperature and humidity levels. The magnitude of response and change depends upon species, breed and physical environment factors. The speed of change in physiological functions (Respiratory frequency, heart rate and energy expenditure) with rise in temperature doubles or trebled for an increase of 10°C in temperature. One of the physiological responses to heat stress is reduction in their heat production, which in turn is caused by reduction in feed intake, thyroid hormone secretion.
5. *Heat Stress*: There does not seem to have been a great deal of work done on the direct impacts of climate change on heat stress in animals, particularly in the tropics and subtropics. It has been noted that significant changes in feed intake and numerous physiological processes do not occur in the range 5-25°C. However, the thermal comfort zone is influenced by a range of factors, and is much higher in tropical breeds because of both better adaptation to heat and the lower food intake of most domestic cattle in small-holder systems. Clearly, hot and humid conditions can cause heat stress in livestock, which will induce behavioural and metabolic changes, including reduced feed intake and thus a decline in productivity. The vulnerability of livestock to heat stress varies according to species, genetic potential, life stage and nutritional status. Increasing temperatures at higher latitudes are generally going to have greater impacts on livestock than at lower latitudes, where local livestock breeds are often already quite well-adapted to heat stress and drought. Increasing intensification of dairy systems in the developing world through the use of temperate-breed genetic stock could lead to greater vulnerability to increasing temperatures. AR4 also summarizes recent literature on heat stress. It confirms the relationship among heat stress, declines in physical activity, and associated (direct and indirect) declines in levels of feed intake. The wide geographic distribution of livestock production is some evidence for its adaptability to different climates.
6. *Affect the Productivity of Pasture*: The dominant influence of climate change on pasture growth is expected to be the change in the amount of rainfall. Variation in rainfall, temperature, water stress affects the photosynthesis rate. Rising temperature could benefit pastures in cooler, southern climates by increasing the length of the growing season and reducing frost damage. However increased plant growth in the cooler months could deplete soil

moisture at expense of pasture growth in the spring. Changes in seasonal patterns of forages availability could pose additional challenges for grazing management. In warmer climates increased heat stress and increased evaporative demand would likely have negative effect on pasture. Pasture growth is sensitive to CO_2 than other climatic factors. The carrying capacity of pasture decreases. It has been observed that in pastures, elevated CO_2 together with increases in temperature, precipitation and N deposition results in increased primary productivity, with changes in species distribution and litter composition. The various experiments that have separated the components of C_3 pasture response to CO_2 have demonstrated that stimulated plant production was almost entirely, attributable to indirect effect of moisture saving rather than directly stimulated photosynthesis. There is growing evidence that C_4 grazing land grasses may not be substantially less responsive to CO_2 than C_3 grasses particularly under field conditions. The effect of CO_2 in stimulating pasture growth may be greatest in ecosystem receiving intermediate amount of rainfall and where water is limited during most period of active plant growth. Effects will depend significantly on location, system and species. In C_4 species, a rise in temperature to 30-35°C may increase the productivity of crops, fodder and pastures. In C_3 plants, rising temperature has a similar effect, but increases in CO_2 levels will have a positive impact on the productivity of these crops. For food-feed crops, harvest indexes will change, as will the availability of energy that can be metabolized for dry season feeding. In semi-arid rangelands where the growing season is likely to contract, productivity is expected to decrease.

7. *Botanical Changes in Vegetation Composition*: The climate change affecting the botanical composition of pasture is demonstrated by past role weather events have played in effecting species changes. Where climate become hotter and drier which result in pasture composition shift to more xeric spp. That may be less suitable for Grazing management practices have to change to match the new vegetation and climate. As temperature and CO_2 levels change due to climate change, the optimal growth ranges for different species also change, species alter their competition dynamics, and the composition of mixed grasslands changes. For example, higher CO_2 levels will affect the proportion of browse species. They are expected to expand as a result of increased growth and competition between each other. Legume species will also benefit from CO_2 increases and in tropical grasslands the mix between legumes and grasses could be altered. The chance of invasion of unwanted weeds increases. In the temperate regions and subtropics, where grasslands often contain C3 and C4 species, some species are more prominent than others in the summer, while the balance of the mix reverts in winter.

8. *Affect the Quality and Quantity of Forage Produced*: As CO_2 increases forage protein content decreases and forage non-structural Carbohydrates increases which decline their digestibility. Carbon dioxide and temperature cause seasonal variability in forage protein content. Increased temperatures increase lignification of plant tissues and therefore reduce the digestibility and the rates of degradation of plant species. This leads to reduced nutrient availability for animals and ultimately to a reduction in livestock production, which may have impacts on food security and incomes through reductions in the production of milk and meat for small-holders. Changes in herbage quality, with changing concentrations of water-soluble carbohydrates and N at given dry matter (DM) yields which hamper the productivity of grazing livestock. Interactions between primary productivity and quality of grasslands will require modifications in the management of grazing systems to attain production objectives.
9. *Effect on Biodiversity Loss*: Modern drivers of change are already having substantial impacts on biodiversity. Losses have been seen in varieties of domestic animals; of the nearly 4000 breeds of ass, water buffalo, cattle, goat, horse, pig and sheep recorded in the 20th century, some 16 per cent had become extinct by 2000, and 12 per cent of what was left was rare. As per the FAO report on animal genetic resources (2007) indicates that 20 per cent of reported breeds are now classified as at risk, and that almost one breed per month is becoming extinct. In developed regions, 20-28 per cent of mammalian species are classified as at risk, and these regions have highly specialized livestock industries, in which production is dominated by a small number of breeds. For developing regions, the proportion of mammalian species at risk is lower (7-10%), but 60-70 per cent of mammals are classified as being of unknown risk status (CGRFA, 2007). Much of this genetic erosion is attributed to global livestock production practices and the increasing marginalisation of traditional production systems and associated local breeds. The drivers of these changes in developing countries depend on the system (Sere *et al.* 2008).

Role of Agroforestry to Mitigate Climate Change

Climate variability is well buffered by agroforestry because of permanent tree cover and varied ecological niches. Resilience or recovering after a disturbance (*e.g.*, extreme weather events, or market failure) is well performed by agroforestry because of diversified temporal and spatial management options.

Today's climate change context confirms the potential of Agroforestry

- Climate-smart agriculture gives trees a large importance.
- Conservation agriculture (no-till + cover crops) mimics the protective cover of trees.

- Sustainability attributes of agroforestry are strong assets for climate change adaptation.
- Carbon sequestration by trees contributes to climate change mitigation.

The double potential of agroforestry to address climate change issues:

Greenhouse gas – mitigation strategy through carbon sequestration because of greater efficiency of integrated systems in resource (nutrients, light, and water) capture and utilization than single-species systems.

Sustainable adjustment to changing conditions because agroforestry systems can be called perennial farming systems. They maintain and develop their root and woody biomass throughout seasons while providing food, fibre, energy and vegetative cover for soils.

Agroforestry for Mitigating Climate Change

- Potential to limit carbon emissions and sequester carbon.
- Microclimate amelioration.
- Protection and stabilization of ecosystem.
- Soil and water conservation.
- Sustainable diversification of agricultural systems.
- Improvement in rain water efficiency.
- Interventions for drought mitigation.
- Agrofoestry plays vitals roles in mitigation of atmospheric accumulation of GHGs.
- Carbon sequestration rates are very encouraging for complex agroforestry, boundary planting, hedgerow intercropping and home gardens.
- Highest carbon storage results are found in multistory/complex agroforestry system.
- *Agroforestry is*
  - Buffering against Temperature variability.
  - Buffering against extreme events: storms and winds.

Agroforestry as a Strategy to Climate Change Adaptation

- *Drought*: Tree components through their deep roots explore a large soil volume of water and nutrients which help to maintain production during drought seasons.
- *High Rainfall*: Pumping excess water out of the soil profile more rapidly by higher evapo-transpiration and maintain aerated soil conditions.
- *Temperature*: Increased soil cover and multi strata cropping pattern system utilize the light resource efficiently and guard the soil from direct sunlight which lead to a reduction in soil temperature.

Agroforestry could Contribute to Climate Adaptation

- *Improve microclimate.*
  - Provide shade → reduce temperatures.
  - Reduce wind speed → reduce evapotranspiration.

Microclimatic improvement through agroforestry has a major impact on crop performance as trees can buffer climatic extremes that affect crop growth. In an agroforestry system trees bring about favorable changes in the microclimatic conditions by influencing radiation flux, air temperature, wind speed all of which will have a significant impact on the rate and duration of photosynthesis and subsequent plant growth, transpiration and soil water use.

- *Improve Soil Quality.*
  - More soil → carbon greater water-holding capacity.
  - Nitrogen fixation → reduce multiple stresses.
  - Promote to combat the threat of soil erosion.
- *Access alternate resources*
  - More efficient interception of rainfall; less runoff.
  - *Hydraulic lift*: bring water to surface from depth.
  - *Nutrient pumps*: access nutrients at depth.

Agroforestry can boost synergy between adaptation mainly a function of soil organic matter content and diversified, multispecies cropping technologies and mitigation mainly takes the form of carbon sequestration, *e.g.*, biomass, either above or below ground. Agroforestry performs well on the 2 above criteria and thus is a preferred approach to develop synergies between adaptation and mitigation. High biodiversity and resulting ecosystem services in agroforestry also contribute to synergy between adaptation and mitigation. As we moved from non-agroforestry (monocropping) system to different agroforestry systems the synergy between adaptation and mitigation for climate change increases.

C. Sequestration Potential of Agroforestry as Climate Change Mitigation Option

Agroforestry system recognized as a carbon sequestration strategy because of its applicability in agricultural lands as well as in reforestation programmes. Agroforestry offers the highest potential for carbon sequestration. Agroforestry systems maintain 22 times more carbon stored above ground when compared to traditional maize. Average carbon storage by Agroforestry system has been estimated to be 63 Mg C/ha in semiarid sub humid, humid and temperate region. Higher level reported in for temperate ecosystem zones, longer cutting cycle result in long-term storage.

Table 9.2: Various agroforestry systems have varying capabilities to sequester carbon in India

	Species Based	Carbon Sequested (t/ha/yr)	Study Area	Reference
Agroforestry System	Leaucena	0.87	Punjab	Mittal and Singh (1998)
	Anogeissus	1.36	Bundelkhand (UP)	Rai *et al* (2002)
	Casuarina	1.45	Tamilnadu	Vishwanath *et al* (2004)
	Poplar	2.06	Uttaranchal	Yadava (2010)
	Gmelina	2.47	Chhattisgarh	Swamy and Puri (2005)
	Poplar	8.92	Punjab	Chauhan *et al* (2010)
	Albizia procera	3.5	UP	Newaj *et al* (2008)
Agrihorticulture	*Emblica officinalis*	\0.73	Bundelkhand (UP)	Ajit *et al* (2011)
Silvipasture	Neem	0.80	Bundelkhand (UP)	Rai *et al*. 2000
	Dalbergia	2.90		-do-
	Terminalia	1.11		-do-
	Eucalyptus and Leucaena	3.41 and 3.6	Himalayan foot hills	Narain *et al*. 1998
Alley cropping	Leucaena	3.4 to 5.51 and 5.51 3.40	In diff. states of india. Himalayan foot hills UP	Narain *et al*. 1998 Bhatia and Kanaujia, 2001

Sajwal *et al*. 2008 studied the carbon sequestration rates of different agroforestry systems in the different regions of the world and found that the carbon sequestration rates highest in the homegarden as compare to the other systems. The different agroforetry systems with their carbon sequestration rates are given as in the Table 9.3 as under:

Table. 9.3: Carbon sequestration rates for selected agroforestry systems

Agroforestry Systems	Carbon Sequestration Rates (tonnes C seq/ha/yr)	Region
Complex Agroforestry	11	Central Africa
Complex Agroforestry	21	Costa Rica
Boundry Planting	35	Central Africa
Hedgerow Intercropping	37	Indonesia and India
Homegarden	145	Panama

(Sajwal *et al*. 2008)

Sequestration Potential of different Agroforestry Tree Species (Kg annum^{-1})

Chambial, 2014 studied that the biomass carbon stock in a particular agroforestry tree species depends upon its total biomass (Table 9.4). A significant variations in the carbon stored in different MPTs. Carbon sequestration potential (kg/tree) of *Acer oblongum*, which was statistically at par with *Bauhinia variegata* found highest among all the species. The carbon sequestration potential of MPTs in Kg., annum^{-1} was found highest in *Acer oblongum*, it was statistically at par with *Bauhinia variegata* due to higher biomass produced by these tree species.

Table 9.4: Sequestration potential of different agroforestry tree species (Kg annum^{-1})

Species	Carbon Sequestration Potential (Kg annum^{-1})
Acacia catechu	08.03
Melia azedarach	14.25
Grewia optiva	04.49
Celtis australis	07.00
Acer oblongum	22.04
Bauhinia variegata	21.78
Morus alba	06.50

Interventions for drought Mitigation

Tree canopies in an agroforestry system lower temperature and increase relative humidity which lower transpiration rate. Tree litter and pruning material act mulch decrease the evaporative loss of soil moisture. Water storage capacity of soil is increase due to improved soil organic matter moisture. Higher survival and biomass generation under Agroforestry is possible due to greater efficiency for photosynthesis, tapping of nutrients water from the deeper layers, efficient utilization of off-season rainfall by perennial tree component and better environmental conditions.

Protection and Stabilization of Ecosystem

Trees give protection from adverse effect of diff. kinds of pollutants like: dust, dirt and other physical air pollutants. Dust level in air is 75 per cent lower on the sheltered side as compared to windward side. It is estimated that one hectare Close forest filters about 50 ton of dust and dirt every year. Trees also absorb some of chemical air pollutants. With the modern day crisis of shortage of land forestry and agriculture, agroforestry is well recognized to provide a balance and a viable solution. Today it has become sustainable method to manage forest and agriculture together, while being becomes an economically and environmentally viable.

Conclusion

The livestock production system is sensitive to climate change and at the same time itself a contributor to the climate change. To counter the adverse effect of climate change on animal production and health, human intervention for physical modification of the environment and improvement in nutritional management practices would be additionally required. Agroforestry has a potential of carbon Sequestration, microclimate amelioration, ecosystem protection and stablization, soil and water conservation and drought mitigation. Livestock production under Agroforestry will be a better choice in near future since it would provide fodder, ameliorate thermal stress to animals and sequester carbon produced from the livestock.

REFERENCES

Ajit, Newaj R., Dhyani S.K, Handa A.K, Alam B., Rizvi R.H., Prasad R. and Singh R. (2011). Standardizing Methodology for Estimating carbon Sequestration of Agroforestry Systems in Bundelkhand Region: Parameterization of CO_2 FIX model in Indian context. *Range Manegement Agroforestry* 32(1): 68-70.

Anonymous. (2001). Technical Summary: Contribution of Working Group I to the Third Assessment Report. Intergovernmental Panel on Climate Change.

Anonymous. (2006). Livestock a Major Threat to the Environment: Remedies Urgently Needed. Food and Agriculture Organization of the United Nations 2006. *Forage Science* 62, 118-126.

Anonymous. (2007). Climate Change: Impacts, Adaptation and Vulnerability. Intergovernmental Panel on Climate Change.

Bhatia S.K. and Kanaujia V.K. (2001). Performance of pearmillet and barley in Leucaena based alley Cropping System on alluvial soil. *Indian Journal of Soil Conservation* 29(1):39-42.

CGRFA (Commission on Genetic Resources for Food and Agriculture). (2007). The State of the World's Animal Genetic Resources for Food and Agriculture. FAO, Rome, 523 pp.

Chambial, A. (2014). Studies on Nutrient Status and Carbon Sequestration Potential of Important Multi-purpose Trees of Himachal Pradesh. MSc. Dr. Y.S. Parmar University of Horticulture and Forestry Nauni-Solan.

Chase L.E. (2006). Climate Change Impacts on Dairy Cattle. Fact Sheet, Climate Change and Agriculture: Promoting Practical and Profitable Responses.

Chauhan S.K, Sharma S.C., Chauhan R., Gupta., N. and Ritu. (2010). Accounting Poplar and Wheat Productivity for Carbon Sequestration in Agriculture System. *Indian Forester* 136(9):1174-1182.

Collier, R.J., Zimbelman, R.B. (2007). Heat Stress Effects on Cattle.

Crutzen P.J., Aselmann I and Seiler W. (1986). Methane Production by Domestic Animals, Wild Ruminants, other Herbivorous fauna and humans. *Tellus* 38 B:271-284.

Garg A. and Shukla P.R. (2002). Emission Inventory of India. Tata McGraw Hill, New Delhi. pp. 84-89.

Johnson D.E, Phetteplace H.W. and Seidl A, F. (2000). Methane, nitrous oxide and carbon dioxide Emissions from ruminant Livestock Production Systems. In GHGes and Animal Agriculture. Proceeding of the 1st International Conference on GHGes and Animal Agriculture, Obihiro, Japan, November 2001 (eds. J. Takahashi and B.A. Young), pp. 77-85.

Johnson, H.D., (1980). Depressed Chemical thermogenesis and Hormonal Function in Heat. In: Yousef, M.K. (Ed.), Environmental Physiology: Ageing, Heat and Altitude. Elsevier North Holland, Inc., New York, USA, pp. 3-9.

Lacetera, N., Bernabucci, U., Ronchi, B., Nardone, A. (1996). Body Condition score, metabolic Status and Milk Production of Early lactating dairy cows exposed to warm Environment. Riv. Agric. Subtrop. Trop. 90, 43-55.

Lacetera, N., Bernabucci, U., Ronchi, B., Nardone, A. (2003). Physiological and Productive Consequences of Heat Stress. The Case of Dairy Ruminants. In: Lacetera, N., Bernabucci, U., Khalifa, H.H., Ronchi, B., Nardone A. (Eds.), Proc. of the Symposiumon Interaction between Climate and Animal Production: EAAP *Technical Series*, No. 7, pp. 45-60.

Mittal S.P. and Singh P. (1989). Intercropping Field Crops between rows of *Leucaena leucocephala* under rainfed Conditionin Northern India. *Agroforestry Systems* 8 (2): 165-172.

Moss A. R., Jounany J. P. and Neevbold J. (2000). Methane Production by Ruminants: Its Contribution to Global Warming. *Annal of Zootec* 49: 231-253.

Murthy I. K, Gupta M., Tomar S, Munsi M. and Tiwari R. (2013). Carbon Sequestration Potential of Agroforestry Systems in India. *Journal of Earth Science and Climate Change* 4: 131.

Nair P.K. R, Kumar B.M, Nair V.D. (2009). Agroforestry as a Strategy for Carbon Sequestration. *Journal of Plant Nutrition and Soil Science* 172:10-23.

Narain P., Singh R.K., Sindhwal N.L. and Joshie P. (1998). Water Balance and Water use Efficiency of Different Land uses in Western Himalayan Valley Region. *Agricultural Water Management* 37:225-240.

Nardone A., Ronchi B., Lacetera N., Ranieri M.S. and Bernabucci U. (2010). Effects of Climate Changes on Animal Production and Sustainability of Livestock Systems. *Livestock Science* 130:57-69.

Newaj, Ram, Dar, S.A., Yadav, R.S. Ajit, Sanker, A.K. and Dhyani, S.K. (2008). Management Effect on Growth, Biomass Carbon and Nitrogen Accumulation in *Albizia procera* at four years in Agroforestry System. *Journal of Tropical Forestry* 23 (3&4):73-80.

Patra A.K. and Behra B.B. (2014). Role of Agroforestry in Adapting and Mitigating Climate Change. ACRIP on Agroforestry Options for Climate Resilient Farming. NRCA Jhansi publ, pp. 58-61.

Rai A.K, Solanki K.R. and Rai P. (2002). Performance of *Anageissus pendula* genorypes under Agrisilviculture System. *Indian Journal of Agroforestry* 4(1): 71-77.

Rai P., Solanki K.R. and Singh U.P. (2000). Growth and Biomass Production of Multipurpose Tree Species in Natural Grassland under Semi Arid Condition. *Indian Journal of Agroforestry* 2:101-103.

Sajwaj T., Harley M. and Parker C. (2008). Eliasch Review: Forest Management Impacts on Ecosystem Services. Report to the Office of Climate Change. EAT/ENN/R/2623/1. pp. 1-31.

Sarmah B.C. (2010). Impending Climate Changes on Animal Production and Health. In: International Conference on "Physiological Capacity Building in Livestock under Changing climate Scenario". Physiology and Climatology Division, Indian Veterinary Research Institute, Izatnagar, 243122, Uttar Pradesh, India, November 11-13, pp. 81-88.

Scheehle E. (2002). Emissions and Projections of non CO2 Green house gases from Developing Countries 1990-2020, p. 73.

Sere, C., van der Zijpp, A., Persley, G., Rege, E., (2008). Dynamics of Livestock Production Systems, Drivers of Change and Prospects for Animal Genetic Resources. *Animal Genetic Resources Information* 42: 3-27.

Singh G.P. (2001). Livestock Production and Environmental Protection. In: Proc. X Animal Nutrition Conference, National Dairy Research Institute, Karnal, India, pp. 211-221.

Singh G.P. (1998). Methanogenesis and Production of Greenhouse Gases under Animal Husbandry System. Final Report A.P. Cess Fund Project, National Dairy Research Institute, Karnal, India.

Singhal K.K, Mohini M. (2002). Uncertainty Reduction in Methane and nitrous oxide gases emission from Livestock in India. Project Report, Dairy Cattle Nutrition Division, National Dairy Research Institute, Karnal, India, p. 62.

Steinfeld H., Gerber P., Wassenaar T., Castel V., Rosales M. and de Haan C. (2006). Livestock's Long Shadow: Environmental Issues and Options. Rome: Food and Agriculture Organization of the United Nations. Supplementation of a tropical grass diet with forage legumes and *Sapindus saponaria* fruits: effect on in vitro ruminal nitrogen turnover and methanogenesis. *Australian Journal of Agricultural Research,* 54, pp. 703-713.

Swamy S. L. and Puri S. (2005). Biomass Production and C-sequestration of *Gmelia arborea* in plantation and agroforestry system in India. *Agroforestry Systems* 64(3):181-195.

Thornton P.K., Steeg J., Notenbaert A. and Herrero M. (2009). The Impacts of Climate Change on Livestock and Livestock Systems in Developing Countries: A Review of what we know and what we need to know. *Agricultural Systems* 101: 113-127.

Topping J. C., Jr. (2007). Summit Aftermath: Study by NASA and University Scientists Shows World Temperature Reaching a Level not seen in thousands of years and raises grave concern of irreparable harm.

Upadhyay R.C., Ashutosh, Kumar Ashok, Gupta S.K., Singh S.V. and Rani Nitika. (2009). Report on Inventory of Methane. National Dairy Research Institute, Karnal, Haryana.

Verchot L.V., Noordwijk M.V., Kandji S., Tomich T., Ong. C., Albrecht A., Mackensen J., Bantilan C., Anupama K. V. and Palm C. (2007). Climate Change: Linking Adaptation and Mitigation through Agroforestry. *Mitigation and Adaptation Strategies for Global Change* 12: 901-918.

Vishwanth S, Peddappaiah R.S., Subramoniam V., Manivachakam P. and George M. (2004). Management of *Casuarina equisetifolia* in wide-row Intercropping Systems for Enhanced Productivity. *Indian Journal of Agroforestry* 6(2):19-25.

Webster A.J.F. (1991). Metabolic Responses of Farm Animals to high Temperature. Animal Husbandry in Warm Climates: EAAP Publ., 55, pp. 15-22.

Yadava A. K. (2010). Carbon Sequestration: Under Exploited Environmental Benefits of Tarai Agroforestry Systems. *Indian Journal of Soil Conservation* 38(2):25-131.

Yousef, M.K., (1987). Principles of Bioclimatology. In: Yousef, M.K. (Ed.), Bioclimatology and Adaptation of Livestock. Elsevier Science Publ., Amsterdam, pp. 17-29.

Pages: 148-161

AGRO-BIODIVERSITY: *CONSERVATION AND SUSTAINABLE DEVELOPMENT*

Edited by: Dr. Pankaj Sharma; Dr. Narayan Singh & Dr. Pawan Kumar 'Bharti'

ISBN: 978-93-5056-782-1

Edition: 2016

Published by: Discovery Publishing House Pvt. Ltd., New Delhi (India)

10 Sacred Plants
Role in Religion and Health Care System

Meenakshi Jalal[1*]; Deeksha Nautiyal[2] and Swati Pathak[3]

ABSTRACT

Peoples of Uttarakhand are highly religious and traditional. Besides the god made up of stone, marble, coconut people highly value and worshipped some of the trees and these are termed as sacred plants by communities. These are referred as god or worship as god because they are used to cure many diseases since time immemorial. Therefore people are worshipping plants and offer their flowers, leaves, fruits, seeds, wood etc., to gods in various religious ceremonies for getting blessings. Sacred plants protections are one of the first instances of traditional conservation Nature worship has been a key force of shaping the human attitudes towards conservation and sustainable utilization of natural resources. Such traditional practices have been invariably operating in different parts of India. Plants provide everything to humans. It is believed that the gods and fairies visit sacred gardens on special occasions on full moon nights with supernatural powers. These traditional beliefs support the sustainable utilization of natural resources. The plants are not only source of holy faith but also a booklet of indigenous medicines. Ayurveda got its place by developing traditional

1. WWF Field Office, Haldwani, P.O. Chakuluwa, Vill. Devipura, Kaladungi, Nainital, Uttrakhand, 263 140, India.

2. Department of Forestry, D.S.B Campus, Kumaun University, Nainital, Uttrakhand, India.

3. Devasthali Vidhyapeeth, Rudrapur, Udhamsingh Nagar, Uttrakhand, India.

knowledge of people. Still in villages of India people treat minor injury by themselves their beliefs and knowledge make their tradition works and it's only these beliefs which are providing a way to conserved biodiversity.

Keywords: Religious, traditional, sacred plants, indigenous, Uttarakhand

INTRODUCTION

India is a land of diverse resource. It is also country with strongest tradition of nature conservation anywhere in the world. Our ancient people lived and spent their life in nature. They had divine thought about nature – 'Nature is our God'. Then they might have started worshipping nature. They had a very strong belief about nature because of 'Panchabutha'. Man protected his life from diseases or bad evils by using plants and through the medicinal values of plants, and they thought anything which gives inspiration to life is God and so worshipped with great respect. So, probably this became the basis of protecting plants and might have started worshipping plants (Sharma Vijay and Joshi, 2010). The human culture, customs, ethos, rites, legends, myths, folktales and folk songs, food as well as medicinal practices are deeply associated and influenced by plants (Badoni and Badoni, 2001). Plants play vital role in the enhancement of socio-economic status of people. It provides to the people food, fodder and building material. Indian culture has cosmic beliefs for all happenings in their life including sickness and sufferings and also has close association and respect for many animals and plants in religious activities (Ranta and Pirta, 2007).

In this world of plants some are use for sacred and ceremonial purposes; to explore the spirit world. The use of these plants derives from native culture. All sacred plants represent a specific deity. They are believed to be homes of certain gods. For *e.g.;* – all trees, which have trifoliate leaves, like the Bael are believed to be associated with Trimurthy, which also represent Shiva's three eyes are offered to him in worship. There are different believes associated with trees. It is believed that during Chaturmasa, gods rest in trees and plants. Therefore if trees are worshipped and boons asked from during this time, the gods are said to be generous. Kalpavriksha, a mythological tree mentioned in Puranas, is believed to be wish granting tree. Threads are tied around certain trees, like the Peepal. It is believed that the thread bothers the tree spirit, which therefore grants the boon (Kumari and Charantimath 2011).

Additionally the sacred plants are use for healing purposes. They had a great importance in ayurveda and are part of indigenous medicine in various states of India. One of the most common offerings in Indian temples is a Coconut. It is also offered on occasions like weddings, festivals, the use of new vehicle, house etc. The coconut is broken and placed before the Lord. It is later distributed as Prasad. Coconut fruit is also offered as Tambulum along with Betel leaves and Areca nuts. Even in Purnakumbha a coconut is part of Kalasha. A brass or copper pot is filled with water. Mango leaves are placed in the mouth of the pot and a Coconut is placed over it. Red or white thread is tied around its neck. Such pot is known as a Kalasha. Kalasha is placed with due rituals on all important occasions like traditional house warming, wedding, daily worship etc. Every part of this tree is useful. The most important occasion of tree worship is during Durga Puja. Along with goddess Durga nine leaves are worshipped with the chanting mantras. In different regions of India certain trees are still worshipped as deities by the tribals of pre-ascutraloid stock. Certain plants, flowers and leaves are offered daily in the worship of God (Bhatla *et al.* 1984). *Azadirachta indica* is worshipped in India and its leaves used to keep away the evil spirits and also associated with the farmers traditional methods of weather forecasting (Narjas and Trivedi, 2003).

Uttarakhand formerly Uttaranchal, is a state in the northern part of India. It is often referred to as the Land of Gods (Devbhumi) due to the many holy Hindu temples and cities found throughout the state, some of which are among Hinduism's most spiritual and auspicious places of pilgrimage and worship. Uttarakhand has a total geographic area of 51,125 km^2, of which 93 per cent is mountainous and 64 per cent is covered by forest. People of the state are highly religious and varieties of rituals related to god are performed in several of ways by locals in which plant play an important role. Traditionally in the hills of Kumaun, some of the villages are named after the caste of the people or single caste occupies the village. The village Minar is located in Bhaikiyasian block of Almora of Kumaunand residements of the village are Adhikari, which are Kshatriya. The caste is neither the tribes nor they are forest dwellers, but they retain their traditional ecological ethic by revitalizing the relic of a scared grove that belongs to the deity Golu Devta. The ideal of deity wasmerely stone which was at the distal end of village. Adjacent to which few of the villagers had their own land and for the restoration of sacred grove the villagers had donate their land.

People with their combined efforts (monetarily and physically) brought the marble idol and established the area as sacred grove. They planted some of the religious plant (Padam - *Prunuscerasoides,* Peepal - *Ficusreligiosa,* Mango - *Mangiferaindica,* Banana - *Musaparadisiacal,* Doob - *Cynodondactylon;* ornamental plants (Morpankhi - *Thuja oriental,* Chirpine - *Pinusroxburghii,* Surai *Cupressustorulosa*) Adhikari and Adhikari 2007. Similarly the sacred mountain of Nandadevi in Almora Uttarakhand is guarded by Peepal tree, a large fig tree with dangling root growing above the Raamjhula foot bridge in Risikhesh, Haridwar, Harkipori a largest holy place is headed by several Peepal tree in surrounding.

Material and Methods

The present study was carried out in Nainital District in the year 2013-14. The findings of the work are; assessment of fodder, fuel wood consumption and socio-economic status of van-panchayat villages. The information regarding traditionally worshipping plants was collected after observing that large no of tree tied with thread and have temples consulting the local people through interviews, discussions and own observations. Several specimens of plants were collected. The collected specimens were identified with the help of Floras. The plant species are arranged with botanical names followed by local names, english names, family and sacred significance of plants. The beliefs and medicinal property associates with are discussed with peoples as well as studied in books. The tabular formation of some species of Kumaun is also highlighted with through light on beliefs and festivals associated with trees.

Result and Discussion

Present study shows that 10 plant species are of great commercial value, associated with sacred beliefs and have religious importance. These plant species are used by local people in various religious activities and traditional healing system. The use of each sacred plant in religion and health care system of people of Nainital district are discussed below:

1. ***Aegle marmelosL.***; *Family* - Rutaceae; *Local Name* - Bael; *Sanskrit* - Sriphla, Bilva; *English* - the Bengal Quince or the Bael tree; *Type*: Tree.

It is the scared tree of the Hindus native to India. Plant mostly present in plains region of district and is used highly by people for its fruit and leaves. The plant mostly preferred dry habitat (Fig. 10.1).

Sacred Value

- The tree is dedicated to lord Shiva the reason behind it might be tri-leaves of tree which resembles three eyes of Shiva.
- Leaves are offered to lord Shiva during fast as prayers. The leaves are also used in enchantments and twigs are used for sacred fire.
- The fruit is sometime use in temples besides coconut.
- Plant is generally cultivated near to temples and cherishes this tree and it is sacrilege to cut it down.

Medicinal Value

- Fruits fleshy part is dried, powdered and given/used to children as anastigmatic for diarrhoea while Fruits pulp used for stomach ache.
- Juice is prepared from ripe fruit used as mild laxative and coolant in summers.
- Researchers had found that essential oil of Bael tree fought against 21 types of bacteria (Pattanaik *et al.* 1996).
- Leaves chewed and swallowed every morning help in healing stomach ulcer and also to reduced sugar of diabetes patient.

2. *Curcuma longa L.*; *Family* - Zinziberaceae; *Local Name* - Haldi ; *Sanskrit* - Harida *English* - Turmeric; *Type*: Herb.

It is believed to originate from south or south East Asia, from western India. It is used widely as an Indian species (Fig. 10.2).

Box 1: Some Important Sacred Plants

(Fig. 10.1)

(Fig. 10.2)

Scared Value

- It is termed as auspicious and holy in India and used for various Hindus ceremonies.
- It is used to make kumkum a tilak of Hindus. Kumkum is a red powder made from turmeric and lime.
- In Hindu marriage ceremonies paste of it applied to bride and groom.
- In Tamil festival Pongal a whole turmeric plant with fresh rhizome is offered.

Medicinal Value

- It is used in liver problem and digestive disorder.
- Treatment of skin disorder.
- It is also used in wound healing and bacterial infection.

3. *Cynodon dactylon (L.) Pers.*; *Family* - Poaceae ; *Local Name* - Doob; *Sanskrit* - Durva; *English* - Bermunda grass; *Type:* Herb.

The species is native to Middle East got its name as Bermuda grass as it is invasive species occur abundantly in Bermuda. The species is fast growing and tough, it property of recover fast made it part of sports ground lawns etc. (Fig. 10.3)

Sacred Value

- This plant is known as second most important Indian sacred herb.
- The plant is sacred for Hindus and niche in the temple of Hindu. Its offers for Lord Ganesh who is said to remove all obstacles in life.
- It is that the gram grass made its appearance when the sea of milk was churned by the gods and demons with the help of mountain Mandera as the remover of all sins as the three gods – Brahmas, Vishnu, and Mahesh reside in the three parts of its body - root, plant body and tips of leaves.
- The plant is worshipped on Durga Ashtami in the month of Bhadrapad Shukla Ashtami.

Medicinal Value

- The whole plant decoction used as juice (Sharbat), it gives cooling effect.
- Washed leaves paste applied on cuts help in quick.
- Home remedies in acidity, fever and stomach pain.

4. *Ficusbenghalensis L.*; *Family* - Moraceae; *Local Name* - Bar, Bargad; *Sanskrit* - Vata; *English* - Banyan *Type*: Tree.

The species is native to Indian sub-continent also known as Bengal fig and Indian fig. It is national tree of India. (Fig. 10.4).

(Fig. 10.3)

(Fig.10. 4)

Sacred Values

- Hindu mythology says that Brahma was transformed into a Vat tree and it is viewed as the male to the Peepal.
- It is considered as a sin to destroy both the trees especially the male.
- The dry twigs of the tree are used as Samidhas for producing sacred fire.
- The women folk worship this tree on Jeshth Shudh 15 (May to June), to water it, to wind a thread around it to worship it with Indian Marigold (Genda) flowers.

Medicinal Value

- Leaf extract given with milk to both men and women as an aphrodisiac.
- Warm paste of the aerial roots together with egg paste is applied in bone fracture and tied with the help of *Dendrocalamus strictus* for 3 days for the treatment of bone fractions.

5. ***FicusreligiosaL.;*** *Family* - Moraceae; *Local Name* - Peepal; *Sanskrit* - Aswaththama; *English*-Bo-tree, Peepal; *Type*: Tree.

Ficus religious is also known as scared fig native to Nepal, India, Bangladesh, Myanmar, Pakistan, Srilanka, South-west China and Indo china. The tree is worshipped by Hinduism, Jainism and Buddhism (Fig. 10.5).

Sacred Values

- The tree is sacred for Hindus, viewed as the female to the Banyan tree.
- The tree is worshipped on every month on which a new moon falls. Among the Hindus five sacred trees [*i.e.* *(i)* Peepal, *(ii)* Gular, *(iii)* Bargad, *(iv)* Pakar, and *(v)* Mango] Peepal ranks first.
- The Peepal is believed to be inhabited by the sacred triad - Brahma, Vishnu and Mahesh (Shiva) of its wood the spoons are made with which to pour ghee on the sacred fire (Home).

Medicinal Value

- Bark paste applied to sores of children (3-4 times a day) to get relief from apathies.
- Leaf bud is used in curing snake bite. Aqueous extract of bark shows anti-bacterial activity.
- Used in 50 types of disorder including: asthma, diabetes, diarrhea, epilepsy and sexual disorder (Singh *et al*. 2011).

6. ***Mangiferaindica L.***; *Family* - Anacardiaceae; *Local Name* - Aam; *Sanskrit* - Amra; *English* - Mango Tree; *Type* - Tree.

Mangiferaindica is found in the wild in India and cultivated varieties have been introduced to other warm region of the world (Fig. 10.6).

(Fig. 10.5)

Fig. 10.6)

Sacred Value

- Plant is sacred by the Hindus, connected with many mythological legends and folk lore. The tree is said to be a transformation of Prajapati (Lord of Creatures).
- The leaves and twigs are employed in adorning mandaps and houses on occasions of various religious ceremonies.
- The twigs are offered to sacred fire.

Medicinal Value

- Bark powder (50 mg) with cumin used for preventing conception.
- Leaf ash with honey used to cures the cough and cold.
- Unripe fruits boiled, given with rice and curd gives from diarrhoea and dysentery.
- It is ant diuretic, ant diarrheal, antiemetic and cardiac herb (National R and D facility for Rasayana).

7. ***Musa paradisiaca* L.**; *Family* - Musaceae; *Local Name* - Kela; *English* - Banana tree; *Type* - Tree.

It is a hybrid of *M. acuminate* and *M. balbisiana*. It is believed that Southeast Asian farmer first domesticated *M.acuminata* when the cultivated plant spread north-west into areas where *M. balbisiana* was native hybrid between two species occurred (Fig.10.7).

Scared Value

- The tree trunk is used to erect gates in several occasions of Hindus.
- Leaves are used to serve Prasad in some festivals.
- Fruit is offered to Lord Vishnu and Lakshmi.
- In Purnima the tree is fruit is worshipped and serve as Prasad.

Medicinal Value

- The high content of iron in bananas increases the production of haemoglobin in blood.
- It regulate bowl movement whether constipation and diarrhea.
- The banana is rich source of potassium which makes it as a good brain tonic.
- It is a good stress releaser.

8. ***Phyllanthusemblica L.***; *Family* - Euphorbiaceae; *Local Name* - Amla; *Sanskrit* - Umrital Amal, Amalki; *English* - Emblic Myrobalan; *Type* - Tree.

It is also known as Emblic myrobalan, Indian goose berry. It is native to large area ranging from Nepal, India and Srilanka. It is holy tree in Indian along with variety of use in allopathic and Ayurvedic (Fig. 10.8).

(Fig. 10.7)

(Fig. 10.8)

Sacred Values

- The Amla is worshipped by the women folk on Amla - navmi in the month of Kartik Shukla.
- Kartik Mahatma orders to worship the tree and a Brahmin couple should feed under it whereby all their sinsare washed.

Medicinal Value

- Powdered fruits of *Phyllanthus emblica*, *Terminalia chebula* and *Terminalia bellirica* are taken in equal proportion (known as 'Triphala) with warm water or milk acts a mild laxative.
- Triphala soaked in water and used for washing eyes.
- It may prove to have potential activity against some cancers (Ngamkitidechakul, C., *et al*. 2010).

9. ***Ocimumtenuiflorum* L.**; *Family* - Lamiaceae ; *Local Name* - Tulsi, Vranda; *Sanskrit* - Tulsi, Manjarika; *English* - The sacred basil; *Type* - Herb.

It is also known as *Ocimum sanctum*, is native to Indian sub-continent and wide spreads as a cultivated plant throughout the South East Asian tropics (Fig. 10.9).

Sacred Value

- Most sacred plant in the Hindu religion, Brahmins held it sacred to Vishnu found in near every Hindu house and it's said that it protects from misfortunes, sanctifies and guides to heaven all who cultivate it.
- The mythological story narrates that the plant is a transformed nymph called Tulsi a beloved of Krishna and for this reason near every house it is cultivated, daily watered and worshipped by all members of the family.
- The leaves make one of the constituents of Charnamrit offered to Lord Vishnu and other holy events.
- It is worshipped by Hindus as Avatar of goddess Lakshmi.

Medicinal Value

- Tea with ginger or black pepper and tulsi cures cough and cold. Decoction of Tulsi (*Ocimum sanctum*), Black pepper (*Piper nigrum*), Adarak (*Zingiber officinalis*) with little salt is good for malaria.
- Balance different process in body and helpful adapting stress. (Botanical pathways article with clinical trials details).

10. ***Saracaasoca* L.**; *Family* - Fabaceae; *Local Name* - Sita Ashoka; *Sanskrit* - Ashoka; Agana Priya *English* - Ashok Tree; *Type* - Tree.

It is important tree in Indian sub-continent. It is distribution in central areas of the Deccan plateau. It is prized for its foliage and fragrant flower (Fig. 10.10).

Scared Value

- It is found in gates of Indian and Buddhist temple gates.
- In Hindus it is worshiped in Chaitra, the 1st month of Hindu calendar.
- It is Ashok Vatika where hanuman meets Sitafirst therefore worship by most Hindus.

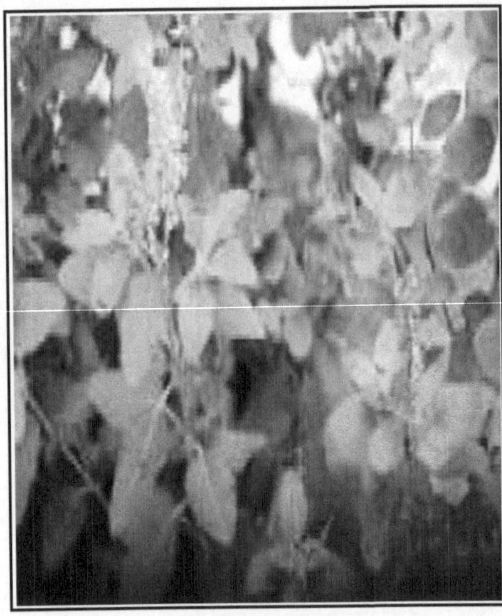

(Fig. 10.9)

(Fig. 10.10)

Source: All the figure are taken online from different websites

Medicinal Value

- It help to teat various problem of menstrual disorder.
- It also helps in maintain cardiac activity as it has a nourishing effect.
- Extract of flower used to treat dysentery.

Conclusion

Since ancient time plants are associated with human beings. Plants provide everything to humans. Indians believe that some plants are represented by gods this is because they are used as to cure diseases of folks from ancient time. Therefore people are worshipping plants and offer their flowers, leaves, fruits, seeds, wood etc., to gods in various religious ceremonies for getting blessings. It is believed that the gods and fairies visit sacred gardens on special occasions on full moon nights with supernatural powers. These traditional beliefs support the sustainable utilization of natural resources. The religious customs protect the forests where deities reside which can be preserved as sacred grooves. The religious activities as well as hypothesis act as conserving tool for biodiversity and nature, which will play an important role in betterment of human being.

Table 10.1: Representing some trees and sacred and medicinal value related with them

Sr. No.	Botanical Name	Family	Sacred/Medicinal Significance
1	2	3	4
1.	*Acacia catechu* (L.f.) Wild	Fabaceae	❖ The fragrance of wood repels poisonous animals like snake and scorpion. ❖ Plant have antifungal property and help in clotting blood in excessive bleeding.
2.	*Azadirachta indica A.Juss*	Meliaceae	❖ The whole plant is worshipped by the people for good health ❖ The leaves are good for maintain sugar and have anti bacterial property.
3.	*Bauhinias variegate* L.	Fabaceae	❖ The twig is carried with new born child in traveling to repel evil spirits. ❖ Bark and bud are alternative to astringent. In many skin disease decoction of bark is given.
4.	*Butea monosperma* (Lam.) Taub	Fabaceae	❖ The trifoliate leaf is represented by Brahma, Vishnu and Shiva. The red flowers are offered to gods for blessings in various religious activities. ❖ Used as a tonic in ayurveda and seeds are anti diabetic.
5.	*Cassia fistula*L.	Fabaceae	❖ The twigs are kept in houses to keep away evil spirits. ❖ Good source of iron and manganese and high in energy.
6.	*Dalbergia sissoo* DC	Fabaceae	❖ It is planted near houses and believed that it protect house from natural lightening. ❖ Decoction of leaves used in gonorrhea and root is astringent.
7.	*Madhuca indica* (Roxb.) A.Chev	Sapotaceae	❖ The smoke of leaves inhaled to ward of the evil spirits. The leaves are used in religious ceremonies. ❖ Bark is used to cure leprocacy and also used in skin problem and constipation.
8.	*Santalum album*L	Santalaceae	❖ The paste derived from wood is given as an offering to the gods and incense made of sandal wood shavings is burnt before them. ❖ It has antiseptic property used in skin diseases.
9.	*Shorea robusta* Gaertn.f.	Dipterocar-paceae	❖ It is offered to god to give prosperity, stability and unity among all the people.

Contd...

1	2	3	4
			❖ Used as astringent in Ayurvedic medicine. It also term as natural remedy for burn, arthritis and joint pain.
10.	*Syzygium cumini* (L.) Skeels	Myrtaceae	❖ It is employed for psychological problems for various superstitious rites to ward off evil eyes and evil spirits. ❖ Used in treatment of chronic diarrhea and other disorder.
11.	*Terminalia arjuna* (Roxb.ex DC.) Wight and Arn.	Combretaceae	❖ These plants are offered to god to protect crops from natural calamities ❖ Herb use for cardiovascular health also helps to maintain hypertension.
12.	*Pyrus malus* Linn	Rosaceae	❖ The fruit is offered to deity. ❖ Juice used to improve digestive system.
13.	*Rhododendron arboreum* Sm.	Ericaceae	❖ Flower offer to deity in all religious function. ❖ Decoction use to treat diarrhea and dysentery.
14.	*Urtica dioica* Linn,	Urticaceae	❖ Twigs are carried with new born baby at travelling to ward off evil spirit. ❖ Root extract is used in case of tooth cavity.
15.	*Zanthoxyllum armatum* DC.	Rutaceae	❖ Twigs kept in house to keep away evil spirit. ❖ Seeds are used to make seed powder.

Table 10.2: List of Sacred plant species of Kumaun Himalaya and belief

Scientific Name	Vernacular Name	Beliefs/Uses
Cynodon dactylon	Doob	Used in rituals
Ficus religiosa	Peepal	Sacred tree
Ficus benghalensis	Bargad	Sacred tree
Ocimum sanctum	Tulsi	Sacred herb
Musa paradisica	Banana	Used in rituals
Aegle marmelos	Bail	Sacred plant
Emblica officinalis	Amla	Sacred tree
Mangifera indica	Mango	Used in rituals
Pinus roxburghii	Pine	Used in rituals
Prunus cerasoides	Paiya	Used in rituals
Cedrus deodara	Deodar	Sacred tree
Zanthoxylum armatum	Timroo	Sacred tree
Azadirachta indica	Neem	Sacred tree
Quercus spp	Oak	Sacred tree

Table 10.3: Religious festivals of Kumaun associated with Sacred trees

Festivals	Month of festival	Species Associated
Sheela Asthami	March	*Azadirachta indica*
Nimb Saptami	April	*Azadirachta indica*
Vat Savitri	May	*Ficus bengalensis*
Bilvamengal	May-June	*Aegle marmelos*
Sawan ke Somvaar	Mid July-Mid August	*Aegle marmelos*
Kadii Vrat	September	*Musa paradisica*
Somvari Amavasya	15 of all months	*Ficus religiosa*

Sacred plants are not only the source of fulfilling holy faith of people but also a source of traditional indigenous medicine. There is a need to spread information relation to tradition and religion to the upcoming generation so that sustainably things are used and protected. It's only the faith in god and religion which can now protect the forest from human greed.

REFERENCES

Adhikari D. and Adikari, S. (2007). Veneration of a Deity by Restoration of Sacred Grove in a Village Minar, Kumaun Region of Uttarakhand: A Case Study. *Journal of American Science.* (3)2, 45-49; (ISSN-1545-1003).

Badoni A. and Badoni K. (2001). Ethnobotanical Heritage. In: Kandari O.P., Gusain (eds.) *Garhwal Himalaya: Nature, Culture and Society*. Trans Media Srinagar (Garhwal). pp. 125-47.

Bhatla N., Mukherjee T. and Singh G. (1984). Plants: Traditional Worshipping. *Indian J. of History of Science*. 19(1)37-42.

Nargas, J. and Trivedi P.C. (2003). Traditional and Medicinal Importance of *Azadirachtaindica* A. Juss. In India. In: Maheswari J.K. (eds.) Ethnobotany and Medicinal Plants of Indian Sub-continent. Scientific Publishers, Jodhpur, Rajasthan, 33-77.

Ngamkitidechakul C., Jaijoy K., Hansakul P., Soonthoroncharenon N. and Sireeeratawong S. (2010). Antitumour Effects of *Phyllanthusemblica*L.: Induction of Cancer cell Apoptosis and Inhabition of in Vitro Tumour Promotion and in vitro of Human Cancer Cells. *Phytotheraphy Research* 24 (9): 1405-1413.

Pattnaik S., Subramanyan V.R. and Kole C. (1996). Antibacterial and Antifungal Activity of Ten Essential oils in vitro. *Microbis*, 86 (349); 237-246. PMID 8893526.

Ranta R.S., and Pirta R.S. (2007). Socio-Ecology and Religious Affiliations in three Himalayan Villages: Implications for Mental Health. *J. of Applied Psychology.* 33 (1):23-30.

Kumari S. and Charantimath A. (2011). Sacred Plants - Their Role in Religion and uses in Health care System of Davangere District. *An International Quarterly Journal of Ethno and Social Sciences. The Socioscanissn*: 2230-99853 (1 & 2): 1-4, 2011.

Sharma V. and Joshi B.D. (2010). Role of Sacred Plants in Religion and Health Care System of Local People of Almora District of Uttarakhand, India. *Academic Arena.* 2(6): 57-60.

Pages: 162-175

AGRO-BIODIVERSITY: *CONSERVATION AND SUSTAINABLE DEVELOPMENT*

Edited by: Dr. Pankaj Sharma; Dr. Narayan Singh & Dr. Pawan Kumar 'Bharti'

ISBN: 978-93-5056-782-1

Edition: 2016

Published by: Discovery Publishing House Pvt. Ltd., New Delhi (India)

SWOT Analysis of Established and Potential Tourism Destinations in Kullu Valley, Himachal Pradesh, India
A Case Study

11

Sagar Sood[1]; **Sarla Shashni***[1] and **Aditi Kohli**[2]

ABSTRACT

In Himalayas, especially in Kullu Valley natural areas with rich biodiversity, scenic beauty, and snow kept mountains and riverine systems have always been the major tourism attraction from historical time. But now-a-day, due to heavy unregulated tourism influx and its activities in these pristine areas are causing a serious threat to the biodiversity and degradation of ecosystem and environment in large extent.

Current study is to explore the status of the established tourism destinations and potential areas which can be developed for alternate tourism in the Kullu Valley. Therefore, the attempt has also been made in the paper analyzing the strengths, weaknesses, opportunities and threats of the tourism industry in Kullu Valley for the sustainable management of resources and its utilization in longer run.

Keywords: Tourism, Alternate tourism, Sustainable management, Environment

1. G.B. Pant Institute of Himalayan Environment and Development, Himachal Unit, Mohal-Kullu - 175 126, District Kullu, Himachal Pradesh, India.

2 Government Post-Graduate Degree College Kullu, District Kullu -175 101, Himachal Pradesh, India.

INTRODUCTION

Tourism is one of an important economic activity in most of the countries around the world. According to World Travel and Tourism Council (WTTC), 2015 this travel and tourism industry contributed USD 2,364.8 billion in 2014 which is 3.1 per cent of total gross domestic product (GDP) and forecasted to rise by 3.7 per cent in 2015. According to Smith, 1989 the word tourism was first introduced in early nineteenth century and since then many attempts had been done on defining what is it? For example World Tourism Organization (WTO), 1993 defines tourism as the activities of the persons travelling to and staying to the places outside their usual environment for not more than one consecutive year for leisure, business and other purposes. Maintosh and Geoldner, 1986 defined tourism as the some kind of phenomenon and relationship which arises from the interaction of tourists, business suppliers, host government, communities in the process of attracting and hosting the visitors.

Ayodele and Falade (1989, 1993), also defined tourism as science, art, business of attracting and transporting tourists, accommodating them and catering their needs. With the increase in concern and understanding of tourism research various parameters were added in the tourism definition with various authors time to time. Such as: Przeclawski, 1993 and Ryan, 1992 emphazized on psychological, social and cultural aspect of the tourism definition as 'the mean by which people seek psychological benefits that arise from experiencing new places, and new situations that are of temporary duration, whilst free from the constraints of work, or normal patterns of daily life at home'. Fletcher and Latham, 1995 highlighted the economic aspect of tourism and Mcintosh and Goeldners, 1996 discussed the effects of these tourism activities on the planet and particularly the physical environment that plays the host. With the passage of time now there are many forms of tourism which are being introduced and studied by different stakeholders and environmentalists to lower down the negative impact of the mass tourism on the environment and community as a whole.

According to Smith, 1977 tourism can be classified in five categories such as: ethnic tourism, cultural tourism, historical tourism, ecotourism and recreational tourism. These tourism category is broadly known as 'Ecotourism' which according to The International Ecotourism Society (TIES), 1993 defined as travel to natural destinations, minimizes impact, environmental awareness building, direct financial benefits and empowerment of local people, respect local culture and support human rights and democrative movements. The principle which separates ecotourism from mass tourism are mainly education and sustainability component, ethical nature of experience, local livelihood generation and a narrow base (Blamey, 1995; Hawkes and William, 1993; Wallace and Pierce, 1996; Goodwin, 1996).

India or *Bharat* is the second largest country (population) in the world. Due to high density of people, it is the most culturally diverse country in the world. It showcases the perfect amalgamation of various cultures, manners, dialects and religions. People of 8 different religions: *(i)* Hinduism, *(ii)* Sikhism, *(iii)* Islam, *(iv)* Jainism, *(v)* Buddhism, *(vi)* Christianity, *(vii)* Judaism and *(viii)* Zoroastrianism resides in this country. The mixture of races produced a large number of languages. Linguists have listed 845 dialects and 225 distinct languages and the constitution of India recognizes 15 major languages including Sanskrit (Singh, 2012). Because of this geographical, religious and cultural varying, India possesses a great potential for various forms of tourism. In the northern region of the country lie The Great Himalayan ranges which have ample potential for adventure tourism, bird watching, eco-tourism etc. In central region of country lies Varanasi, oldest inhabited city of world (previously known as *Kashi* -) attracts cultural tourists from all around the globe. The southern region of country (Deccan Plateau) have some of the most beautiful and sacred beaches of world (Rameshwaram, Pamban Island) and also houses some of the most wealthy temples of country (Padmanabhaswamy, Kerala) which caters religious tourists from all corners of country and world, thus making India a perfect host for various forms of tourism.

India's recognition as one of the four mega-diversity countries of Asia is mainly due to the two of its major hotspots one of which is Himalayas (Ramakrishnan, 2000). According to Negi, 1990 tourism is an economic and industrial activity in which many organizations, individuals, firms, co-operation's and associations are engaged or in directly concerned to many other for the socio-economic and socio-environmental impacts in the developing countries. In India tourism industry is associated with many problems and for the removal of these problems various measures have been suggested and analyzed (Singh, 2003). In tourism industry local residents are seen as key resources in sustaining the local product and its management and their participation ensures the level of sustainability (Hardy *et al.* 2002; Woodley, 1993). It also ensures the benefit to the local community, positive attitude and local resource conservation (Tosun, 2006). Sebele, 2010 viewed that increase in the involvement and participation of local in tourism will help in empowerment and conservation and local resources. According to Babu, 2010 conservation projects and training programmes should be promoted by the government through fund generation through this tourism industry. Besides other forms of development tourism is a less environmentally destructive.

Indian Himalayan Region starting from the Jammu and Kashmir in the North to the Sikkim, Arunachal Pradesh in the east provides varieties of destinations for the tourists. North-western state of Himachal Pradesh, popularly called as *Dev Bhumi*, is believed to be abode of gods. Himachal is a hilly state of India, rich in its natural resources, is bounded on the north by Jammu and Kashmir, south west by Punjab, south by Haryana, south east by Uttrakhand and north east by Tibet. The geographical setting of Himachal Pradesh is also very sublime. Himachal represents western Himalayan ecosystem concealing a variety of flora and fauna. Endangered species like snow leopard, musk deer, western tragopan etc., resides in this beautiful state. As the elevation of state varies from 450 to 7026 above mean sea level (amsl), so Himachal owns some great peaks like: Shilla peak (7026 amsl, Kinnaur), Reo Purgil (6,816 amsl, Kinnaur), Deo Tibba (6001 amsl, Kullu), Manimahesh Kailash (5,660 amsl, Chamba) etc. According to archaeological survey conducted by Prof. B.B. Lal and R.V. Joshi, the early history of Himachal Pradesh, dates back to later stage of Paleolithic period (Verma, 1995). Indus Valley Civilization also provides the traces of existence of human race in Himachal Pradesh. The migration of people from different regions of country to Himachal makes it a culturally diversified state.

Hinduism and Buddhism are the most followed religions in the state. Buddhism is the most followed religion in The Great Himalayan region. As Hinduism is largest followed religion, so there is high concentration of temples in the state. Some of the prominent and ancient temples are Brajeshwari Temple (Kangra), Jawalaji (Kangra), Hadimba Devi Temple (Kullu), Chaurasi Temple complex (Chamba), Bhimakali Temple (Shimla), Parashar Rishi Temple (Mandi) etc. As concentration of Buddhists are also high in tribal region of state, so there are also prominent Buddhist structures in the state like Tabo Monastery (Spiti), Kye Monastery (Spiti), Thekchen Choeling (Dharamshala), Rewalser Monastery (Mandi). Due to this assortment of culture, religion and geography, Himachal offers plentiful opportunities for tourism. Shimla (erstwhile summer capital of British India) for heritage tourism, Kullu for adventure tourism, Kangra for religious tourism, Kinnaur and Lahaul and Spiti for Cultural tourism. Not only Himachal showcases variety in its culture and religion, but also in tourism aspect. According to Himachal Pradesh Tourism Department the number of tourists visiting the state increased from 71.36 Lakhs in 2005 to 151.30 Lakhs in 2013 which is futher less than 10 lakhs as compare to 161.46 lakhs in the year 2012. The main reason for lowering the number was mainly natural calamities in the year 2013.

Study Area: Kullu Valley

Kullu is a district of Himachal Pradesh state of India. According to 2011 census of India, total population of the district is around 437,903 and lies at latitude 31.9156° N and longitude at 77.2242° E. Kullu derived its name from a tribe of upper valley of river Beas '*Kulutah*'. Kullu, famously known as 'Valley of Gods', reference of its origin could be traced back to *Ramayana* and *Mahabharata* period. The Chinese pilgrim monk 'Xuanzang' visited the

Kullu valley in 634 A.D. and mentioned it as a fertile region. The history of Kullu comprises two phases – pre independence and post independence period. The pre independence period states that Kullu was probably the most ancient state next to Kashmir and Kangra. Post independence Kullu was made Sub-Division of Kangra district. In 1963, Kullu was separated from Kangra district and was made a separate district. Located on the western Himalayan Mountains, Kullu boasts one of the most beautiful passes and peaks of Himachal Pradesh like Rohtang La Pass, Chanderkhani Pass, Hamta Pass, Friendship peak, Deo Tibba peak etc. The unique *Kathkuni* architecture is believed to be originated in Kullu valley. Also kullu is divided into various valleys like Upper valley (Manali and nearby regions) Lug Valley (Britishers horse road from Kullu to Jogindernagar), Parvati Valley (gateway to pin valley of Spiti), Rupi Valley (least explored valley of Kullu), Tirthan Valley (famous for its biodiversity). Also The Great Himalayan National Park (June 2014, UNESCO World Heritage Site) pertains itself to Kullu district. The oldest democracy of world (Malana village) is also situated in this pristine district.

As Kullu is dispersed into different valleys, so there is difference in culture, rituals, geographical setting and dialect of residents of these valleys, so it gives this district an ample opportunity for different forms of tourism. In upper valley there is opportunity of leisure and recreational tourism, in Tirthan valley there is opportunity of ecotourism, in Parvati valley for adventure tourism, Rupi valley for cultural tourism. Thus if there is proper co-operation and coordination between local community, stake holders and government agencies, tourism in a sustainable way can be widespread and strengthen in already developed tourism sites and potential tourist sites.

Established tourism Destination in the Kullu District

Kullu district is one of the most promising tourism destinations of Himachal Pradesh state. According to Himachal Pradesh tourism statistics there is a continuous trend of tourists flow in the valley. It was observed that during the year 2005 total 17.09 lakh tourists visited the valley which grows to 32.26 lakh in the year 2012.

1. *Kullu (1,278 amsl):* Kullu was not a popular tourist destination among the domestic and inbound tourists until the emergence of terrorism in Kashmir. As the terrorism flourished in Kashmir valley, tourists started to diverge towards Himachal Pradesh and other Himalayan regions. Thus the tourist destinations started to develop in Kullu valley. Kullu town is the district headquarters of the Kullu district and chief deity of Kullu is Lord Raghunath Ji, the famous International Dussehra festival (7 days) is held in his name. The idol is same which was used by Lord Rama himself at the time of Ashwamegh Yagya. Raghunath Ji temple was built in 1660 AD in mixed Pahari and Pyramidal style architecture.

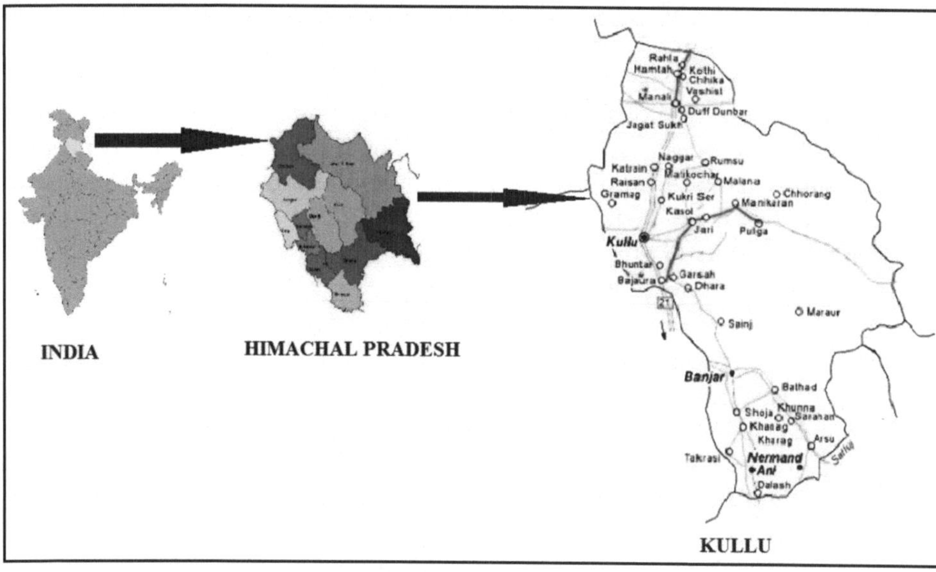

Fig. 11.1: **Map showing Tourist Destinations of Kullu district**

Kullu also houses the residence *Rupi Palace* of present Kullu king. Kullu is also the hub of white water rafting in the district and many co-operative weavers' societies are present in kullu, which provides variety of Kullu shawls, caps etc., for the tourists.

2. *Manali (2,050 amsl):* Manali, erstwhile known as Manu-allaya meaning abode of Manu, is the adventure capital of India. There are many historic and natural places in vicinity of the town. Hadimba Devi Temple located in Dhungri is the most visited place in Manali. This temple portraits the Pagoda style architecture. The Manu Rishi Temple in old Manali and is dedicated to Rishi Manu (Manali derived its name after him), Mall road (shopping hub of the town), Manali Sanctuary (Famous for Western Tragopan and Monal). Manali caters second highest number of tourists in the state (first Shimla) and numbers of tourists are increasing year after year, which is decreasing the carrying capacity of the city, thus increasing the stress on the physical and natural resources of the town.
3. *Naggar (1,851 amsl):* The heritage village Naggar is located 20 kms., from Kullu on the left bank of the valley. It was capital of Kullu kingdom for about 1500 years before it was shifted to Raghunathpur (presently in Kullu town). The infamous Naggar Castle (Erstwhile residence of Kullu king) is also situated in this village. Roerich art gallery founded by Nikolai Roerich in 20th century is also a popular place among the tourists. A less famous Krishna temple located on the top of Naggar village caters tourists from Russia and Europe. Thus Naggar provides ample opportunities for cultural tourism and ecotourism.

4. *Solang Valley (2,560 amsl):* The second most popular tourist destination among tourists who visits the Kullu valley. Tourists can enjoy various adventure activities like: paragliding, skiing, zorbing, rock climbing, rappelling etc. Various trek routes depart from this place. The famous one is trek to Beas Kund (13 km., from Solang valley), the startup point of river Beas. Some important peaks like Hanuman Tibba, Friendship peak and Patalsu peak get accessible through this valley. The famous Rohtang Tunnel (9 km.,) also gets its way through solang valley towards the tribal district of Lahoul and Spiti.
5. *Manikaran Sahib (1,760 amsl):* A Sikh and Hindu pilgrimage centre, Manikaran is located in the eastern part of the district. It derived its name Manikaran *i.e.*, 'jewel from the ear' from a Hindu mythological legend. It is famous for its hot water springs. Manikaran is the starting point of famous Pin Parvati trek which ends at the Pin valley of Spiti region. Enroute Pin Parvati trek lies the Pin Valley National Park which is famous for endangered snow leopard. If anyone is a fond of nature and spirituality, this valley is a perfect getaway.
6. *Rohtang Pass (3,978 amsl):* Rohtang derived its name from Bhoti word (Ruh-Tang) which means 'pile of dead'. It acts as a gate of Lahaul and Spiti from Manali side (Bajpai, 2002). Rohtang not only divides Kullu from Lahual Spiti, but also separates the cultures and religions of the two districts. In the foothills of Rohtang lies the source of river Beas *i.e.*, Beas Kund. Thousands of tourist visits Rohtang every year to enjoy the snow capped mountains in and around Rohtang. Various adventure activities like skiing, snowboarding, only vehicles registered in Himachal Pradesh are allowed to go to Rohtang pass, outstate vehicles have to take special permission from S.D.M. Manali to go to Rohtang Pass.
7. *Kasol (1,680 amsl):* A small settlement situated on the bank of river Parvati is famous destination among foreign tourists. The majority of tourists are Israelis and Italians. The town is located amid of lush green cedar forests. The town is divided into two regions by a bridge, old Kasol on Bhunter side and old Kasol on the Manikaran side. Reggae bars, traveller restaurants, internet cafes and cheap guest houses make it a perfect off beat Himalayan destination.

Potential Tourism Destinations in Kullu Valley

Kullu is an established tourist destination both in national and international context. It showcases the distinctive forms of tourism within its realm. But its real potential has not been yet discovered by both local communities and government. There is ample opportunity of alternative forms of tourism within in the region. Some of the off beat destinations which have potential for alternative forms of tourism are described below.

1. *Tirthan Valley:* The most biodiverse valley of Kullu, Tirthan Valley is famous for Great Himalayan National Park (GHNP) and trout fishing. GHNP became first UNESCO World Heritage Site in Himachal Pradesh (Natural Importance) in June, 2014. Tirthan Valley derived its name from Tirthan River. The GHNP in this valley houses some of endangered species like Western Tragopan, Musk deer and snow leopard. The Ecozone is an area adjacent to the park; it separates the buffer zone from the rest of the region. The residents of Ecozone are directly or indirectly dependent on the park. The valley is famous for angling in Tirthan River. There are many trout fishing farms in the valley and they also runs the angling training programme for beginners. Tirthan is a rich valley for its culture and biodiversity, but still it is not able to attract large number of tourists.
2. *Diyar:* A hilltop village located 24 km., in south-east of district headquarters, Diyar is famous for its Triyugi Narayan temple. This 'Pagoda' style temple is dedicated to Lord Vishnu. The temple was built in 800 A.D. A local fair called Kayka is celebrated every third year in the village. Diyar is a gateway to less explored Rupi valley which still sustains the original Kullvi culture. The reserved forest near Diyar village can be developed as a site for Ecotourism. Many medicinal herbs and plants are found in wild form in the forests of this region, so local people can be encouraged to generate sustainable livelihood from it. Also the places around Diyar provide some decent ascents like Bir Billing for paragliding. So being such a diverse region Diyar can be promoted as a perfect destination for alternative forms of tourism like community based ecotourism (CBET), cultural tourism and adventure tourism.
3. *Bijli Mahadev:* Located at a height of 2,460 amsl, Bijli Mahadev is a wooden temple constructed on Pent Roof style of architecture. The place derived its name after village deity Bijli Mahadev (Shabab, 1996). It is said that light strikes the Shiva Linga and it breaks into pieces, then the priest (Pujari) collects the fragments and joins them will the help of butter and Shiva Linga comes to its original form (Chaudhry, 2003). As temple is located on a very open ridge, so there are many panoramic sights all around it, Rohtang Pass to right, Pin Parvati in the back, Kaisdhar in front and down below lies the confluence of Beas and Parvati rivers. There are many campsites around Bijli Mahadev. A rocky muddy road connects Bijli Mahadev from kullu valley. This road offers a variety of flora and terrains and also enroute one can visit Kais wildlife sanctuary which is famous for brown bear. So Bijli Mahadev holds a great potential for day hikes, jeep safaris and camping in and around its vicinity.
4. *Shanghar:* A majestic grassland located in the Seraj Valley of Kullu. The place distances 57 km., from district headquarters. It is one of the finest

pine savannas in the state. It falls in Great Himalayan National Park's (GHNP) western boundary. In middle of the grassland there is temple of, Sangchul Mahadev. The village is believed to be nestled by Pandva's during their exile. The grassland of Shanghar is so smooth that it is literally free from bumps and stones. Because of the natural and cultural bounty of the village and surroundings, it can be a perfect host for sustainable tourism.

5. *Jalori pass, Raghpur garh and Saryolsar:* Jalori Pass (3350 amsl) links the inner and outer Seraj valleys of Kullu district (Betts and McCulloch, 2014). It is located on the majestic Pir Panjal ranges of Himalayas. It is the nearest pass to national capital of India, Delhi (approx. 600 kms). It is the earliest pass in India to open after the winters. In opposite sides of pass lies the Raghupur Garh and Saryolsar Lake. In west of the pass lies the ruins of Raghupur Garh fort, grasslands of which offers majestic views especially of Pir Panjal ranges. In the east of Jalori Pass is the tranquil Saryolsar Lake (pure water Lake), where woman worship the snake goddess, *Burhi Nagni Devi*. As there are so many places in and around Jalori Pass, so it can be promoted as a destination for day hikes and short treks and visitors can enjoy the virgin beauty of Pir Panjal ranges.
6. *Malana:* A lost utopia in Himalayas, Malana is regarded as the oldest democracy of the world. Its inimitable culture and the temple of Jamlu Rishi differentiate the village from rest of the World. It stands out a sovereign self-reliant contingent whose ancestor claims Greek ancestry (Bangroo, 2002). People of Malana consider all non Malani inferior and literally untouchable. Rishi Jamlu is the chief deity of the village and also responsible for justice in the village. The village is surrounded by lush green forests, rough mountain ranges and difficult tract. That is why the traditions of village were not influence by outsiders for thousands of years. Most of the residents of Malana were uneducated in the past but now the complexion is changing in the village and people are getting educated. Thus with education the host people have started to understand the importance of their culture. So these people can be encouraged to showcase their culture and tradition to outer world and alternate livelihood generation in sustainable manner.

SWOT Analysis in Context of Established and Potential Tourism Destinations of Kullu Valley

It is one of the most frequently used methods of strategic management and environmental analysis. This technique gives the effective strategy maximizing business strength and opportunities in one hand and minimizing its weaknesses or threats in other hand. According to Gierszewska and Romanowska, 2002 SWOT is not the method of strategic method but is a unique algorithm of a strategic analysis process, a systematically prepared and a wide ranging evolution of external and internal factors which specify a company's current status and future developmental potentials. It is also used for a tourism destination for the account of its tourism potential in totality of the natural and anthropogenic resources and infrastructure etc., the detail of the term SWOT is as follow:

- *Strengths:* It is a unique characteristic of an area which gives an advantage over others. Its comparative advantages like skill, available resources, goodwill, market leadership and buyer/seller relationships are the examples of strength of an organization.
- *Weaknesses:* It is a limitation or deficiency in resources, skill and capabilities that impede effective information. Facilities, financial resources, management, capabilities, marketing skills and brand image could be the cause of these weaknesses.
- *Opportunities:* It is a major favorable situation and element that the proposed area could exploit to its advantages.
- *Threats:* Those elements which could cause trouble in a particular proposed area.

Strengths

- Kullu holds strong potential to develop ecotourism because of the cultural and natural diversity of the region.
- Kullu is considered to be a peaceful and tranquil place.
- The unique *Kathkuni* architecture style adds traditional flavor to the destination.
- Kullu is a collection of wealth of culture, customs, cuisines, clothes and souvenirs.
- The people of Kullu are courteous by nature, which is one of the sacred aspects of the society.
- Kullu has good weather and climate and it is usually cooler than other regions of country so it attracts tourists' especially in summer months *i.e.,* May to July.

Weaknesses

- Lack of co-ordination and co-operation between local community, governmental organizations and stake holders.
- Lack of Infrastructure in the region like poor condition of roads, less or no air travelling facilities to the region, no rail connectivity, etc.
- Lack of basic communication such as: internet, phone network, good hygienic toilets, disposal system, etc.
- Lack of proper waste management in tourism concentrated areas like: Manali, Solang Valley etc.

- Inadequate promotion of the region in national and international markets.
- Lack of professionalism among the people associated in tourism industry in the region.
- The concentration of stake holders are only on mass tourism in the region, alternate forms of tourism are not promoted by them.
- Monopoly of locals in tourism concentrated region *i.e.,* localite factor, overcharging for the services rendered.

Opportunities

- Kullu is a highly diverse region both in biological and natural aspects, so it can be promoted as destination for alternate forms of tourism like community based ecotourism (CBET), Cultural tourism, heritage tourism, rural tourism, etc.
- Kullu is famous for its temples and culture, so it can be promoted in national and international level in such a way that it generate interest in people interested to travel to regions of religious importance.
- The spectacular view of Kullu valley has strong potential to boost photography tours.
- Participation of host community will give a new perspective to their community assets.
- The region can be promoted as year round destination by promoting different forms of tourism. In winters for snow sport activities, in summers for leisure and recreation, in monsoon for photography and orchard tourism.
- Kullu houses various medicinal plants and herbs in wild form. So local community can be encouraged to cultivate these plants and herbs so that they can generate alternate income source.
- Each unexplored site of this valley holds a unique story that can be used as a marketing tool for promotion of Kullu district at international level.
- Develop or establish enterprises of value added products or locally available resources through women's group and linking them with tourism activity can further strengthen the activity in the region.

Threats

- Tourists are affecting quality of life of host community as host society is facing major problem like addiction to alcohol and drugs.
- Deforestation for personal motives has lead to loss of various flora and fauna species of this region.
- Due to demonstration effect, the youths of host community are forgetting their cultures, ritual, dialects and customs.
- Over consumption of resources at major tourist destinations in the region, beauty and serenity is decreasing day-by-day.

- Mass tourism is disintegrating the culture values of this valley.
- Improper waste management is continuously toxicating the native air and water resources of the region which is hazardous both for local community and tourists.

Conclusion and Recommendations

Kullu valley is a region which holds potential for variety of tourism. The valley is endowed with the lot of treasure of beautiful natural spots which attracts a number of tourists in the region. This tourism industry holds a great potential to flourish the area provided its cultural, traditional and historical legacy is properly taken care of. As tourism industry is highly dynamic and is linked to other industries also, so tourism cannot be enhanced and sustained by the efforts of governmental organizations alone, but participation of local community and stake holders are must, in a sustainable way. The only way to do so is by the proper coordination and cooperation between the government, local people and people indulged in the tourism industry. The thrust should not only be on the mass tourism, but alternate form of tourism should also be developed in the region because it can provide local residents an opportunity to promote their homeland to the outer world along with a permanent employment resource for their coming generations and at the same time conservation of biodiversity, culture and tradition. If Kullu has to maintain its charm in near future, the focus should be shifted to alternate tourism such as: ecotourism only through which it can remain in its colors in times to come.

Based on the SWOT analysis of the available and potential sites of the valley it is also recommended to build the capacities of the local community, development of the basic infrastructural activities and ecotourism model for the sustainable livelihood pattern and environmental conservation. It is also recommended that the state government should pay more attention to the ecotourism and income generation through development of the alternative tourism destination involving local communities and women entrepreneurs in particular. More efforts should be given to livelihood generation and awareness for biodiversity conservation among the stakeholders.

REFERENCES

Ahluwalia, M.S. (1998). Social, Cultural, and Economic History of Himachal Pradesh. India: Indus Publishing, pp. 1-200.

Ayodele, I.A. and Falade, G.O. (1989). Essentials of Tourism Management. Elshadda Elobal Ventures Ltd, pp. 1-90.

Ayodele, I.A. and Falade, G.O. (1993). Wildlife and Tourism Development in Nigeria. *Journal of Tropical Forest Resource Management*, 5: 1-8.

Babu, S. (2010). Ecotourism in the Mudamalai Wildlife Sanctuary. *Southern Ecotourists,* Banglore, India.

Bajpai, S.C. (2002). Lahaul-Spiti: A Forbidden Land in the Himalayas. India: Indus Publishing, pp. 1-176.

Bangroo, V. (2002). MALANA - A Lost Utopia In: The Himalayas. The IGNCA Newsletter, Volume (V) (November-December).

Betts, V. and McCulloch, V. (2014). Delhi and Northwest India Footprint Focus Guide: Includes Amritsar, Shimla, Leh, Srinagar, Kullu Valley, Dharamshala. United Kingdom: Footprint Travel Guides, pp. 1-176.

Blamey, R. K. (1995). The Nature of Ecotourism. Occasional paper no 21. ACT: Bureau of Tourism Research, Cambera.

Chaudhry, M. (2003). Guide to Trekking in Himachal: Over 65 Treks and 100 Destinations. India: Indus Publishing, pp. 1-247.

Chaurasiya, R.S. (2002). History of Ancient India. India: Atlantic Distributors and Publishers, pp. 1-308.

Fletcher, J. and Lantham, J. (1995). Databak: The Global Picture. *Tourism Economics*, 1(1).

Gierszewska, G. and Romanowska, M. (2002). Analiza Strategiczna przedsiêbiorstwa, PWE, Warszawa.

Goodwin, H. (1996). In Persuit of Ecotourism. *Biodiversity Conservation*. 5:277-291.

Hardy, A., Beeton, R.J.S. and Earson, L. (2002). Sustainable Tourism: An Overview of the Concept and its Position in Relation to Conceptualization of Tourism. *Journal of Sustainable Tourism,* 10:475-496.

Hawkes, S. and Williams, P. (1993). The Greening of Tourism, from Principle to Practice: A Casebook of Best Environmental Practice in Tourism. Centre for Tourism Policy and Research, UK, pp. 1-104.

Mcintosh, R. and Goeldner, C. (1996). Tourism: Principles, Practices and Philosophies. New York, Willey.

Negi, J. (1990). Tourism and Travel-Concept and Principles. Gitanjali Publication House, New Delhi.

Przeclawski, K. (1993). Tourism as a Subject of Interdisciplinary Research. In D. Pearce and R. Butler eds., Tourism Research: Critiques and Challenges. London, Routledge.

Ramakrishnan, P.S. (2000). Biodiversity, Land Use and Traditional Ecological Knowledge, Ramkrishnan, P.S., Chandrashekara, U.M., Guilmoto, C.Z. Maikhuri, R.K., Rao, K.S. and Sexena, K.G. (eds.). Oxford and IBH publication, New Delhi, India, pp. 3-13.

Ryan, C. (1991). Recreational Tourism: A Social Science Perspective. London, Routledge.

Sebele, L.S. (2010). Community based Tourism Ventures, Benefits and Challenges: Khama rhino Sanctuary Trust, Central district, Botswana. *Tourism Manage,* 31: 136-146.

Shabab, D. (1996). Kullu: Himalayan Abode of the Divine. India: Indus Publishing, pp. 1-136.

Singh, K. (2012). India an Introduction. India: Harper Collins, pp. 1-320.

Singh, S.P., Pathan, D. and Singh, R. (2002). Hydrobiological Studies of Two Ponds of Satna (M.P.) India. *Econ. Environ. Cons.,* 8: 289-292.

Smith, S. (1989). Tourism Analysis: A Handbook. New York, Longman.

Smith, V. L. (1977). Hosts and Guests: The Anthropology of Tourism. University of Pennsyvalnia press inc. USA, pp: 2-3.

The International Ecotourism Society. 'TIES' (2009) TIES Fact Sheet. www.ecotourism.org/ fact sheet.html Internet; accessed 11 January 2014.

Tosun, C. (2006). Expected Nature of Community Participation in Tourism Development. *Tourism Mange*, 27:493-504.

Varanasi Travel and Tourism - Destinations, Hotels, Transport. http://www.varanasi.org.in/facts-about-varanasi Internet; accessed 15 May 2015.

Verma, V. (1995). The Emergence of Himachal Pradesh: A Survey of Constitutional Developments. India: Indus Publishing, pp. 1-285.

Wallace, G.N. and Pierce, S.M. (1996). An Evolution of Ecotourism in amazonas, Brazil. *Annals of Tourism Research*, 23: 843-873.

Weaver, D. (1998). Ecotourism in less Developed World. Wallingford: *CAB* International, pp. 1-258.

Woodley, A. (1993). Tourism and Sustainable Development: The Community Perspective. In Nelson, J.G., Butler, R. And Wall, G. (eds.). Tourism and Sustainable Development: Monitoring, Planning, Managing. 135-147. University of Waterloo, Heritage Resources Centre. Waterloo, ISBN-13: 9780921083443.

World Tourism Organization (1993). Recommendation on Tourism Statistics. Madrid.

Index

□□□□